Praise for *Into the Story*

"Filled with many outstanding portraits, starting with Clinton and extending to Roberto Clemente . . . Throughout this collection, Maraniss proves himself to be a relentless reporter and a solid writer . . . these are journalistic journeys well worth taking."

—*The Christian Science Monitor*

"Regardless of the level of fame of his subjects, Maraniss's reportage is always sharp and sympathetic."

—*Kirkus Reviews* (starred review)

"These 32 pieces cover a lot of ground—family, grief, politics, sports. Some were written at a leisurely pace, while others are fine examples of reporting and writing under intense deadline. All show the writer's core skills of deep reporting and detailed writing."

—*Star Tribune* (Minneapolis)

". . . demonstrates his ability to capture, with a few well chosen words, people and events with photographic clarity."

—*Booklist*

"There are many journalists skilled at crafting political profiles, and sportswriters aplenty in this country. Rare are those who combine formidable talent in both fields, the sort Pulitzer Prize–winning *Washington Post* reporter David Maraniss demonstrates in this eclectic collection of more than 25 years of his work."

—ShelfAwareness.com

ALSO BY DAVID MARANISS

Rome 1960: The Summer Olympics That Stirred the World

Clemente: The Passion and Grace of Baseball's Last Hero

They Marched Into Sunlight:
War and Peace, Vietnam and America, October 1967

When Pride Still Mattered: The Life of Vince Lombardi

The Clinton Enigma

First in His Class: A Biography of Bill Clinton

The Prince of Tennessee: Al Gore Meets His Fate
(with Ellen Nakashima)

"Tell Newt to Shut Up!"
(with Michael Weisskopf)

Into the Story

A Writer's Journey Through Life, Politics, Sports, and Loss

DAVID MARANISS

Simon & Schuster Paperbacks

New York   London   Toronto   Sydney

For Heidi and Ava,

little odes to joy

Simon & Schuster Paperbacks
A Division of Simon & Schuster, Inc.
1230 Avenue of the Americas
New York, NY 10020

First Simon & Schuster trade paperback edition January 2011

SIMON & SCHUSTER PAPERBACKS and colophon are registered
trademarks of Simon & Schuster, Inc.

For information about special discounts for bulk purchases,
please contact Simon & Schuster Special Sales at
1-866-506-1949 or business@simonandschuster.com.

The Simon & Schuster Speakers Bureau can bring authors
to your live event. For more information or to book an event,
contact the Simon & Schuster Speakers Bureau at
1-866-248-3049 or visit our website at www.simonspeakers.com.

Designed by Elliott Beard

Manufactured in the United States of America

10 9 8 7 6 5 4 3 2 1

Library of Congress Cataloging-in-Publication Data is available.

ISBN 978-1-4391-6002-2
ISBN 978-1-4391-6003-9 (pbk)
ISBN 978-1-4391-6752-6 (ebook)

Photo credit for page 157: Suero, Orlando. Text by Anne Garside. *Camelot at
Dawn: Jacqueline and John Kennedy in Georgetown, May 1954.* Cover photo
© 2001 The Johns Hopkins University Press. Reprinted with permission of
The Johns Hopkins University Press.

CONTENTS

Part III
SPORTING PASSIONS

Part IV
THE ARC TOWARD HOME

INTRODUCTION
———

Common Sense and Sensibility

I came to writing the old-fashioned way, as an apprentice in the family trade. My mother was an editor at the University of Wisconsin Press, and my dad was a newspaperman who spent most of his career at the *Capital Times* of Madison, a progressive afternoon daily that no longer exists, except online, which is to say that it has passed away into the future. With the exception of Cleveland's *Plain Dealer,* all the newspapers that employed my father before he reached Madison (in Detroit, New York, and Bettendorf, Iowa) are dead and gone. His father, my paternal grandfather, ran a print shop in Brooklyn's Coney Island, churning out flyers for ancient amusements like the traveling circus that will undoubtedly outlive most broadsheet newspapers. Journalists are trained to find what is hidden, yet for most of us, when it came to the transformation, if not demise, of our own profession, the obvious became obvious only after it was obvious. Perhaps I am ignoring the obvious one more time, but even as bookstores disappear and electronic reading devices kindle their way into the culture, I still cling to a naïve belief that hardback books will last for another generation, until I am through writing.

But this is not an elegy to the newspapers, magazines, and books that have published my work over several decades. As much as I love the printed word, and adore the aesthetics of typefaces, book jackets, and cleanly designed front pages, the means of delivery is not as important to me as the interplay of two larger ideas. The first is that the sifting of fact and truth from the chaff of unprocessed information or misinformation will always be essential. The second is that humans will always have a need to explain themselves through story. It is that combination that makes up what I do as a nonfiction narrative writer. This book is offered as a journey through a diverse collection of stories that in their totality represent my perspective on that craft. It is also, inevitably, an expression of my personal sensibility and outlook on the world.

I chose a little story titled "A Bus Named Desire" to open the collection because it introduces some of my core beliefs about writing, reporting, and life. I was in New Orleans in 1985 to cover the trial of the governor, Edwin Edwards, and happened to be standing on a busy corner when a bus approached with that evocative one-word destination flashing in the electronic sign above the front windshield—DESIRE. I had other things to do at that hour, but my reporter's curiosity took hold of me. I had to board the bus and go along for the ride. As soon as I got on, I knew I would write something. I had no idea where the bus was headed, literally, but I had a concept about where it could go, figuratively—connecting fact and fiction, past and present, prosaic and romantic, on a journey into the mind of Tennessee Williams and toward the house of Stanley and Stella Kowalski. In the making of this brief story, as I rode the bus and then traced the geography and literature of Desire, I followed the tenets of my journalistic mantra: Be open to any possibility, remain flexible, look for connections, let the story take you where it will and yet always use detail for a purpose, with a larger design in mind.

The concluding thought in the story—Tennessee Williams reflecting in a letter that human frictions are caused more by misunderstanding than malice—is one that I share and that has influenced my writing. There is certainly evil in this world, and some human monsters cannot have their deeds explained away as the product of misunderstanding, but I agree with Williams that most people are a combination of good and bad and that it is always worth the effort to try to understand them. That idea has driven my work in biography, and is especially important to my writings in the political realm. Like all humans, I carry a set of biases—people with whom I agree or disagree, policies that I admire, and policies that I abhor. But my obsession as a biographer goes in a different direction, not toward molding subjects so they fit into my worldview, but trying to comprehend theirs—the forces that shaped them, why they think and act the way they do.

I remember a C-SPAN book event more than a decade ago when I was on a panel with Christopher Hitchens, the brilliant essayist whose distinct tastes included a profound aversion to Bill Clinton, one of my biographical subjects. When Brian Lamb, the moderator, asked me whether I liked or disliked Clinton, I stammered for a moment, and Hitchens swiftly filled the void by answering for me, declaring that I disliked Clinton. My first response was: If only I could face the world with such certainty. Here is someone not only dead certain of what he thinks, but of what I think as well. It took me a moment to regain my equilibrium and remember that my hesitation had a reason behind it. My view of the world was not uncertain, nor was my perspective on Clinton. It was just that to reduce him to a like-or-dislike choice was to negate the value of biography.

From the three stories on Clinton included in this collection, one might reasonably deduce that there were times when I liked him and times when I did not, but neither sentiment is particularly useful. What was of more value, I believed, was that my study of his life showed that you could not separate the good Clinton from the bad one, that his impulses for better or worse arose from the same well of need and desire, and that there was a repetitive cycle of loss and recovery in his life: When he was down, he would find his way back, and when he was on top, he would find a way to screw up again. My role as biographer was not that of propagandist or columnist; it was to report his life as deeply as possible and explain how and why he developed as he did.

There is a difference between that idea and the false argument that often arises in journalism and politics about fairness or balance, two words that have been deadened in any case by the Orwellian abuse of them by the Fox News Channel. I've always believed that a writer's mission, whether as a newspaperman or a biographer, is to search for the truth and to use deep reporting and common sense in its pursuit. If two people I interview make statements that directly contradict each other, it does not mean that they carry equal weight and that I should present them equally. It does not mean that I cannot analyze the comments and reach a conclusion about which one is true or closer to the truth. But what it does mean is that I probably have more work to do, more people to talk to, more documents to search for, more thinking about the context of their accounts and what makes the most sense. It is not quite a science, but it is a serious endeavor with the same respect for evidence and rational thought.

It also requires patience, directness, and honesty in dealing with subjects. In one of the stories in this collection, I go to Vietnam with an old veteran named Clark Welch. Many decades earlier, as a young lieutenant, Welch had commanded a company of soldiers who suffered horrible losses in a battle that is one of the two central events of my book *They Marched Into Sunlight*. Welch is a charismatic figure, more Gary Cooper than John Wayne. If not the main character in the Vietnam book, he is certainly the most unforgettable. Not only did he walk the long-ago battlefield with me, and endure countless hours of questions, he also gave me an invaluable batch of documents—a shoe box full of long, detailed, revealing letters that he had sent home from Vietnam to his wife, Lacy. But it was uncertain at first that he would deal with me at all. All these decades later, he was holed up in the mountains of Colorado, still haunted and angered by the death and destruction his company had endured on October 17, 1967, and the way the U.S. government had lied about it. Finally, a year into my research, he agreed to meet me at a hotel in Denver. As we shook hands and took seats in the lobby, his first words to me were, "David, I'll talk to you if you promise to be good to my boys."

I knew how important Welch was to my book. There were many other characters and story lines, I could write it without him, but it would not have as much depth and power. After all the work that had gone into tracking him down, I did not want to lose him. Still, I realized that I could be walking into a trap that would do neither of us any good. Some people believe that a writer will say anything to get a story. Janet Malcolm wrote an entire book about what she argued was the inherently duplicitous relationship between writer and subject. Truman Capote, in his classic reportage for *In Cold Blood*, might have sold his soul to wring information out of his murderous Kansas characters. I'm not perfect, but I've held myself to a vastly different standard during my decades of work in the nonfiction vineyard. If you manipulate your subjects, you end up manipulating yourself.

"I can't make you that promise," I told Welch. "I can promise you that I will research the story as thoroughly as I can. I'll try to find the truth of what happened. I'll let you know what I'm finding along the way. But I can't promise you that I'll be good to your boys because I don't know what I'll find."

Welch pushed on the arms of his chair, signaling that he was about to get up and walk away. "You have to promise to be good to my boys," he said again.

"I just can't make that promise," I repeated. "I can only promise you that I will search for the truth, wherever that takes me." If I made the promise to be good to his soldiers, meaning write about them only in a positive light, I would either have to keep it, which might taint my story, or break it, which would destroy our relationship.

Welch decided not to leave, and that made all the difference. I was able to pursue the truth without worrying about being duplicitous. I was able to tell him what I was finding, good or bad, and as our mutual trust built, he eventually shared virtually everything with me, including his deepest feelings as well as his letters.

In writing history, even recent history, it is always important to bear in mind the limits of human memory. Bill Clinton could remember thousands of disparate facts (a telephone number he hadn't dialed in thirty years; the name of a friend's little sister that he was seeing for the first time in decades), though he had a striking tendency to forget important things about his own life. Vince Lombardi, for all his attention to detail as the great football coach of the Green Bay Packers, proved terribly frustrating for W. C. Heinz, who wrote the classic *Run to Daylight!* under Lombardi's byline, because of his inability to bring back incidents from his past.

"You have no audiovisual recall!" Heinz, one of the great sportswriters of all time, complained to Lombardi after spending a week trying to interview him.

"What the hell is that?" Lombardi asked.

"Well, I just made it up," Heinz responded. "But you don't remember what anybody said or what they sounded like. You don't remember what anything looked like."

"Whaddaya mean?"

"Well, you told me that you decided that football was what you wanted to do in your life when you had a great game at St. Francis Prep."

"You already got that!" Lombardi said proudly.

"I know I have it, Coach," Heinz said patiently. "Now, as you pulled your jersey over your head . . . I asked you what color the jersey was and you said you didn't know."

"That's right, I didn't know."

"That's what I mean," said Heinz.

Most people have worse memories than Bill Clinton and better memories than Vince Lombardi. But their memories generally fail when they try to recount the precise chronology of events, something particularly important to writers of nonfiction narrative. When I was writing the three chapters that comprise the battle scenes of my Vietnam book, I found that I could not rely on interviews with the survivors about the timing of what happened as they marched into the jungle that fateful day. First of all, in a time of trauma, like a battle, seconds can feel like hours and hours can feel like seconds; everything is distorted. Second, as any cop will tell you, you can ask four witnesses to a traffic accident what happened minutes earlier and you will get four different versions of the same event. The differences only become exaggerated with time, and the accounts less reliable. When someone says this happened, then that, then that, usually they get it wrong. It is best to go back to contemporaneous documents—letters, logs, calendars, diaries, after-action reports, internal investigations, and oral histories—to piece together a reliable chronology.

What you can usually depend on from interviews, Lombardi notwithstanding, are sharp and random fragments of memory. When a soldier recalls that just before the first enemy shot was fired in a jungle ambush, he had stopped to cop a smoke, and the guy next to him was opening a can of peaches, and another guy was taking a piss, I believe it. Those are the vivid little things—the sensations—that are etched permanently in the mind. And though the shards of memory may be random, they can be used for a larger purpose. I did that many times for the stories in this collection, including "September 11, 2001" and "The Desk I Chose to Die Under."

When the World Trade Center Twin Towers were attacked in Manhattan, and again six years later, when a student gunman went on a rampage at Virginia Tech, editors at the *Washington Post* asked me to write chronological narratives of what happened. As different as the two events were, they presented similar problems and common themes. In each case, I had only a few days to compile and analyze a raft of material from my own reporting and memos filed by an army of world-class *Post* reporters. I knew that some aspects of the story, especially those involving the actions and motivations of the perpetrators, would change hour by hour, day after day, with fresh information, while other aspects would not change. I wanted to write something that would have both immediacy and permanence, that would be of value to readers not just then but years later, so I decided to build each story around enduring themes.

The first theme is how ordinary life is until it is not. I wanted to capture the transition between the prosaic poetry of everyday life and the moment when it is changed forever. To do that, I had to accumulate the sharp, random memories of survivors, memories that might seem trivial but do double duty as bits of reality and symbolism. The office worker stopping for an iced coffee and a scone and noticing the exact time—8:09—on the digital clock on a building outside the Fulton Street subway exit as he makes his way to the Twin Towers. The passenger reaching his seat aboard American Airlines flight 11 in Boston and leaving the simple message "Hi, hon, I made it." The kid walking into his German class at Virginia Tech and bantering with his instructor about what college players their favorite NFL teams, the Falcons and Saints, should select in the draft. We can all relate to these moments; all of us have done things like that day after day. In stories of this sort, they are the details I search for first—details that will evoke the universal in the particular. How ordinary it all feels, until . . .

The second theme is the odd, chaotic mixture of banality and horror in the tragic experience itself. I wanted to make readers feel what it was like for victims and survivors. Again, the smallest details do the heaviest work. A man counting the floors on the way down the South Tower stairwell. A woman examining a cloud of papers that have blown across the river to Brooklyn, the detritus of disaster including a rental car form from Broken Arrow, Oklahoma. A young man wondering what he sees on the street. A slab of meat? No, a body. A student unable to repress one thought as the shooter enters his classroom: What does a gun wound feel like?

This collection is separated into four sections that I chose arbitrarily, based on my sense of flow rather than on the years the pieces were written or the chronology of events. The first and last sections are more personal, to give the reader a feel for how I view the world. In the middle are my works about sociology, politics, and sports, the central concerns of my writing career.

People often assume that I am first and foremost a political writer who occasionally dabbles in sports, turning from serious work to play. I've never looked at it that way. There is much about politics that is utterly trivial and boring to me, and much about sports that is inherently dramatic or sociologically interesting. It is not the general subject that draws me, but the possibilities of a particular story. From a little piece about my father ("Dad and Ron Santo") one can see the roots of my fascination with sports and issues of race in American life, and how that led me to stories about Roberto Clemente, Larry Doby, Wilma Rudolph, Rafer Johnson, and Muhammad Ali. With Clinton and Obama, I was drawn to the dramatic arcs of their biographies, each emerging from nowhere to become president and dealing with family dysfunction in a very different way. Clinton was a creation of rural Arkansas, Obama a creation of the world, yet each had to remake himself as an adult to get where he wanted to go.

After the book about Lombardi came out, I was flooded with suggestions to write about Woody Hayes, Bear Bryant, Joe Paterno, and any number of other notable football coaches. But I didn't write *When Pride Still Mattered* because I loved football, or because I had a thing about coaches. I saw in Lombardi a chance to write about reality and mythology, the meaning of competition and success in American life, the cost of winning, and the obsessive pursuit of perfection by a decidedly imperfect man. I was also drawn to the arc of his life. Lombardi reversed the geography of the traditional American success story. Here was a creature of the big city, born and trained in New York, who struggled until he finally made it in little Green Bay, coaching there for nine luminous years in which he won five world titles, culminating with a classic penultimate game known as the Ice Bowl, played on a frozen field in subzero weather and won by his team on the final play of the game.

Everything in Lombardi's football career was in preparation for that game, as was everything I had done in researching his life. My first rule in reporting is *Go there,* wherever *there* is. In this case it meant turning to my wife and uttering the loving phrase "How would you like to move to Green Bay for the winter?" Her response was, "Brrrr," but we went. It had to be winter because I had to experience the season in a company town, the company being the Packers, and for the Ice Bowl chapter ("Ice" in this collection) I needed to know firsthand what it took to endure a Saskatchewan Screamer on a dark, frigid midwinter afternoon. By the time I reached that game in the writing process, I felt so in tune with Lombardi, his team, the place, the weather, the moment, that I sat down at six in the morning and wrote nonstop until midnight—a full chapter in a single day. I never set word-total goals for a single day—every day is different—but I do set a goal for words in a week, and this time I had written two weeks' worth in one sitting.

I never met Lombardi. He died in 1970, when I was twenty-one. Had we met, his first words might have been, "Maraniss, get your goddamn hair cut!" We came from vastly different cultures and generations. It would have been easy for me to portray him as a caricature, a madman who fit the saying most widely attributed to him, "Winning isn't everything, it's the only thing." Easy, but to my mind not only wrong (he didn't coin the phrase; it was first uttered publicly by a young actress in a John Wayne movie), but pointless. To return to one of my earlier points, what could I learn, or teach anyone, simply by taking Lombardi and making him mine? Not much. I wanted to comprehend the way he encountered the world.

This has to do with differentiating between sensibility and ego. My sensibility is always there, whether I'm writing about Vince Lombardi, or a congressman returning to his district ("Back Home in Indiana"), or the sight of animal carcasses lining a roadway in south Louisiana ("Roadside Distraction"), or something deeply personal, like the accidental death of my sister ("Losing Wendy"). It is sensibility that takes nonfiction beyond stenography, providing it with a frame of thought and context. But I try to keep my ego out of it. Ego tends to dominate the modern culture, and much of today's writing, but usually it only gets in the way of the story. Someone with Norman Mailer's brilliance can do it, but most writers cannot. Ego serves too often, not as a form of revelation but as a cover for writer's block or for a paucity of research. Figuring things out is not easy.

My argument runs counter to the way things are trending. With the advent of blogs, the spread of the Internet, the deadening of political rhetoric, the onslaught of television blab mongers, the reader's diminishing attention span—with so much information presented in television crawls and Web site links without context or story—there are fewer ways for a writer to become noticed and a greater temptation to make the most of ego and attitude. I enjoy a snarky take on something (usually, to be honest, only if I agree with the snarker) as much as anyone, now and then. But for a nonfiction writer, all-attitude can give you short-term gain, a momentary buzz, but lead to long-term frustration. What do you do after you become sick of your own contrived persona? What have you learned? I grew up in a family of scholars ("The Sensations of Jim"), and was a distracted student myself when I was supposed to be a student, but my job has allowed me to spend the rest of my life making up for it. The world of nonfiction writing is a continual graduate school. But only if you avoid the easier path, the lure of assumption and attitude, and open yourself to what can be an educational and fulfilling lifelong journey.

Part I

RIPPED APART
AND SEWN TOGETHER

1

A Bus Named Desire

New Orleans
It mattered not at all that it was a monstrous city bus with green plastic seats shaped to the contours of fat people, or that it was belching dark smoke, or that the electronic marquee above the bubble-glass windshield displayed destinations in dot-matrix letters that flashed by like time and temperature readings at a suburban bank. All that mattered was the designation of this bus approaching the curb near the corner of Canal and Royal, at the border of skyscraper and French Quarter, reality and fantasy. It was a bus named Desire.

It was not a streetcar: The only one still operating is named St. Charles. It probably was not coming from the railroad station, and it certainly was not carrying any broken Mississippi belles like Blanche DuBois, with dainty beauty that must avoid strong light. Still, when a bus named Desire pulls over and opens its doors, the temptation is to pay the sixty cents and ride. There is something oddly profound when history, literature, and life conspire that way, when a simple name on a bus evokes the haunting internal lives of misunderstood souls in the postwar New Orleans of playwright Tennessee Williams.

Williams was born in Mississippi, grew up in St. Louis, took his pen name from his ancestors in Tennessee, and lived out his years in Key West, but it was in New Orleans that his surroundings were most in harmony with his sense of life—ambiguous, isolated, decayed, sensuous, sympathetic. This city, like Blanche, has a dainty beauty, but it must avoid direct light. The sweet sound of its place-names, the blend of French, Spanish, Cajun, Creole, and black, the grillwork, gardens, and courtyards; the brown Mississippi, the bananas and coffee, the cemeteries—all these are authentic, but they betray a deep anxiety. The bus named Desire passes glistening new hotels and office buildings barely half full, built on false premises and undeserved arrogance; passes warehouses and wharves boarded up since the World's Fair collapsed last year amid grand jury investigations and a $120 million bankruptcy. The bus turns away from a port steadily losing markets and rumbles toward a housing project named Desire where there is far more of that than of hope.

It is not the route that Williams prescribed to Blanche when she got to town. "They told me to take a streetcar named Desire," she said, "and then transfer to one called Cemeteries and ride six blocks and get off at Elysian Fields!" But it is close enough. The bus comes within a few blocks of the address where Blanche's sister, Stella, lived with her earthy husband, Stanley Kowalski. In *A Streetcar Named Desire*, the Kowalskis lived at 632 Elysian Fields Avenue. There is such an address. It is a white clapboard house, two stories, deteriorating, part of a duplex of sorts with three apartments on one side and a barbershop on the other. The barber advertises in a peculiar way. "No New Customers, No Children, and No Loitering." Then again, the shop is closed most of the time. No one is home at the Kowalskis'. The screens are down but the windows are open about six inches, and a breeze blows gently against white curtains made of the material Williams dressed Blanche in, with something about it "that suggests a moth."

Across the avenue, one can only imagine what goes on inside the Teamsters Local 270 building or Pino's Private Club. And down at the Washington Square Park, winos share one another's company on the sun-warmed benches. The market from which Stanley brought home his bloody meat is still there. But where did he go bowling?

Of course, one should never try to bring too much real life into literature; it has a life of its own. "It is only in his work that an artist can find reality and satisfaction," Williams wrote, "for the actual world is less intense than the world of his invention, and consequently his life, without recourse to violent disorder, does not seem very substantial." Williams's life had enough violent disorders, as his various biographers have revealed, but it was rather tame during the years he was writing *Streetcar*. He started writing it in Chapala, Mexico, with the working title "A Poker Night." Then he moved to New Orleans, changed the title, and worked with a fury, waking each morning with Blanche, "this lascivious, demonic woman who possessed me."

At mid-afternoon he would leave his second-story apartment in the French Quarter, near the corner of Royal and St. Peter, and walk over to Victor's, a long-gone bar, where he would drink brandy alexanders and listen to the Ink Spots sing "If I Didn't Care" on the jukebox. All the time he was writing the play, which won the 1948 Pulitzer Prize, he thought he was dying of pancreatic cancer. He lived another thirty-five years. The streetcar named Desire, or at least one of them, sits quietly behind the iron gates of the old U.S. Mint at the end of the French Market. Another landmark, a letter from Williams to Elia Kazan, who directed the play and movie, can be found at the New Orleans Historic Collection on Royal Street near where Williams once lived. "There are no 'good' or 'bad' people," Williams wrote. "Some are a little better or a little worse but all are activated more by misunderstanding than malice. A blindness to what is going on in each other's hearts."

2

Losing Wendy

My little sister, Wendy Maraniss, said goodbye to her eleven-year-old son, Dave, who was practicing at the grand piano in their front room. Play a little slower, she gently instructed him, and then she bounced out the door to go to work on the morning of November 16, 1997. She was driving from one college town to another in upstate New York, from her home in Ithaca to her teaching assignment in Geneva, about an hour's commute. To Wendy, neither the journey nor the destination seemed burdensome. She loved to drive—it was her time alone to think—and she thoroughly enjoyed teaching piano and accompanying her students, one of whom had scheduled a session with her at Hobart and William Smith Colleges that Sunday afternoon.

Winter had already descended into the gorges of the Finger Lakes. Only two days earlier, a snow flurry had forced her to stop halfway to Geneva, and she returned home, much to husband Brian's relief. But now the worst of the early storm had cleared, the sun was shining, and Wendy was on her way. She was driving the same flimsy subcompact, seemingly made of tin and cardboard, that had served the family's needs for fourteen years. Brian's vigilant concern for his wife's safety had only intensified that fall, when Wendy added the commute to Geneva to her already overflowing list of assignments. He had recently prepared the car for winter with a new set of snow tires. Wendy never seemed as concerned about her well-being as he was, and at times would chafe at his cautious nature, but she followed his most persistent request: Call when you get there.

She always called. Soon after Wendy left, wending north out of Ithaca on Route 96, Brian took their two boys, Dave and big brother Max, fourteen, on a long walk up the hill to his office at Cornell's School of Industrial and Labor Relations, where he was managing editor of the *ILR Review.* While doing some catch-up work and watching the boys play computer games, he waited anxiously for word from

Wendy

Maraniss family collection

Wendy. An hour went by, then two. No call. He tried to calm himself by thinking, I've worried about her hundreds of times over the years and everything turned out okay. Finally, he and the boys returned the mile and a half down the hill. It was after five when they reached the front porch steps of the old wood house on Lake Avenue. Already dark. Wendy should have been back by then, but the car was not in the driveway. Brian walked through the shadowed hallway to the kitchen and around to the dining room, where the phone sat atop a bookcase. Messages blinked on the answering machine. Brian hoped to hear Wendy's voice. Instead, he stood and listened as the tape played out his most dreadful apprehension.

It was unbelievable, yet irrefutably true. A call from someone at Hobart and William Smith. So, so sorry. How horrible. Wendy killed like that. In a car accident. At 12:25 p.m., Wendy, forty-two, had been approaching the small town of Varick in Seneca County, about fifteen miles north of Ithaca. She was driving on a straightaway stretch of two-lane highway. The road was 90 percent clear, according to the state police report, and 10 percent windblown, slippery in spots. Wendy hit a patch of "black ice"—glassy ice the color of the roadway and almost impossible to detect. Her little car went into a skid, swirling into the other lane, where it was hit broadside by a big Buick. Wendy died immediately of a ruptured aorta; literally, a broken heart.

It took all of my twenty-five years of newspaper training to report even that much about her final seconds of life. Maybe someday I will feel the need to learn and memorize every detail, but not now. Now I feel the details do not matter. My little sister is dead. She died in an accident. Accidents happen. They are random acts of physics. There are a million "if onlys" to every random act, but not one of them changes a thing.

Wendy came along at a low point for the Maraniss family. My dad was temporarily out of the newspaper business then, an unhappy salesman at a variety store in Detroit with a lovely, intelligent, and underappreciated wife and three, now four, kids. We called her Little Red when she arrived on June 27, 1955, with her fuzzy orange hair. For some reason my mom let me name the baby, and I named her after a cute kindergartner named Wendy. Everything started to turn for the better after her birth, and though it surely might have been coincidence, Dad never thought so, and neither did I. Wendy made the family whole:

two boys, two girls, the oldest and youngest with red hair, the middle two with brown. She was not just a distraction from tough times, she illuminated the way out. Within two years of Wendy's birth we had moved to Madison, and my dad, after struggling for a decade, began his long and rewarding career as a newspaperman at the *Capital Times.* Wendy was our good-luck charm. She helped the Braves win the World Series in 1957, and sat at my father's side in the living room of our house on Regent Street, putting a hex on the opposition as the Green Bay Packers started their 1960s dynasty. She was my protector. Whenever I was in trouble with my parents—getting bad grades or losing my gloves or forgetting to go somewhere important—Wendy would stick up for me, even crying if that got Dad to lay off.

Little Red followed me to Randall School, and then to West Junior High. We shared the same childhood landscape: Vilas Park, Camp Randall Stadium, and the Field House, the cluttered newsroom of the *Cap Times* downtown. Her intelligence was far keener than mine, yet she never got her high school diploma. Wendy quit the public school system after ninth grade and attended Madison Community School during the early 1970s. It was an alternative institution, and Wendy's alternative was mostly to stay home. No conscientious parent ever homeschooled a child better than she homeschooled herself. Wendy spent several hours a day in our back room, playing the piano intensely, and an equal amount of time sprawled on our living room couch, wrapped in a blanket, reading Russian novels. She aced the GED and earned degrees in piano performance at the University of Wisconsin and Yale School of Music.

A despairing year in New York followed. I cannot say what the arbiters of musical talent there were looking for, but I am sure that whatever it was, Wendy offered something deeper. The world is full of artists who present themselves empathetically onstage, then step back into the real world and behave like jerks. Wendy felt everything she played. Her intense love and understanding of texture, nuance, clarity, beauty, and her hatred of bigotry, false adulation, mob psychology—all of that somehow came out in her music. It got her nowhere in New York. She ended up working as a bank teller. One day, near her apartment on the Upper West Side, some lowlife tried to mug her. She was stunned. "I don't know why you're bothering with me. I don't have anything!" she yelled. She packed her bags and headed home to Madison.

There, while working as a census taker, she met Brian Keeling, a shy, acutely perceptive English major, and married him in 1981. He came along at a crucial time, when she was struggling with self-doubt, and his uncommon honesty and practical nature helped her recover. Within two years, when Wendy was twenty-eight, she left Madison with her husband and first son for a new life in Ithaca. She was the last of the Maraniss children to leave town. My parents hated to see her go, and soon moved away themselves.

We were a family that for four decades, since Wendy had come along, considered itself exceedingly lucky. You are lucky until you are not, and then you start to think that you never were. Death not only changes the future, it reshapes the past. After Brian got the news of her death from a disembodied voice offering condolences on the answering machine, he undertook a task requiring unimaginable courage. He called my parents in Milwaukee and told Elliott and Mary Maraniss that their youngest child was dead. Then Mom and Dad, with their own sudden weight of grief, had to pass it along to my sister Jean in Pittsburgh and my brother, Jim, in Amherst and me in Washington. No sound I have ever heard could reach the depth of emotion of my father's wail on the telephone that night. I will hear it for the rest of my life.

I had been thinking about fate and odds and random acts of physics for months before Wendy's accident. One joyous day the previous summer, I took the subway from Manhattan out to Shea Stadium with my friend Blaine Harden to watch the Mets play the Atlanta Braves. We sat in the upper deck down the left-field line, barely in foul territory, some four hundred feet from home plate. Late in the game, Andruw Jones, a young Braves slugger, cracked a ball that came soaring higher, higher, closer, closer—right at us. Blaine ducked and everybody else scattered and the ball hit me smack in the hands and bounced away. All night long, and for days and months afterward, I was obsessed by the randomness of that event. How was it possible that the baseball found its way exactly to me, so far away, in that very seat in the upper deck? I could go to the stadium every day for the rest of my life and sit in that seat and never touch another baseball.

Someone could drive up Route 96 every day for decades and never find that patch of black ice and skid into the southbound lane and hit a big Buick and die. But the ball found me and the ice found Wendy and a random act broke the hearts of everyone in the family.

The memorial service for Wendy was held at the First Unitarian Church in Ithaca. The church was full. Our family sat in the first two rows. My mother wore a locket with Wendy's picture inside. The best musicians in Ithaca, a city of music, all performed—including Wendy. The service opened with a tape of her playing a Bach partita, my brother Jim's favorite. Wendy's colleagues from the Ithaca Piano Trio, her practice partners and Cornell friends, her comrades in the vanguard of contemporary music—alone and in pairs they rose to play selections from Bach, Mozart, Shostakovich, Olivier Messiaen, and Jules Massenet. Trudy Borden, a mentor of Wendy's, played "At the Base of a Great Mountain" and "The Little Rondo," selections from *Twenty-Four Little Pieces* by Wendy Maraniss.

The music and testimonials went on for two hours, and I learned as much about Wendy as I had in the forty-two years before. As a sibling, you know your brothers and sisters instinctively, intuitively, subconsciously. You know them in ways that words cannot describe. But you cannot know their daily lives. I learned that Wendy was a beloved piano teacher who infused her students with a passion for music. I learned that she never yelled at those students (she had at least forty, ranging in age from five to thirty, when she died). If one came to her having decided to give up piano, she had nothing but sympathy, explaining that she too had stopped playing at one point but came to regret it later. I learned that she would not charge students who could not afford to pay. I learned that once a year, on New Year's Eve, she would drink too much wine and get giddy and then get sick.

I had sensed that the last few years were the happiest of her life, and now I discovered why. She had reached a point where family life and career were moving in the same direction. She had managed to be, at once, a loving mother and wife, a respected teacher, and the center of Ithaca's music community. All the musicians wanted to play with her. They said she could play anything, and get it right, and fill any room with beauty and intensity. Despite her modesty, her family had always known her genius, and now we discovered that others had come to see her in the same light. The realization was at once thrilling and painful.

All of those thoughts washed over me as I listened to the music celebrating her life and mourning her death. It made me think about the people our modern celebrity culture honors. To peer into the fetid life of a dysfunctional public figure, we buy books by the millions.

We weep and throw flowers at the memory of a distant princess. We scream in delight and tear at the clothes of immature frauds. We tune in to hear experts with bloated egos talk about how they are right and how wrong everyone else is. We pay young men millions of dollars to hit or shoot or catch a ball, watch them buy fleets of luxury cars, and listen to them whine about feeling underappreciated. And yet we all know people who are the real thing, teaching glorious music to our children, appalled by self-righteousness, searching not for status but for meaning, driving off to work on Sundays in their old cars. People like Wendy, my little sister.

3

The Sensations of Jim

My brother, Jim, stood outside the gates of Pratt Field at Amherst College one November football Saturday and waited for me to arrive with my pal Jimmy Warren. We had come up to western Massachusetts from Washington that morning ostensibly to take in the season finale against archrival Williams. The "biggest little game in America" that season had the bonus attraction of a Cajun quarterback who wore No. 4—our very own "little Favre" leading the way for the Lord Jeffs. But mostly we were there just to hang out with my big brother, who had been Warren's Spanish professor decades ago at Amherst. The game was incidental. "Daaave!" Jim said when our eyes met, sounding exactly like our father, Elliott, who had a way of greeting family and friends as though he were surprised and overjoyed every time. My brother and I adored our dad, but Jim was more overt about it; to him, everything seemed to have a family subtext. Then, when he saw who was with me, he smiled and lowered his voice to acknowledge, "Jimmmee!"

He had been stationed outside the stadium for quite a while before we got there, warmed less by the autumn sun than by the constant recognition of former students who had flocked back to campus for game-day reunions. Jim had been a tenured professor at Amherst since the early 1970s (when he was in his midtwenties), was consistently voted one of the most popular professors on campus, and had a well-known soft spot for students from Wisconsin, anyone who took his classes, and most jocks. As the unofficial gatekeeper at Pratt Field, he was in his element, although putting it that way leaves room for misinterpretation. This was not Bill Clinton working a campaign rope line as a means of self-gratification. My brother is the furthest thing from a glad-hander or striver. But the game, the setting, the students, our arrival—all combined to make him contagiously happy. Warren and I brightened at the sight of him, rocking slightly on his spindly legs, his pants riding high above his waist, his pale, bespectacled face protected by a wide-brimmed hat.

The secret about Jim is that he is too cool to care about appearances. Or, as one of his Amherst colleagues recently described him, at once joking and accurate, "He's so laid back, he's prone."

We had special seats awaiting us up in the rickety press box, but as much as Jim looked forward to watching the action from there, he seemed in no hurry to abandon his pregame position. "Life is sensations," he explained as the three of us loitered outside, chatting. "I'm just soaking in the sensations."

Warren cast a quick glance my way, and we shared an unspoken appreciation that I can't fully explain. It's not just that you never know what Jim is going to say, it's more that whatever he says will have several levels to it. In this case, it helps to know that Jim is a Calderón and Cervantes scholar who wrote his doctoral thesis on *Life Is a Dream* and is now working on a translation of *Don Quixote*. Whatever I might say about those seminal works of Spanish literature would sound embarrassingly superficial compared with Jim's deep understanding of them, but I sensed that my brother, as he luxuriated on a Saturday afternoon outside Pratt Field, was in a frame of mind to blissfully mistake a barber's basin for a knight's helmet or an innkeeper's hunchbacked daughter for a princess—or a kid named Marsh Moseley for Brett Favre. Of course, I don't mean that literally. Jim is rarely literal. I mean it in the sense that at that moment he was ready and able to experience the illusions of life with two loyal Sancho Panzas at his side.

"Life is sensations," he said. The sensation of life with Jim takes me back to another story, a few years earlier, with Jimmy Warren again bearing witness along with my wife, Linda, my sister Jean and brother-in-law Michael, and me. On the evening of January 30, 2000, 130.7 million Americans were at home watching the broadcast of Super Bowl XXXIV between the St. Louis Rams and the Tennessee Titans. But in

Cambridge, Massachusetts, we plodded through the slush and snow to join a sports-snubbing scrum of literati and music devotees, most of them gray-haired, elegant, and sophisticated, for a singular operatic performance of *Life Is a Dream*. Twenty-two years earlier, Jim had written the libretto for the work by his Amherst friend Lewis Spratlan, a professor of composition, and now it was being performed for the first time. Many in the audience arrived an hour early to hear Jim lead a discussion on Calderón and the meaning of the play on which the opera was based. I forget everything he said except one line that I'll remember the rest of my life. Someone in the audience asked a question comparing Pedro Calderón de la Barca to William Shakespeare. Without missing a beat, Jim rummaged through his massive and eclectic brain to dredge up an apt quote from that famed literary critic George "Sparky" Anderson, former manager of the Detroit Tigers and the Cincinnati Reds. "As Sparky Anderson said when asked to compare Carlton Fisk to Johnny Bench . . ."

This was not a crowd expected to know its major-league catchers, but for those few of us who followed the allusion, it was classic Jim. He can talk golden age literature and minor-league prospects for the Tampa Bay Rays; new wave French cinema and 1970s pro soccer players from the Netherlands; World War II fighter planes and linemen from the Coach Bart Starr era of Green Bay Packers football. It is typical of Jim that he would focus on Starr as the coach of mediocre teams rather than as the legendary quarterback of the glory years Packers. As for those anonymous linemen from the lost years between Lombardi and Favre, his favorite was Ezra Johnson, who was once delayed lumbering onto the field because he hadn't finished eating a hot dog—or was it bratwurst? Jim was certainly the only member of his Harvard class who, for an alumni magazine in which they were asked to provide capsule summaries of their lives after college, wrote not about himself but about Sweet Lou Whitaker, an African American Tigers second baseman who had declined to stand for the national anthem because worshipping the American flag contradicted his religious beliefs as a Jehovah's Witness. That essay, in its own poetic and indirect way, said more about Jim than any account of his advanced degrees and book translations.

James Elliott Maraniss is my only brother, four and a half years older than me, and he skipped a grade in elementary school, so he was gone to college by the time I reached seventh grade. We shared a bedroom until then, but we were not uncommonly close. He was redheaded and skinny, and his ankle and knee joints snapped, crackled, and popped loudly when he walked up the stairs. I was even skinnier and noisier, an asthmatic who wheezed all night, not only keeping him up, but drawing more attention from our mother. I was a little tattletale who squealed on him and his friends when I spotted them stealing a baseball from a variety store. One of my strongest memories as a five-year-old in Detroit is of Jim playing the role of a Nazi SS interrogator, sitting on top of me, my arms pinned to the ground by his legs, as he assumed a German accent and asked me what my name was and where I lived and slapped my face, shouting, "Oh, you lie!" after every answer. A few years later, when we were at our grandparents' farm outside Ann Arbor, he fired his BB gun at me from about forty paces. I was facing the other way, down past the peach trees. He hit me behind the right knee. I presume he was shocked by his accuracy, and more shocked by the fact that our dad happened to be looking out the picture window and saw the whole thing and came running out to punish him while I whimpered in disbelief. The BB didn't penetrate the cloth of my pants, as I remember it, but still I had a story forever. The time my brother shot me!

During Jim's college years, when he was coming home to Madison from Harvard for the summers, I was at my adolescent worst, a brain-less borderline delinquent who read little beyond the sports pages and knew nothing about the wider world. Jim got migraine headaches and listened to Sonny Terry and Brownie McGhee and read García Lorca and had an exotic Radcliffe girlfriend named Pamela and wore cool jeans and herringbone sport coats and must have thought he had a loser of a little brother. "Dave, don't be a boor," he admonished me one day in front of my friends, who mocked me, and I suppose him, by repeating that line for years.

My brother was so much smarter than me that I didn't know how to handle it. On the surface, utterly outmatched academically, I stopped trying to compete with him, and pretended that I was happy to be a dumb jock, even though I was better at playing dumb than at being a jock. But deep inside, at some point I started to feel proud and lucky that he was my brother. The taunts of our early days left no lasting trauma. I knew that he did not want to kill me with that BB gun, and that the rest of it, the slapping and the condescending, was just what big brothers tend to do at certain stages, and by age sixteen I was bigger than he was in any case. If family circumstances and my own laziness had left me trapped in a persona I didn't want, I came to realize as I approached adulthood that Jim was showing me the way out. I couldn't do it his way, by succeeding in academia, but I could draw on the traits we had in common, especially a shared sense of feeling different. He instructed me in what he thought it meant to be a Maraniss, apart from the crowd, not brazenly or predictably nonconformist but nonchalantly so, and made me feel that I could live up to the name as much as he did. For the past thirty years, that is something we talk about between ourselves, but rarely with anyone else, because even to talk about it is to do it a disservice.

A few years ago, at a wedding reception in Washington, a guest in his late twenties came up to me and said he had been one of my brother's students at Amherst. "Man, I love Jim," he said. "In fact, I always wanted to *be* Jim." This well-dressed black guy who had played intercollegiate sports at Amherst always wanted to be Jim? What was that about? I can't imagine that he wanted to have Jim's fragile body—his chronically wobbly legs and various psychosomatic ailments. And there are a lot of people who look bolder and more self-assured. But Jim, he said, seemed so easy, natural, unburdened by the normal pressures of success, so different from the other professors and the white upper-class ambiance of Amherst. "Jim, man, he was the coolest."

Actually, I had heard it many times before. Jim's former students had been coming my way for more than three decades with some variation of that pronouncement. Part of it is easy to explain. Jim didn't abide by routines. He lectured for as long as he had something to say, then stopped and dismissed class, ignoring the standard schedule. He played pool with his students, and talked football with them, or movies, or small towns in the upper Midwest, or church suppers, or Slovakian surnames. He knew something about everything. He taught what he wanted, his classes ranging from Spanish to Cervantes to the Spanish civil war to French cinema to Nazi propaganda. He was a notoriously lenient grader. He had a fantasy baseball team called the Rojos, and was always inquiring about American League prospects. He was inces-

santly curious, constantly learning something, and then never forgetting it. His big white house, overloaded with books and newspapers,
dirty dishes in the sink, kids everywhere, classical music or reggae playing, and amazing wife, Gigi, offering wisdom and a sympathetic ear to
anyone who dropped by, became a sort of off-campus student union.
Who wouldn't want to be Jim?

But part of it is more complex. He hides his vulnerabilities in plain
sight. As the oldest of four children, Jim had the most complicated
relationship with our mother, Mary, who was brilliant, beautiful, musical, gentle, frustrated, mildly depressed, and the most sensitive person
I've ever known. I don't fully understand the dynamics of their relationship, but it seems that her hypersensitivity was difficult for him
because he felt it tamped down his ability to enjoy life. I won't go any
further than that; it's something he should write about, if he wants to,
not me. In the old Smothers Brothers routine, Tommy always complained that Mom liked Dick best. In our family, partly because of my
childhood asthma, and partly because I lacked the intellectual powers
of Jim and my older sister, Jean, and had to find some other means of
parental approval, I became the child most sympathetic to our mother.
I've never been quite sure how Jim felt about that, but she is gone now
and all love is equal in memory.

The affection of our dad, a crusty old newspaper editor, was more
easily shared. On the surface, he could seem as insensitive and crude
as our mother was sensitive and refined. He smelled of raw onions and
hard salami. He rarely ate without a piece of food sticking to his chin
or mustard spotting his shirt. He once slammed a car door on his hand
and didn't feel it until someone told him his hand was caught in the
car door. But Elliott was equally positive with all his children, he saw
the best in each of us, and you always knew where you stood with him.
While Jim inherited our mother's intellect, he and I both got our love
of sports and journalism, and in some sense our life force, from our
dad. Bending the nepotism rules slightly, we both worked at his newspaper, the Madison *Capital Times,* during the summers of our college
years, though Jim did it more as a diversion and I saw it as my lone way
out. We worshipped the p.m. daily of the pre-computer age—the copy
paper and pneumatic tubes, the cigarette butts on the linoleum floor,
the smell of ink and paste, and the lineup of old-fashioned newspaper-

men. One of the many things that Jim and I share is a love of names—place-names, given names, surnames. To us, names are poetry, evoking more feeling and memory than any adjective.

Few things give Jim more pleasure than to recite the names of the old newspapermen at the *Cap Times:* Art Marshall, Irv Kreisman, Cedric Parker, Frank Custer, Harry Sage, John Sammis, Aldric Revell, John Patrick Hunter, Elliott Maraniss.

The defining story of his summers at the paper involved a tragedy at the Henry Vilas Zoo in 1966, when Winkie the elephant seized a three-year-old girl by the trunk, yanked her through the cage bars, and stomped her to death in front of her horrified parents—the sort of unspeakable story that no journalist, no matter how grizzled, could enjoy. Dad, as city editor, looked around his newsroom, saw that Jim was the only reporter available at that moment, and instructed him to go find the grieving mother for an interview.

"Dad! I can't do that!" Jim said, recoiling at the very idea.

Jim recounted this story at our father's funeral, pausing here for the desired effect, before offering the quintessential city editor's punch line:

"Then you're fired!"

Another pause.

"And don't call me Dad!"

The love with which Jim told that story is hard to overstate. When Elliott was dying in a Milwaukee hospital, Jim came out and sat by his side for days and read him chapters of *War and Peace.* He would call me up and moan into the telephone . . . "Dad! Daaad! Dad!" In many ways, Dad was our strongest bond, and still is, the touchstone for our love and our shared sense of being different. Elliott loved nothing more than to lie on the living room couch or a cot on the side porch in his shorts and T-shirt and talk about sports while listening to a ball game on the radio. It is no coincidence that many of my sweetest moments with Jim are retakes of that scene. For many years, back when I lived in Austin, we would share a hotel room in Washington every April for the annual baseball draft in our *Washington Post* (Ghost) rotisserie league. It was usually the same weekend as the Masters golf tournament, and after the draft we'd go back to the room and lie on our beds in our shorts and watch the final round and talk about our favorite players.

It was all about Dad. Sometimes my son, Andrew, would be there, passing it down another generation. It sounds stupid, perhaps, but the glow in the room was spiritual.

With Dad gone, those moments with Jim are even more special. At Andrew's wedding in Nashville last year, a weekend filled with emotion, one of my favorite moments came late one night when Jim and I and two of his sons, little Elliott and Ben, along with our friend Jimmy Warren, gathered in Jim's hotel room and talked. He sprawled on the bed in the style of our father and announced that his favorite NFL coach was Jack Del Rio of the Jacksonville Jaguars. "Jack Del Rio!" he said, and Jimmy Warren and I looked at each other with the same unspoken understanding we shared that day outside the gates of Pratt Field. Though I must say I'm still trying to figure out the connection—and I know there must be one—between Jack Del Rio and Calderón and Cervantes.

One final story about my big brother brings this full circle. On April 14, 2000, Jim hosted a conference on Spanish literature at Amherst. Attendance was paltry, and Jim's spirits were even lower as he left for home that night. He felt out of it. Over the hill. Out of the zeitgeist. No one cared about what he did. The world seemed mean, empty, superficial. If life is sensations, this was a sensation he could do without. Inside the big white house, the message light was blinking on his telephone answering machine. It was full of messages—from me, from Jimmy Warren, from our father. All ecstatic. All saying versions of the same thing: Hey, Jim! You won't believe it! The opera. You and Lew Spratlan. Performed only that one Super Bowl weekend up in Massachusetts twenty-two years after you guys wrote it. It won the Pulitzer Prize.

Life is a dream.

4

Connections

When Cathay Pacific flight 765 from Hong Kong touched down at Ho Chi Minh City on the morning of January 27, 2002, here I was, finally, decades late, the FNG—fucking new guy. This was my first visit to a country that I had only imagined, for better and worse. With my wife at my side, I looked out the window from seat 45C as the airplane rolled toward the terminal. Everything seems exotic the first time: guard towers, machine guns, uniforms of deep olive green and dark red; motorbikes racing our jet on a parallel dirt road, three-packs of teenage boys clinging to each seat; a hive of gray hangars, giant, culvertlike cement half-moons that once provided cover for U.S. helicopters; patient queues of travelers at the checkpoints inside; more soldiers, stone-cold serious, born after the war was over; a clattering, expectant sea of people waiting outside, fingers gripping the chain-link fence, heads straining for the first glimpse of arriving relatives bringing appliances and cardboard boxes full of other material wonders from the world beyond. Then into the sunlight and a surprising jolt of exhilaration in the steamy Saigon heat.

Connections are what fascinate me, the connections of history and of individual lives, the accidents, incidents, and intentions that rip people apart and sew them back together. These interest me more than ideological formulations that pretend to be certain of the meaning of it all. I came to Vietnam looking for more connections. And I brought some connections with me.

I grew up in Madison, where half the events recorded in *They Marched Into Sunlight* would take place. During the days in October 1967 when the Black Lions were fighting and dying in the jungle of the Long Nguyen Secret Zone and antiwar protesters were staging a sit-in at the Commerce Building on the University of Wisconsin campus, I was a naïve freshman at the school. I observed the protest against Dow Chemical, makers of napalm, from the edge of the crowd, and felt the sting of tear gas, and saw a few things that I mostly forgot. Three years later I received a low number in the draft lottery (114) and rode the bus to Milwaukee for an induction physical but was declared 4-F because of chronic asthma that I'd had since childhood. Campus demonstrations were still going on, and I began covering them in newspaper and radio reports. None of this was enough to warrant making myself a character in a book of history. I had no intention of including myself in any case, beyond the extent to which all authors of nonfiction or fiction are hidden characters in anything they write. But I was of Madison. I was steeped in its progressive tradition, honoring the right to dissent, and I carried that with me wherever I went, and in that sense I was making a connection as soon as I landed in Ho Chi Minh City (formerly Saigon), bringing the Wisconsin side of the story to the Vietnam side.

In the lobby of the Hotel Continental a few hours later, there stood Clark Welch, the great soldier of Delta Company, at age sixty-two his stomach filled out and his crew cut turned gray, but still with his characteristic forward lean and disarmingly sheepish smile. He was back in Vietnam for the first time since the war, and he looked exactly like what he was: American veteran and tourist, wearing a short-sleeved striped shirt and fanny pack, his keen blue eyes occasionally darting around the room, always scouting the territory. And next to him was Consuelo Allen, the oldest daughter of Lieutenant Colonel Terry Allen Jr., the battalion commander who was killed thirty-five years earlier on that bloody autumn day. People had always commented that Consuelo was the spitting image of her father, and the resemblance was now stronger than ever.

For more than three decades after the battle, Clark Welch burned with hostile feelings about Colonel Allen and the flawed leadership decisions that sent the 2/28 Black Lions battalion into the jungle on the morning of October 17, 1967, on a search-and-destroy mission that ended up destroying *them,* with sixty men killed and an equal number wounded in an ambush that the U.S. government lied about and described as a victory. Welch had questioned the decision to march into the jungle that day, suspicious of a trap, and had fought valiantly as so many of his "boys" had died. He had thought about that battle every day since, and as he rose through the ranks to captain, major, and colonel, he committed himself to the promise that no one who trained under him would get caught in a similar situation. He knew that Allen had three daughters but was wary of meeting them. He was afraid that they would not like him and that seeing them would bring him pain. But in the final few years of the twentieth century, after he had retired, he was tracked down by an old comrade, Jim Shelton, who had been Terry Allen's closest friend in Vietnam. Shelton had told him about the Allen girls and how bright and curious they were, and it started Welch on the path of wondering.

"I'm going to ask you something: Where are Terry Allen's daughters and what do they think of me?" Welch had asked me at the end of our first long interview, conducted in the lobby of a Denver hotel.

I told him the daughters were in Texas—El Paso and Austin—and that they did not know enough about Welch to think much about him at all, except that he was a soldier with their father and that he had lived and their father had died.

"I dream about them," Welch confided. "I want them to be wonderful people."

Now here they were, together, Clark Welch and Consuelo Allen, connected for this mission in Vietnam. Consuelo came with questions. Where did her father die? What did it look like? What must it have felt like? How has it changed? Welch had fewer questions; he thought he knew the answers. He anticipated that the experience would be difficult, that his mind would ricochet endlessly from present to past to present to past.

Once, long ago, on an early summer evening in 1967, after he had flown over his little section of Vietnam in a helicopter, Lieutenant Welch wrote to his wife:

This place can be beautiful! The winding rivers, the little hamlets, the neat rice paddies, and little gardens are very tranquil looking.

And the rivers are either bright blue or brown, the fields and forests
are deep green, and the shallow water on the rice looks silver from
up there. Riding in the chopper with the doors off—there's a nice
cool breeze too. Maybe we could come back here some day when it's as
peaceful and beautiful on the ground as it looks from the sky.

Nothing is that peaceful, ever, and certainly not the Democratic Republic of Vietnam, but now the war was long over and Clark Welch was back. He was eager to see the beauty of the country again; and to reflect on what happened in 1967 and how things might have gone differently, in the battle and the war; and to be there when and if I found soldiers who had fought that day for the other side, the VC First Regiment. And he and Consuelo would come with me to walk the battlefield in the Long Nguyen Secret Zone south of the Ong Thanh stream. Big Rock, as his young soldiers once called him, was ready. He had his old army pictograph map with the coordinates of the battle and a little Global Positioning System location finder that dangled from his neck like a good-luck pendant.

In the summer of 2001, my wife and I had returned to Madison for three months of research on the Wisconsin side of the book. On my first day back I walked into the offices of the *Capital Times,* my home away from home. My father, Elliott, had been an editor of the *Cap Times,* and I had begun my journalism career there covering high school football games and antiwar protests. Ron McCrea, the city editor, saw me approaching and said, "Hey, Dave, isn't that an amazing coincidence about your book?"

"What coincidence?" I asked. I had no idea what he was talking about. One of McCrea's best friends was Dave Wagner, a veteran journalist who worked at the paper in the early 1970s before moving on to editing jobs in Waukesha and Phoenix. Before that, Wagner had been part of the antiwar movement at the University of Wisconsin and a founding journalist at the alternative newspaper *Connections.* More writer and intellectual than activist, he was not one of the people inside the Commerce Building when the Dow confrontation began on October 18, 1967, but he got there in time to see the scrum with the baton-wielding Madison police on the plaza outside the building and he felt the tear gas—and afterward edited a special edition of his paper headlined "The Great Dow War."

Wagner and his wife, Grace, who had witnessed the Dow protest, watching in shock as the cops entered the building and broke up the sit-down protest with their clubs, have two adult children. Their son Ben was born a year after Dow. He came back to Wisconsin in the late 1980s to get a degree in philosophy, then returned to the Phoenix area in 1991. He found a job at the AT&T call center in Phoenix, where he sat next to a vibrant young woman named Theresa Arias. They had a constant patter going, and Ben thought Theresa was "a terrible smart-ass" contradicting him all the time. In other words, he was taken by her. They started dating and never stopped and were married on October 19, 1996. Two days before the wedding, as he did every year on October 17, Theresa's father, Michael Arias, visited a cemetery in Phoenix to pay respects and place a can of beer at the gravestone of his old Vietnam buddy Ralph Carrasco. This was the same Michael Arias who had served as a radiotelephone operator for the 2/28 Black Lions and who had taken the compass to lead his wounded band of survivors out of the jungle in the battle of Ong Thanh, the battle that took the life of Consuelo Allen's father and led Clark Welch back to Vietnam.

After visiting the grave before his daughter's wedding, Arias went to dinner at a Chinese restaurant in Scottsdale with Ben's father, Dave Wagner. The two men were meeting for the first time. Wagner had told his father about the military decorations on the wall at the Arias home—an M-16 and various pictures and awards. Theresa Arias knew a bit about the Wagner family history—white, liberal, antiwar agnostics from the North. Ben and Theresa were worried about how the meeting would go. It went fine; the war did not come up. Years later, at a family gathering, Arias and Wagner got to talking about Vietnam and found that they agreed more than they disagreed. Theresa mentioned that a writer for the *Washington Post* had recently interviewed her father about an awful ambush his battalion had marched into on October 17, 1967. Wagner said that he knew one reporter at the *Post,* David Maraniss. That's him, Michael Arias said.

The odds were infinitesimal, but there it was, a marriage connecting the worlds of war and peace in 1967, the Black Lions soldiers of Vietnam and the student demonstrators of Wisconsin. There were no great lessons to be drawn from this improbable marriage except a reminder of how people and groups are shaped and reshaped. This has less to do with the overwrought notion of healing than with the unpredictability of life and the relentless power of the human spirit.

Here we sat, across from one another at a long conference table in a quiet room inside the offices of the foreign ministry in Ho Chi Minh City: Clark Welch and I on one side, Vo Minh Triet and two interpreters on the other. Two days earlier, I had given the Vietnamese press office Triet's name, which I had seen on U.S. military documents: intelligence reports from the late 1960s and more recent reports regarding MIA searches in Vietnam. Now Clark and I were looking at Triet in the flesh, the officer who had commanded the First Regiment in 1967. I was afraid that he might not remember anything about the battle, and I wanted to learn as much as I could from him, so I asked questions that had nothing to do with October

Clark Welch and Vo Minh Triet

Linda Maraniss

17. Clark thought this was a waste of time, although he was polite enough to tolerate it.

Then, finally, after a lunch break, we pulled out our maps of the area north of Lai Khe in the Long Nguyen Secret Zone, and I started to say a few things about the Black Lions battalion and what they were doing on so-called search-and-destroy missions in the weeks leading up to the battle. Triet rose from his chair, examined the maps for a few minutes, which seemed like forever, and at last put his finger right on the coordinates of the battlefield and said something in Vietnamese, which was translated by my interpreter, Kyle Horst. The words gave me chills. "Of course I remember," Triet said. "We weren't supposed to be there. Let me tell you how it happened."

For the next two hours he talked about the battle and the days before and after: how his regiment was starving, in desperate search for rice. They had been subsisting on bamboo shoots and boiled stink grass for days, and had entered the Long Nguyen Secret Zone because they knew there was a rear service supply group for the Vietcong there, not far from the Ong Thanh stream. But when they reached Rear Service Group 83 headquarters, there was no rice there either, and they decided to wait there for the next shipment. They were supposed to make their way north and west for the start of an offensive in War Zone D. But as Triet waited, he received news that an American battalion was in the jungle, rumbling around looking for action. His reports said it was a battalion, a few hundred men. He had a regiment, more than twelve hundred soldiers. He decided to set up a three-sided ambush and lure the Americans into it.

The more Triet talked, the more it seemed that Clark Welch's comprehension of Vietnamese, which he had studied briefly before being sent to Vietnam in 1967, came back to him. The two old soldiers were talking the same language, communicating, even when they did not understand everything the other was saying. At the end of the interview I asked whether Colonel Triet would be willing to ride with us the next day to the battlefield. He said why not, he had nothing better to do. He was seventy-two years old and retired; he spent his days now as a functionary in Ho Chi Minh City's Ward 14, promoting population control.

At eight the next morning our entourage piled into a van for the bumpy ride north up Thunder Road. Triet was there, and Clark Welch, and Consuelo Allen, and her friend Rob Keefe, and Kyle Horst, my guide and interpreter. Also my wife and I, and a driver and our Vietnamese minder, Madame Ha. Before the van pulled away from the Hotel Continental, Triet turned to Welch, soldier to soldier, and said of that long-ago battle on the ground we were visiting, "No one won that day."

It was a statement with several levels of meaning, but above all, it was a grace note, a way of connecting men who had once tried to kill each other. Triet later made the same comment to Consuelo Allen.

Kyle was fluent in Vietnamese and seemed to know everyone in the country, having lived there off and on since the early 1980s, when he worked on refugee issues for the United Nations. He had been to the battle area several months earlier on a scouting mission. Clark Welch had tried to get there a few days earlier, before I arrived in Ho Chi Minh City, and had gotten close but couldn't quite find it. He had encountered a friendly family that farmed a small plot of land a few miles away. From them, using his basic Vietnamese, he had learned that they had supported America and South Vietnam and had fled to the village of Chon Thanh during the war and that after, the father had been sent to a prison reeducation camp for many years.

This time, executing a few turns at intersections that were not apparent on every map, we made it to an unmarked road closer to the battlefield. We drove down that road until it became impassable, then got out and walked. Our destination was the bamboo-and-tin house of Nguyen Van Lam, another local farmer. He had served as a company commander in Rear Service Group 83 and fought in the October 17 battle. When we arrived at Lam's, he was out. A son said he was attending a wedding, but Lam showed up shortly thereafter, the word having spread quickly about the appearance of the bearded American (Kyle) and some other strangers with big noses.

Nguyen Van Lam had ten sons, the youngest ten years old. At the entrance to his house they kept squirrels in a cage. In a muddy little enclosed pond in the side yard, they raised eels. There were several framed portraits and certificates on the walls of his living area, some honoring Lam for his war service, others honoring his wife's brother, who was considered a martyr, killed "opposing the Americans to save the country."

When Lam arrived from the wedding, Triet immediately recognized him, even though they had been together only for a few days thirty-five years earlier. "Oh, my God," Lam said. "You are still alive?"

They hugged and sat down in the shaded opening to the house, clasping hands much of the time as they talked. When Triet heard that Lam had ten children, he chastised him. "You give birth like chickens," he said, and asked whether Lam and his wife had ever heard of population control.

Are you sick at all? Triet asked.

No, Lam said. He had some hearing loss from air strikes and a cluster bomb pellet in his lung, but other than that he was fine.

Do you have AIDS? Triet asked.

Lam laughed. Triet was still ribbing him for his prodigious family.

Soon we were off, walking tentatively across a creaking bamboo monkey bridge over the Ong Thanh stream, following a narrow path through the manioc fields, passing a herd of water buffalo, and moving south toward the battlefield. Our first stop was where the Black Lions had set up their night defensive perimeter on October 16. There were still a few holes in the field, remnants of American bunkers. The open land we walked through next had been dense jungle in 1967. Clark Welch, checking his GPS, said we were right on target, but he kept repeating, "It looks so different. Everything has changed."

Lam said that after the battle, the area was heavily bombed and then defoliated until there were no trees left. Years later everyone in the area started getting headaches, he said. Not long ago a few local people in their forties and fifties had terrible headaches for three days and then died. The villagers thought it was because of Agent Orange.

As we moved closer to the battlefield, Triet and Welch seemed like they were in their own world again, the two proficient soldiers reliving the battle. They would walk off together and point and say a few things, describing the line of march of the American companies and the positioning of Triet's three battalions. At one point Nguyen Van Lam stopped and pointed to a depression in the ground and said this was where he and his men, on the morning after the battle, had found the torso of an American soldier that had been ripped apart by wild pigs. A hundred meters farther, Clark checked his GPS and his maps and said we were nearing the ground of the battle. We had to move to our right, or west, a few hundred meters, he said, so we turned and walked in that direction.

In 1967 this had been dense jungle; now it was a government rubber plantation, a grove of medium-height trees planted in neat rows. It was refreshingly cool, away from the ninety-degree heat, and sunlight dappled gently through the grove. The ground was covered with dry brown leaves that crunched softly as we walked. It felt as though we were walking into a cathedral. And then Clark pointed to a spot that matched the coordinates of where Terry Allen and the battalion command were killed.

An anthill happened to be there, just as there had been during the battle. A different anthill, obviously, but it served as a fitting memorial nonetheless. I asked our Vietnamese companions to keep quiet so we could pay our respects. Clark Welch bit his lip and winced, memories of that day cascading through his mind. Tears streamed down Consuelo Allen's face as she studied the lonely spot where her father died. The moment he was killed and this moment, as she stood on the same ground, separated by thirty-five years, now seemed as one.

A few days later, Clark Welch and I returned to talk to Nguyen Van Lam. There had been too much going on that first day walking the battlefield for me to interview him in depth, but on the return visit we sat down and talked at leisure. When the interview was done, Lam introduced us to his family—all of the boys, his wife, a daughter-in-law, and a grandchild. His seventh son was maimed, one hand cut off at the wrist. He had been weeding around the family rubber trees in their garden across the road, and an old grenade from an American M-79 came out of the ground and exploded, shattering his right hand. There was still a lot of ammo around, Lam said. He pointed to a pile near the squirrel cage. "My, my, my," Clark said, looking at a collection of bullets and pieces of shrapnel hidden under a banana tree. Lam reached down and picked up some shrapnel. "You left these behind," he said.

5

September 11, 2001

A few minutes before eight, Tuesday morning. The day had broken clean and clear and sweet on the East Coast. Summer was over mentally, if not officially. It was time to get to work, and people were up and at it. The saddest and most relentlessly horrific day in modern American existence started in the most ordinary of ways.

American Airlines flight 11 had backed away from gate 26 of terminal B at Boston's Logan International Airport and was rolling toward the runway for a six-hour flight to Los Angeles. Edmund Glazer, in seat 4A, first class, heard the flight attendant instruct passengers to put away their cell phones and computers, but could not resist punching in his wife Candy's number anyway. He had left her in the darkness of their Wellesley home and driven away in their black SUV. He was a top financial guy for a high-tech firm, and though business was rough, life seemed good. He had lost forty pounds. He and Candy were feeling close. He was on board. "Hi, hon, I made it," he said.

A few minutes later, Steve Miller was getting off the subway at the Fulton Street exit in Lower Manhattan. The digital clock on the side of the Century 21 building read 8:09. He stopped at a deli for an iced coffee and a scone and moved on, passing a farmers' market. He made a note to himself: Get back here later to buy veggies for dinner. Then into Two World Trade Center at the Liberty Street entrance and up the elevator to the seventy-eighth floor, out again, across the lobby to another elevator, and off at the eightieth, and over to his desk for Mizuho Bank, where he was a computer systems operator. He was a married man of thirty-nine, thinking of starting a family, but not surrendering to middle age. On his two large computer monitors he had taped a photo of Britney Spears and an old tabloid headline: "Die You Vile Scum."

A red bag was taped over his seat, a survival pack that had been distributed to each of Mizuho's employees after the World Trade Center bombing in 1993. Inside: flashlight, glow stick, and a hood you can slip over your head to help you breathe. Miller sat down and took off his shoes, a new pair of brown leathers that he was still breaking in. He looked out at the glorious view east toward the heart of the financial district and the East River and the Brooklyn Bridge. The office's telephone systems manager came by, a spirited young woman named Hope Romano. "Hi, Hope," he said.

Across the skyscraper chasm, up on the 106th floor of One World Trade Center, the northern of the Twin Towers, Adam White was already at work. He liked to be in place by 7:30 after making the hour-long subway haul from his industrial loft in east Brooklyn. He was one of the eager kids at the huge bond brokerage firm Cantor Fitzgerald. Blue-eyed and upbeat, only twenty-five and a few years out of the University of Colorado, where he climbed mountains and acted and took environmental studies. He was using that interest in his job, traveling around the world for a program that helped power plants broker and trade emission credits. He had told his mother in suburban Baltimore that he would be in the office all week before leaving Friday for business in Rio.

The prosaic poetry of what passes for workaday life, all around, even in places and among people accustomed to danger. Sheila Moody had reported for her first day on the job as an accountant at the Pentagon, off the Metro and inside her office—first floor, E Ring, corridor 4, room 472—before sunrise so that she could fill out reams of administrative paperwork. Matt Rosenberg was down in corridor 8, a medic at the health clinic in the massive military headquarters, grateful for an uninterrupted hour in which he could study a new medical emergency disaster plan based on the unlikely scenario of an airplane crashing into the place. At Dulles International Airport, Captain Charles Burlingame, who had been a navy F-4 pilot and once worked on antiterrorism strategies at the Pentagon, was steering his 757, American Airlines flight 77, down the runway for the long flight to Los Angeles. Plenty of empty seats in his cabin, like several other cross-country trips at that hour.

Real people, not characters in a movie, yet all of them soon to be caught up in surreal scenes of dread and death and horror organized by perpetrators who seemed to understand perfectly the symbols and theatrics of American culture. People surviving or dying in ways at once shudderingly alien and hauntingly familiar, if only on celluloid. People rendered speechless by what they witnessed. People making selfless choices, some leading to death. People allowed only the choice of how to die, reduced to a hand or a limbless corpse on the street. People in their own isolated hells yet somehow connected to one another and to the entire world by spectacular technology that could spread their voices and their images and do everything but save the doomed among them.

"American, this is Boston Center. How do you read?"

The flight carrying Edmund Glazer to Los Angeles was about twenty minutes out of Logan when the call of concern came from air-traffic control. They had given the go-ahead for the flight to climb to thirty-one thousand feet, but nothing happened, no word from Captain John Ogonowski or his copilot, Tom McGuinness. Nothing from the transponder, a device that sends an airplane's airline identification, flight number, speed, and altitude to the radar screens. Somewhere above Albany, the plane veered off its flight path, heading south down the Hudson River, the water gleaming in the morning sun.

What happened next is to a large degree unknowable. Anyone who saw any of it is dead. But a few voices apparently made their way to the outside world first. Betty Ong, a flight attendant, was able to call her supervisor in Boston and report that the plane had been hijacked. There were five hijackers, she said, and one person aboard the plane had been stabbed. Then, intermittently, traffic controllers were able to pick up snatches of conversation from AA-11's cockpit. A push-to-talk button that allows pilots to communicate with air-traffic control while their hands are on the controls was going on and off. Among the alarming snippets of conversation heard: "We have more planes. We have other planes."

Then nothing again, as the jetliner buzzed toward Lower Manhattan. Rob Marchesano, a construction foreman, was working at a site at La Guardia Place and West Third Street. He heard a roar overhead, and saw a plane flying by, low and fast and at an angle that at first made him fear that it would hit his crane. He and his coworkers watched in astonishment and then horror as the plane approached the North Tower of the World Trade Center. He noticed that the plane seemed to tilt at the last second, as though someone wanted the wings to take out as many floors as possible.

At 8:47 a.m., Steve Miller was leaning back in his chair, trying to figure out ways to avoid the drudgery of work. He could hear traders across the floor talking loudly into their phones. Disembodied voices from the Chicago Mercantile Exchange were coming over the loudspeakers. A television was turned to MSNBC. Then came a sound. High-pitched. Whoosh! He walked to the window and saw an enormous swirl of paper and dust. It looked to him like a ticker-tape parade, except that made no sense.

A man burst onto the floor and shouted, "Get out! Get out!" Something had struck the other tower. Miller didn't know what to think. He sat down and put on his shoes, then followed his colleagues out.

"Everyone get out!" a woman shouted in the hallway, arms flailing. They filed down the stairs, three across, without speaking, the only sounds at first their breathing and the shuffle of shoes hitting cement steps. After a few floors, the pace slowed and more people joined the descent.

"What's going on?" a man asked.

"I don't know," said another.

"Shut up!" said a third.

There was a faint sour odor. Miller concentrated on getting down the stairs and keeping his breathing steady. He thought of his wife, Rhonda, back in Brooklyn. Call her, he thought. The floors were passing slowly. Seventy-seven . . . seventy-five . . . seventy-two . . .

"Move it!" someone shouted.

"C'mon!"

"Shut up!"

Sixty-seven . . . fifty-nine . . . fifty-five . . . fifty-three.

Everyone stopped. Miller was not sure why. He was tired, and saw an open door. He stepped out of the hallway into a trading office and heard a voice over the building's loudspeaker: "There's a fire in Tower One. Tower Two is unaffected. If you want to leave, you can leave. If you want to return to your office, it's okay."

Miller walked to the elevator bank, where he found a group of people, including his friend and colleague Hope Romano.

"This is so scary," he said, hugging her.

"Yeah, it really is," she said.

The elevator door opened, going up, and they got on with the crowd, ten or fifteen people. Miller felt uneasy about it; what if the elevator broke down and they were all stuck? He slipped out, and looked back at his friend. "Hope, I don't think you should go up," he said. The door closed before she could answer.

He walked into an office to find a telephone and saw a cluster of people over by the window, looking out. "Oh, my God!" one shouted. "They're jumping. People are jumping!"

Inside the North Tower, there was the same stairwell exodus, though the intensity was perhaps tenfold, even among those who were as yet unaware of exactly what had happened. Bomb? Earthquake? Their building was on fire, and shaking. Fire marshals were on the stairwells, urging people to walk on the right and keep moving. People were fainting, collapsing, being passed along overhead so they wouldn't slow the escape too much. Down in the lobby of the Marriott hotel that straddled the towers stood Ron Clifford, a businessman from New Jersey, the appointment that was to take him upstairs suddenly rendered irrelevant. In the haze he saw a woman coming toward him with hideous burns all over her body. He found some water to put on her wounds and tried to comfort her, not leaving her side.

High above, on those floors in the nineties and hundreds, including the floors of young Adam White's firm, Cantor Fitzgerald, there were no stairwells to reach, no ways out, except the windows and freefalling down a thousand feet. Some were in the inferno itself, others were just above it, the walls and floors crumbled, the heat rising. They had time to contemplate their fate, to call their wives and mothers and best friends, but then what? From the window of his condominium on North Moore Street in TriBeCa, author Chip Brown had a clear sight line to the top of the building. He saw the profile of the plane's wing and orange flames burning along entire floors above and below. Each window, to him, looked like the window into a kiln.

Scott Pasquini was standing in the doorway of his apartment building along the West Side Highway, three blocks away. He thought the noise he heard a few minutes earlier was a car bomb. The doorman turned ghastly pale. Was it a meat truck? He pointed to a big slab out on the street. There, in the middle of the northbound lane, was a twisted torso, without limbs. Pasquini was not the overly squeamish sort; he had wrestled for four years at Princeton before coming to New York to start life in a brokerage firm in building 4 of the trade center. He walked to the corner and saw two young women crying, pointing to something on the sidewalk outside the Marriott. It was part of a human hand. A man from the hotel took his jacket off and threw it over the horrific sight.

"Hi, Jules," Brian Sweeney was saying into his cell phone. "It's Brian. We've been hijacked, and it doesn't look too good." His wife, Julie, was not at their home in Barnstable, Massachusetts, so he was talking into the answering machine. His voice sounded calm, but his message was fatalistic for a big guy, six-foot-two and 225 pounds, who had flown F-14s for the navy. "Hopefully, I'll talk to you again, but if not, have a good life. I know I'll see you again someday." The time was 8:58 a.m. Sweeney was aboard United flight 175, which had left Boston for Los Angeles and crossed over Massachusetts and the northwest tip of Connecticut and lower New York State into New Jersey before the five terrorists took it on a different path, pounding toward Manhattan at low altitude.

Cell phones again conveyed the dreadful situation and the sense of impending doom aboard the 767. If anything could have been prevented, pilots Vic Saracini and Michael Horrocks and passengers such as Sweeney and two tough professional hockey scouts, Ace Bailey and Mark Bavis, would have been the ones to do it. Saracini was another former navy pilot, and Horrocks had been a star quarterback at West Chester University before learning how to fly in the marines. He never got rattled when the big linemen came at him. But by the time of Sweeney's call, it was too late.

At the air-traffic control center in Garden City, Long Island, which tracks and manages traffic flow in high-level airspace over the New York area, controllers had caught sight on radar of this aircraft as it made its descent. Its identification was still unknown to them. At this point, they were still searching for American flight 11. They knew it had been hijacked but were unaware that it was the first plane to hit the towers. Now as this other craft lowered toward the city, they wondered whether it was another hijacked plane or a troubled aircraft rushing for a runway at either Newark or La Guardia. Then, in the dark and windowless control room lit only by a bank of radar screens, one controller stood up in horror.

"No!" he shouted. "He's not going to land. He's going in!"

"Oh, my God! He's headed for the city," another controller shouted. "Oh, my God! He's headed for Manhattan!"

Every eye in the room was now trained on one radar screen, a roomful of professional controllers frozen by the electronic rendering of a hideous sight they could not control. A single controller counted down the hits of the radar as it turned. "Two more hits . . . one more hit . . . That's the last. He's in." It meant gone.

And here came flight 175 searing its image forever into the consciousness of the millions who by now were watching the tragedy unfold on television—here it came into view in the last second of its approach to the South Tower of the World Trade Center. On television it seemed small, artificial, like one of those re-creations of a bullet entering a body or going through jelly. Then the fireball. It was 9:05 a.m. One of the passengers who died in that instant was a woman named Ruth McCourt, the sister of Ron Clifford, the New Jersey businessman who was nursing the badly burned woman in the lobby of the hotel below. Soothing a stranger and losing a sister in the same horrible interconnected mangled moment.

Scott Pasquini had by now walked down toward Battery Park, along the river, and was standing in a crowd of people looking up at the North Tower when he heard a sound overhead and watched the second plane hit the other tower. Everyone started to run. He headed toward the river, then gathered his wits and started looking for a pay phone. As he waited in line, looking up, he saw the twin horrors, the monstrous billowing of orange flame from the South Tower and people jumping from the top floors of the North. He saw a man who seemed to have created a makeshift parachute; it slowed him down for about ten stories, then fell apart and he accelerated and was lost.

Melvyn Blum, a wealthy executive whose real estate company had tried to buy the Trade Center leases the previous year, was watching through a telescope from his forty-fourth-floor office on Seventh Avenue a few miles away. He saw people waving towels and hanging out the windows of the upper floors and jumping. Chip Brown was now on the roof of his TriBeCa condominium, his binoculars trained on the same sight. He too saw a man waving a white flag, and then chairs and debris falling and then people. "A man in khakis and an open blue suit jacket, feet up in the air, falling down the side of the building facing the river . . . three, four, five seconds, gone . . . then more out the front, where they fell against the backdrop of windows, almost in sequence, like paratroopers bustling out of an aircraft." He stopped counting after a dozen, but there were so many more.

The collision in the South Tower knocked Steve Miller off his feet. Everyone was racing for the stairs again. He stepped into the hallway, saw the logjam, and went back to a bathroom, then found another stairwell. There were no outward signs of panic. A woman in her fifties stopped in front of him. "Are you okay?" he asked. She nodded and moved on. They reached a landing where a maintenance man said he wanted to go up to help people. "Don't go," someone yelled. "It's not your responsibility."

They had yet to reach the fortieth floor. Miller was sweating, feeling dizzy, but kept going . . . thirty-five . . . thirty . . . twenty . . . seventeen . . . ten and the lobby, where there was another crowd waiting to take two escalators down to a concourse. Through a picture window he could see the huge modernist sculpture in the plaza, normally a gleaming silver, now shrouded in dust and debris. Finally, he was down and out the double doors on Church Street and into daylight and fresh air, and he was so happy he wanted to hug the sky. There were firefighters everywhere, and barricades, and he joined the throng moving east and looked up at the building and saw a big hole on the side of his tower, very close to his office. How did it get there? he wondered.

Rita Ryack, a costume designer and cartoonist, was then leaving her apartment in south Brooklyn to move her car and looked up to see what she thought was glitter fluttering from the sky onto Clinton Street at Second Place. No, not glitter, but papers, by the hundreds, all blown by the wind from the towers across the river, singed but still readable. She started gathering them out of curiosity. *A rental car claim adjustment from Broken Arrow, Oklahoma. A financial statement from Osprey*

Partners. A statement noting that the gross short futures and interim haircut was a negative number. A reference guide for SNA dial equipment. Two pages from a novel about paratroopers in southern France in World War II. A printout of the daily run of trades for Lehman Brothers customers. Expenses for Carr Futures. A fax from South America. And coded pages of sales comparisons for Cantor Fitzgerald, which had found their way over from the 106th floor, where Adam White worked.

The modern world might seem all digital and electronic, millions of facts stored in a thumbnail, but business still runs with paper everywhere, recording everything, and here it was on Ryack's street. She thought of it as a hideous art form—"the banality of evil."

Two planes gone, targets hit. Two more in the air, taken over by terrorists. American flight 77 had more than an hour earlier pulled out of gate D26 at Dulles and was reaching its normal cruising altitude at thirty-five thousand feet when it became apparent that hijackers were turning the plane around. By 9:25 a.m., one of the passengers, Barbara K. Olson, a television commentator, was on her cell phone with her husband, U.S. Solicitor General Theodore B. Olson. Can you believe this? We're being hijacked, she said. The call was cut off, but she reached him again. He told her about the other hijackings and how the planes had been flown into the World Trade Center. She said the passengers had been herded into the back of the plane by hijackers armed with knives. How could they stop something similar from happening? Captain Burlingame and the first officer, David Charlebois, might have been back there, overpowered by five terrorists, for Olson's last words to her husband were to this effect: "What do I tell the pilot to do?"

Soon controllers at Dulles spotted an unidentified aircraft heading east-southeast toward restricted airspace over the White House. It was flying low and hard, perhaps more than five hundred miles an hour, plowing near Arlington Cemetery, where Burlingame's parents were buried, and on toward the U.S. Capitol and then banking in a circle and coming around again toward the Pentagon from the west.

About 9:40, Alan Wallace had finished fixing the foam metering valve on the back of his fire truck, parked in the Pentagon fire station, and walked to the front of the station. He looked up and saw a jetliner coming straight at him. It was about twenty-five yards off the ground, no landing wheels visible, a few hundred yards away and closing fast.

"Runnnn!" he yelled to a pal. There was no time to look back, barely time to scramble. He made it about thirty feet, heard a terrible roar, felt the heat, and dove underneath a van, skinning his stomach as he slid along the blacktop, sailing under it as though he were riding a luge. The van protected him against burning metal that was flying around. A few seconds later he was sliding back to check on his friend and then race back to the fire truck. He jumped in, grabbed the radio headset, and called the main station at Fort Myer to report the unimaginable.

The sun hung low in the sky, obscured by the Pentagon and the enormous billowing clouds of acrid smoke, making it hauntingly dark. The ground was on fire. Trees were on fire. Hot slices of aluminum were everywhere. Wallace could hear voices crying for help and moved toward them. People were coming out a window headfirst, landing on him. He had faced incoming fire before—he was with the hospital corps in Vietnam when mortars and rocket shells dropped on the operating room in Da Nang—but he had never witnessed anything of this devastating intensity.

Sheila Moody, in room 472, heard a whoosh and a whistle and she wondered where all this air was coming from. Then a blast of fire that left as fast as it came. She looked down and saw her hands aflame, so she shook them. She saw some light from a window but could not reach it and could not find anything to break the window with in any case. Then she heard a voice. "Hello!" a man called out. "I can't see you."

"Hello," she called back, and clapped her hands. She heard him approach and sensed the shoosh of a fire extinguisher and then saw him through a cloud of smoke, the rescuer who would bring her out and ease her fear that she would never get to see her grandchildren.

Into the soothing calm of the Pentagon's health clinic, with its lavender carpets and travel posters, rushed a man screaming, "Evacuate now! Evacuate now!" This was not part of the disaster drill plan Matt Rosenberg had studied earlier that morning. He stopped a biopsy on a patient in Minor Surgery Treatment Room 2 and started evacuating patients. A naval officer ran in and said they had a patient in the courtyard where some people, confused and scared, had rushed to escape the collapsing inferno inside corridor 5. Rosenberg, twenty-six, armed only with a penlight, trauma scissors, and a stethoscope attached to his belt, dashed down a hallway across four inner rings, pushing through hundreds of people escaping in the opposite direction. "Get out of my way!" he screamed, until finally he reached the center courtyard, where he saw smoke billowing and people staggering out from the area that had been hit on the opposite side. He grabbed his radio and called back to the clinic. "You need to initiate MASCAL [the disaster plan] right now! We have mass casualties! I need medical assets to the courtyard!"

Carl Mahnken and his colleague in the army public relations office, David Theall, had been in a first-floor studio only a few dozen feet from where the plane hit. A computer monitor had blown back and hit Theall in the head, but he was conscious and led the way out for his buddy. They were walking over electrical wires, ceiling panels. They could see no more than five feet in any direction. After the initial whoosh and blast, it had seemed eerily silent until they reached the D Ring hallway, where they heard other people crying, moaning, talking. They coaxed some stunned colleagues to follow them. One woman was frantic about her daughter, who was at a child-care center on the other side of the building. They persuaded her to come along. As they struggled down the hallway, Theall called out for people until they made their way outside.

The enormity of the tragedy was answered by the simplest of gestures. There was the woman with a head injury carried out of the gashed building by two men, a third man carrying her infant child behind them. The colonels and lieutenant colonels and captains dropping hats, ties, and ranks and becoming Jim, Cynthia, Joe, and Frank as they formed four-person litters to rescue the wounded, litters that would not be used that day. The American flag waving in the burning third-floor office next to the gaping hole where the jet crashed. The cheers that went up when a firefighter was taken from a window, placed on a gurney, and rolled away. The three-star army general thanking the volunteers. The tall, thin chaplain saying prayers. People who managed to get a cell phone working amid the jammed circuits offering to pass messages on to husbands and wives.

Over in his office at 1D-525 on the first floor of D Ring, Robert Snyder, an army lieutenant colonel, had been surfing the Web to check on the World Trade Center horror. He heard a crack and a boom and then, instantly, he saw flames and felt engulfed. The lights went out and his digital watch stopped. It read 00:00:00. He hit the floor, having been taught in military training that staying low was the best way to avoid smoke. The only light came from a series of small fires burning around the room. He bumped into someone, a civilian secretary, and together they moved ahead until they saw some light and heard voices and made their way through a mangled doorway to corridor 5 and toward safety.

His wife, Margaret, at that moment was caught in her own personal hell. She was an elementary school teacher in Springfield, Virginia, where coworkers had told her about the explosions at the World Trade Center, and she was frantically trying to phone a brother-in-law who worked on the eighty-second floor of one of the towers and her brother who worked across the street. She dialed and dialed but could not get through. A teacher came in and asked, "Where does your husband work?"

"Not my husband," she responded. "My brother and brother-in-law."

"No," came the answer. "Where does your *husband* work?"

Scott Pasquini was still down near Battery Park, looking up, when the next unthinkable thing happened. At 9:51 a.m., the South Tower collapsed and fell, floor upon floor, down a thousand feet, shooting out another hideous billow, this one of soot and dust and ash, crushing and burying all the firefighters and rescue workers and fearless souls who had charged up stairwells on missions of hope.

Pasquini and the crowd around him were momentarily paralyzed by the awesome sight, but then as the massive cloud of debris seemed to be falling toward them, they ran toward the Hudson. Some jumped onto a police boat. Pasquini moved toward another building, a harbor restaurant with a large glass wall facing the water. His face was pressed against the glass when the debris reached ground level, thickening the air with ash. He took off his shirt and wrapped it around his face and head and started banging on the window with two other men, trying to figure out a way inside the restaurant. Now he could barely breathe and could not see. His eyes felt as if they were on fire.

On the other side of the glass, he saw a hand pointing to the left, and he and the others moved that way toward a door. He had made it inside. Tablecloths were being ripped off tables and glasses of water passed around. He took a pitcher and tried to help people flooding in.

One man had a bloody leg; he said he had jumped through a window. They washed the blood and tied a tablecloth around the leg.

Steve Miller, free from the South Tower, had been moving in another direction, in a parade of survivors walking east, toward the Brooklyn Bridge. He worried about whether that was the safest way home. Could the bridge be another target? But he could not think of a better alternative, so he kept going. The sidewalk was packed, everyone speed walking, but not panicking, when the sound washed over them, another tremendous roar. Miller turned around and saw his office building, Two World Trade Center, coming down in an avalanche, and then the outrageous cloud of smoke and ash and confusion.

"Oh, my God!" he said. His office was falling out of the sky. His mind went immediately to his office friend, the telephone systems manager, delightful Hope Romano, who went up when that elevator door closed. She must be dead, he thought.

People were now bumping against his back. He feared a stampede. A woman put her hand over her mouth and bent over at the waist. Then everyone turned and headed toward Brooklyn again, walking even faster. Miller found himself in lockstep with another man.

"I worked in that building," he said.

"I'm sorry," the man said. "I saw the plane hit it."

A plane? Until that moment, Miller had not known what exactly had caused the calamity.

There was one plane of terror still in the sky then, one more commercial jetliner turned into a giant missile loaded with transcontinental fuel and only forty-five passengers and another band of methodical and suicidal hijackers, four of them. This was United Airlines flight 93 to San Francisco, which had backed out from terminal A, gate 17, at Newark International Airport at 8:01 a.m. but was apparently stuck in runway traffic for forty minutes before getting airborne. The plane had followed the designated path west across Pennsylvania and into Ohio toward Cleveland, according to radar, but then started doubling back south and east, taking a series of sharp turns.

Here again, the plane was at once a lonesome vessel, the people aboard facing their singular fate, and yet somehow already attached to the larger drama, connected again by cell phones. People on the plane learned about what had happened in New York and sent word back the other way about what was happening to them.

Thomas E. Burnett Jr., a California businessman, called his wife, Deena, four times. In the first call, he described the hijackers and said they had stabbed a passenger and that his wife should contact authorities. In the second call, he said the passenger had died and that he and some others on board were going to do something about it. She pleaded with him to remain unobtrusive, but he said no way. Mark Bingham, in the rear of the first-class cabin, called his mother near San Francisco and said the plane had been taken over by three terrorists. Bingham was a rugby player, calm and fearless enough to run with the bulls in Pamplona. He sounded calm but scared, as though he knew how this might end.

Jeremy Glick called his wife, Lyzbeth, in Hewitt, New Jersey, with details of the hijackers: Middle Eastern, wearing red bandannas, with knives and a box they said was a bomb. He said some of the bigger men were talking about taking on the hijackers. They would try to storm the cockpit and take on their captors. As Glick talked, Lyzbeth could not stand the anxiety, and passed the phone on to her father. A final call came into the Westmoreland County 911 Center in Pennsylvania from a man who was locked in the lavatory. We're being hijacked, he said. This is not a hoax. The recorded time was 9:58 a.m.

Ten minutes later, in the hamlet of Shanksville, Pennsylvania, Rick King sat in his gray clapboard house watching the disaster coverage on television and talking with his sister, Jody Walsh, on the telephone. "Rick," said Jody. "I hear a big plane . . . I think it's going to crash!" The words seemed implausible to King, the assistant chief of the volunteer fire department. What did Shanksville have to do with any of this? But he dashed to the porch to get a look for himself, and now his sister was more insistent. The plane was nose-diving, falling like a stone. "Oh, my God, Rick . . . it's going to crash!" King heard a shattering boom in his right ear, over the phone, and in his left ear, he heard the rumblings from four miles distant, where United 93 fell.

There were no people around, no symbols; this was not a monument to American capitalism or military might, this could not have been where the plane was supposed to go down—in Shanksville, population 250, in the cornfields eighty miles from Pittsburgh. The destination was thought to be Washington, perhaps the White House, or the

U.S. Capitol—something that would shake the nation again. The passenger revolt must have succeeded for a reason, or more likely a string of reasons, that will never be fully known—the heroism of pilots and other people aboard, the awareness they had of what had happened to the other planes, perhaps some hidden makeshift weapon, perhaps the relative vulnerability of this band of hijackers.

Rick King, in his shorts and T-shirt, hung up the phone and ran to Ida's Country Store, the convenience store and deli he owns with his wife. Moments later he had the Shanksville emergency siren wailing. He suited up in firefighting gear with three other men, jumped into Big Mo, the nickname of their 1992 truck carrying a thousand gallons of water, and screamed up Lambertsville Road. "This is going to be something we haven't seen before," he told his men. "Just prepare yourself." Big Mo turned off Lambertsville onto a gravel road leading to a defunct strip mine that was now a large field of gold grass surrounded by woods. It was 10:20 a.m. King braced himself again for awful carnage. But what he saw left him feeling strangely calm and vacant:

Obliteration to the point of almost nothing. A few scattered fires. Some debris hanging from trees. Small chunks of yellow honeycomb insulation. No pieces of fuselage. No bodies, one piece of charred flesh no larger than a piece of bread. Over in the woods, fifty yards away, he could see some shirts, pants, loose papers. Farther in the distance, out of sight, some farm lawns were scattered with mail.

By 10:25 a.m., Melissa Turnage had left her teaching job at St. Paul's School and was home in Cockeysville, Maryland, watching television with her husband, an Episcopal priest, along with other friends and family. She had not heard from her son, Adam White, the young mountain climber and Cantor Fitzgerald broker. Much of the television coverage had been so calm and distant that even with such an intense focus, it was not completely clear how awful it was, or had been, for people trapped on those tower-top floors.

Melissa had visited Adam at his office there, and had never felt comfortable with him working in that place—so high up, surrounded by glass. The thought had unavoidably crossed her mind: How in the world would you get out of there? She had mentioned that fear to him, and Adam, so full of energy and goodwill, had put his arm around her shoulder and laughed and said, "It's okay, Mom."

She was watching television at 10:28 when the North Tower collapsed, the steel giving way in thousand-degree heat, her son's office and all the others folding down one upon the next, and then, again, the giant evil cloud of ash. She wanted to believe that he had somehow already made it out.

Looking out from her seventh-story SoHo loft, artist Sigrid Burton had a clear view twenty blocks down West Broadway. The World Trade Center used to be *the* view. Now it looked as though the second building had just melted, like a sand castle under a wave, but there was no wave, and then there was a hole, and the smoke blew away on the eastward wind, and she saw blue sky where the tower had been and she could not believe it. She was on the phone with her brother and told him, "The building isn't there. It just isn't there." More firefighters and rescue workers entombed in the debris. But from her distance, it appeared to Burton almost normal again, though her sensory perceptions were heightened and colors seemed brighter and clearer, which only made it stranger.

Scott Pasquini was still in the harborside restaurant when the second tower collapsed. Some firefighters tromped in and instructed people to make their way down the river to a ferry that could take them to New Jersey. When the dust settled, police led the troop of ash-covered evacuees out of the eerie darkness on the trek to the tip of the island. They boarded a police tugboat, full to the brim. Pasquini found a seat near the back, and the boat shoved off, away from Manhattan. Looked like an illegal immigration scene, he would later reflect, so many piled on the boat it could hardly float. He stared back toward the Financial District in utter disbelief.

"I need a plastic surgeon! I need a plastic surgeon!" a young woman kept screaming as she was loaded off the ambulance into St. Vincent's Hospital. Craig Tenenbaum, an emergency room doctor, quickly assessed her needs as more serious than that. He could tell she was a businesswoman, and she had burns over 70 percent of her body. What little remained of her charred clothing had to be cut off. He tried to reassure her. "It's okay," he said. "You made it. You got out. You're going to be all right." But he was not so sure. The burns were horrific.

He intubated her to help her breathe, and to silence her: Screaming, even just talking, could cause her airway to swell shut.

From 10:30 to noon the ambulances kept coming in a frantic parade. Under normal circumstances, dispatchers would alert the emergency room en route so the waiting medical teams would know what kind of trauma was coming, but there was no time for that. Doctors and nurses waited anxiously in the ambulance bay, not knowing what to expect. Burns, heart attacks. A firefighter came in on a stretcher, an older man, wearing the uniform of a unit from Jersey City, across the river. He was in cardiac arrest from the smoke and debris he had inhaled. No active heart rate or electrical activity, which meant that every minute down decreased his survival odds by another 10 percent. Precious time had been lost at the disaster scene and on the ambulance ride. Tenenbaum didn't think he had much of a chance. The ER team decompressed the firefighter's lungs and abdomen. *Breathe! Breathe! Breathe!* Tenenbaum jammed a needleful of atropine into his heart. They put him on a ventilator. Then a heartbeat, a pulse, life's wonder, it seemed.

In the struggle for life, though, age makes a difference as well as will. The young female burn victim survived. The old firefighter died. It turned out that he was not even supposed to be there. He was sixty-four, retired, had a bad heart, his family did not even know that he had put on his uniform again and gone out with his old crew. He died on the day that firefighters died, hundreds of them.

By the time Steve Miller reached Brooklyn, whitish flakes were falling from the sky. Not papers like the ones Rita Ryack scooped up on Clinton Street, but ash concentrate from the blast. His hair and clothes were soon covered. The image of his office building collapsing kept playing like a film loop in his mind. He passed a construction crew of guys all wearing masks and asked whether they had an extra. Nope. He passed Atlantic Avenue, by his dentist's office, and then down another dozen blocks or so until he reached home. Now what? His street was roped off. Bomb scare, an officer told him. He kept walking until he saw a buddy running east along Union, away from the roped-off area.

"Will!" Miller shouted. "Will!"

Will stopped, turned around.

"Where's Rhonda?" Miller asked.

Around the corner. He ran ahead and saw her running toward him. They hugged and kissed.

"Oh, my God, you're alive," she said. "I thought you were dead!"

"I'm alive. Here I am. I love you." Now she was crying and hugging him and kissing him all over his face.

A few hours later, he was back home and talking to his boss, Wayne Schletter. Was everyone at the office okay? It seemed so. And Hope? Did Hope get out? That haunting sight of the elevator closing, going up.

Yes, his boss told him. Hope was alive.

Melissa Turnage would wait and wait but get no such news about her ebullient young son, Adam White. A phone call at mid-afternoon gave her a glimmer of hope that some Cantor Fitzgerald people had made it down, but there was nothing after that, and slowly the resignation of unspeakable loss set in. She imagined how he might have reacted in those minutes of terror. He was resourceful and dexterous, and she saw him in her mind's eye doing everything possible for the people around him. She grieved, not as a war victim seeking vengeance but as a mother in search of some deeper human understanding.

Carl Mahnken and David Theall, after escaping from the Pentagon inferno, worked all day helping other victims, loading burned women onto helicopters, helping nurses put in IVs, until finally they were told that they had gone through enough and should leave. But leave what and for what? They started walking, first to a Crystal City hotel, and then kept going, mile after mile until they reached Theall's house in Alexandria, and once they were there, they did not want to leave each other. Theall said to Mahnken, "Buddy, I ain't going to let you go. We have survived this. This force that drove us through walls."

The awareness and acceptance of life-changing news often comes in stages. As Candy Glazer watched the news reports all morning, it only gradually entered her consciousness that a plane had come from Boston, that it was American Airlines, that it may have been—and then, it was—the flight her husband of eleven years had called her from at eight o'clock with those simple, reassuring words, "Hi, hon, I made it." When reality hit, she screamed. She became hysterical, overcome for two hours until an airline employee called with the official word. The Glazers were new to their neighborhood, but neighbors came over quickly and stayed with her and put up yellow ribbons. She was exhausted, but kept watching television until well after two in the morning, finding it somehow therapeutic to see the pictures from New York, where her husband actually was. She dozed off for a time and awoke feeling lonely to her soul, and then her four-year-old son, Nathan, came bounding into the room and jumped on his father's side of the bed. She hadn't told him anything yet.

"Honey," she said, pierced with pain she had never imagined possible. "Daddy's been in an accident."

Nathan looked at her. "What do you mean?"

"Daddy's dead."

The boy started sobbing. "Can't we fix him?" he asked.

(With help from Paul Schwartzman, Marc Kaufman, Ellen Nakashima, Susan Okie, Tamara Jones, Michael D. Shear, Steve Vogel, David Snyder, Katherine Shaver, Don Phillips, Sally Jenkins, Bill O'Brian, David S. Fallis, Davis Hilzenrath, and Alice Crites.)

I wrote this story in one day, starting at six in the morning, after figuring out its structure in my sleep the night before and coming to work with a one-page outline that I taped above my computer screen.

6

"The Desk I Chose to Die Under"

The roommates crossed paths near the bathroom door at five in the morning. In the Monday darkness, another school week at Virginia Tech was about to begin. Karan Grewal had pulled an all-nighter to finish his accounting paper. His eyes were bleary as he saw Seung Hui Cho, in boxer shorts and T-shirt, moving around him to get into the bathroom. No words were exchanged, but that is how it always was with Cho, or Seung as his suite mates called him. He never looked you in the eye, rarely changed expression, would just walk right on by.

Grewal returned to his room and collapsed on his bed, falling into a deep sleep. He would not stir until mid-morning, awakened by an uncommon sound on campus, the wail of sirens.

Cho left the bathroom, got dressed, pulled a stocking cap over his head, and set out from his dorm room on his way to kill thirty-two students and teachers and then himself in the bloodiest mass murder by a lone gunman in American history.

The malevolent force that emerged from suite 2121 in Harper Hall that morning set in motion a day of enormous tragedy. There was one murderous villain on the Blacksburg stage with all the familiar characteristics: lonely, angry, mentally unstable, desperate, uncommunicative. But with the world watching, scores of people were drawn into the unfolding drama, from a brave Holocaust survivor who tried valiantly to save his students and died in the trying, to the kid in German class who became an eloquent voice of the survivors, to the quick-thinking student in the computer class who placed a heavy table to block the doorway just in time, to the young man in mechanical engineering who made it through by pretending that he was dead.

April 16, 2007: another date of death for people to absorb, if not fully comprehend. Another unthinkable worst in this violent world. This time it was a college campus tucked away in southwestern Virginia, but the heartache was familiar and universal. Like a string of little jewels, one upon another, came the stories of priceless lives cut short: Alameddine, Bishop, Bluhm, Clark, Cloyd, Couture-Nowak, Granata, Gwaltney, Hammaren, Herbstritt, Hill, Hilscher, Lane, La Porte, Lee, Librescu, Loganathan, Lumbantoruan, McCain, O'Neill, Ortiz, Panchal, Perez Cueva, Peterson, Pohle, Pryde, Read, Samaha, Shaalan, Sherman, Turner, White.

The first call came in to the campus police at 7:15 that morning. A female resident assistant on the fourth floor of West Ambler Johnston Hall, a short walk from where Cho lived. She said there had been a shooting. She had heard screams, then more screams, then a pop, pop, and went down the hall to discover two bodies, a male and a female, near room 4040 in what was known as the elevator section, an area in the middle of the dorm between the men's side and the women's side.

Police later identified the female as Emily Hilscher, a freshman from Woodville, Virginia. The male was one of the dorm's resident assistants, Ryan Clark, from Georgia. The officers began interviewing other students. Most had not heard or seen anything, even though there was a trail of bloody footprints down the hallway.

Among the first medical responders were student leaders from the Virginia Tech rescue squad. Matthew Lewis was brushing his teeth at the squad office on the northwestern perimeter of the sprawling campus when the first alarm went off. Moments later, another alarm sounded, and both EMT ambulances were on their way. One of the victims had been taken away by the time Lewis arrived. His group took the second victim. The dorm's fourth floor was nearly empty. All the students had been taken down to a common room a floor below, where resident assistants and counselors talked with them. Rumors were flying about shootings and death. Most of the students on those floors were freshmen, and they were visibly distraught. They were ordered to stay put;

the hall was under lockdown. After a year on campus, they had finally started to think of their hall as home, said Sarah Peet, a student from Columbus, Ohio. Now all they were talking about was getting out of there, going home. Investigators, in their initial interviews with those who knew Hilscher, learned about her boyfriend, a student at nearby Radford University. Maybe it was a domestic incident, they concluded. Most are. Some officers were dispatched to go find the boyfriend, operating under the assumption that they had the problem contained.

Two hours later, another 911 call came in, this one from Norris Hall.

It was supposed to be an easy week for Trey Perkins, a sophomore from Yorktown, Virginia: "No tests or anything, kind of a laid-back week." He had stayed up late Sunday night at his off-campus apartment with three friends, watching a National Hockey League playoff game between the Dallas Stars and the Vancouver Canucks. He got up at seven, plenty of time to make his eight o'clock class in Engineering Dynamics at Randolph Hall. It was a lecture, going over material for a test, and the professor let them out a few minutes early. Randolph is right behind Norris Hall, where Perkins had a 9:05 in Elementary German. He walked over and sat in the second-floor hallway outside room 207.

When the previous class let out, Perkins was the first one in, greeting his instructor, Christopher James Bishop, known as Jamie to his friends, Herr Bishop to his students, a bespectacled thirty-five-year-old with a long ponytail and a perpetual smile. They enjoyed a comfortable relationship that revolved more around sports than German. Bishop, from Georgia, was an Atlanta Falcons fan, and Perkins, who lived in New Orleans before his family moved to Virginia, rooted for the Saints. Just because the Falcons had the most famous Virginia Tech player ever, quarterback Michael Vick, did not mean that Perkins could switch allegiances. As classmates slowly filtered into class, Bishop and Perkins bantered about whom their two teams should pick in the NFL draft.

Next door in room 211, Kristina Heeger had arrived from her off-campus apartment for her Intermediate French class, taught by Jocelyne Couture-Nowak. Heeger, a sophomore from Vienna, had spent much of the night before with a group of friends who had made a habit of gathering to watch *Planet Earth* on the Discovery Channel and then *Entourage* on HBO. Ten or twelve of them would meet at Ross Berger's place next to a frat house on Roanoke Street, then hang around and talk for a few hours after the shows.

Monday morning, before leaving for French, Heeger had been on her computer, exchanging instant messages with Berger, who had been up since six writing a paper for his Global Ethics class on what he called the totalitarianism of Hugo Chávez, the president of Venezuela. Most of the messages were quick little contacts: "Hello, how are you, good morning, how's your day, cold and crappy outside." The last IM from Berger read, "Have a good day, be safe, and don't let the wind blow you away."

Up and down the hallways, things were getting under way. Haiyan Cheng was preparing to start her Computer Science class. She was filling in for the professor, who was away at a conference. Liviu Librescu, one of the renowned veterans of Tech's professorial academy, a seventy-six-year-old Holocaust survivor, was launching into his course on Solid Mechanics, and next door to him, G. V. Loganathan was getting into Advanced Hydrology. One floor above them, Kevin P. Granata, a professor of biomechanics, was working in his office, where he had developed some of the country's most advanced thinking on movement dynamics and cerebral palsy. And down on the first floor, his brother-in-law, Michael Diersing, whose wife was the identical twin sister of Granata's wife, was chatting and checking e-mail alongside Granata's doctoral assistant, Gregory Slota.

At 9:26 a.m., the first e-mail alert went out to the Virginia Tech community—faculty and students—about the earlier incident at West Ambler Johnston. The university leadership team had been meeting for nearly an hour by then, going over what they knew and didn't know, and how they should handle the situation. The university police chief, W. R. Flinchum, had come in with the latest news on the investigation. It still looked to them like an isolated incident. The e-mail popped up on computers across the campus. John Ellerbe, a senior history major from Woodbridge, Virginia, had just emerged from the shower and was preparing for his ten o'clock class when he read it:

A shooting occurred at West Ambler Johnston earlier this morning. Police are on the scene and are investigating. The university commu-

nity is urged to be cautious and are asked to contact Virginia Tech Police if you observe anything suspicious or with information on the case. . . . We will post as soon as we have more information.

Not long after the posting, the world of Virginia Tech changed forever. Life is ordinary until it is not, and then the ordinary can look serene.

The first attack came in room 206, Advanced Hydrology taught by Loganathan. There were thirteen graduate students in the class, all from the civil engineering department. There was no warning, no foreboding sounds down the hallway. The gunman entered wordlessly and began shooting. Students scattered to get as far away from the door as possible. One bullet hit Partahi "Mora" Lumbantoruan, an Indonesian doctoral student. His body fell on top of fellow grad student Guillermo Colman. Then the shooter aimed his two guns around the room, picking off people one by one before leaving. Colman, protected by his classmate's prone body, was one of only four in the room to survive. The professor and many of his disciples, most of them international students, were dead. Along with Colman, the three who survived were Nathaniel Krause, Lee Hixon, and Chang-Min Park. Two other members of the class lived because they didn't make it that morning.

In Jamie Bishop's German class, they could hear the popping sounds. What was that? Some kind of joke? Construction noises? More pops. Someone suggested that Bishop should place something in front of the classroom door, just in case. The words were no sooner uttered than the door opened and the shooter stepped in. He was holding guns in both hands. Bishop was hit first, a bullet slicking into the side of his head. All the students saw it, an unbelievable horror. The gunman had a serious but calm look on his face. Almost no expression. He stood in front and kept firing, barely moving. People scrambled out of the line of fire. Trey Perkins knocked over a couple of desks and tried to take cover. No way I can survive this, he thought. His mind raced to his mother and what she would go through when she heard he was dead. Shouts, cries, sobs, more shots, maybe thirty in all. Someone threw up. There was blood everywhere. It took about a minute and a half, and then the gunman left the room.

Perkins and two classmates, Derek O'Dell and Katelyn Carney, ran up to the door and put their feet against it to make sure he could not get back in. They would have used a heavy table, but there were none, and the desks were not strong enough. Soon the gunman tried to get back in. The three students pressed against the door with their arms and legs, straining with their lives at stake. Unable to budge the door, the gunman shot through it four times. Splinters flew from the thick wood. The gunman turned away, again. There were more pops, but each one a bit farther away as he moved down the hall. The scene in the classroom "was brutal," Perkins recalled. Most of the students were dead. He saw a few who were bleeding but conscious and tried to save them. He took off his gray hoodie sweatshirt and wrapped it around a male student's leg.

The French class next door was also devastated by then. Couture-Nowak, whose husband was a professor of horticulture at Tech, was dead. Most of Kristina Heeger's classmates were dead. Reema Samaha, a contemporary dancer from northern Virginia, was dead. And Ross Alameddine from Massachusetts and Daniel Perez Cueva from Peru and Caitlin Hammaren from upstate New York. Heeger was among the few lucky ones. She and Hilary Strollo were wounded. Heeger was hit in the stomach. A bullet sliced through Strollo's abdomen and frayed her liver. Clay Violand, a twenty-year-old junior from Walt Whitman High in Bethesda, also survived.

Like those in other classes, the French students had heard the banging, or pops. "That's not what I think it is?" asked Couture-Nowak.

Violand, feeling panicky, pointed at her and said, "Put that desk in front of the door, now!" She did, and then someone called 911. The desk could not hold back a push from outside. The first thing Violand saw was a gun, then the gunman. "I quickly dove under a desk," he recalled. "That was the desk I chose to die under."

He listened as the gunman began "methodically and calmly" shooting people. "It sounded rhythmic-like. He took his time between each shot and kept up the pace, moving from person to person." After every shot, Violand thought, Okay, the next one is me. But shot after shot, and he felt nothing. He played dead.

"The room was silent except for the haunting sound of moans, some quiet crying, and someone muttering, 'It's okay. It's going to be okay. They will be here soon,'" Violand recalled. The gunman circled again and seemed to be unloading a second round into the wounded. Violand thought he heard the gunman reload three times. He could not hold back odd thoughts: "I wondered what a gun wound feels like. I hope it doesn't hurt. I wonder if I'll die slow or fast." He made eye contact with a girl, also still alive. They stared at each other until the gunman left.

The small group of ten in Haiyan Cheng's computer class heard the loud banging outside. She thought it was construction noise at first, but it distracted her. Then silence, then more pops. Cheng and a female student went to the door and peered out. They saw a man emerge from a room across the hall. He was holding a gun, but it was pointed down. They quickly shut the door. More popping sounds, getting louder, closer. The class was in a panic. One student, Zach Petkowicz, was near the lectern, "cowering behind it," he would say later, when he realized that the door was vulnerable. There was a heavy rectangular table in the class, and he and two other students pushed it against the door. No sooner had they fixed it in place than someone pushed hard from the outside. It was the gunman. He forced it open about six inches, but no farther. Petkowicz and his classmates pushed back, not letting up. The gunman fired two shots through the door. One hit the lectern and sent wood scraps and metal flying. Neither hit any students. They could hear a clip dropping, the distinct, awful sound of reloading. And, again, the gunman moved on.

There was more carnage in the hallway. Kevin Granata had heard the commotion in his third-floor office and ran downstairs. He was a military veteran, very protective of his students. He was gunned down trying to confront the shooter. His brother-in-law, Michael Diersing, down on the first floor, heard the awful sounds and realized that the building was under attack. Diersing stepped out into the hallway with Greg Slota and noticed that the entry doors had been chained and padlocked. No way out. They shuddered to think that sometime earlier, as they were chatting or working or drinking coffee, the murderer must have walked right past their room on his way to chain the doors. Their room had a lock on it. Several students came rushing toward them, and they let them in and then locked up.

Room 204, Professor Librescu's class, seems to have been the gunman's last stop on the second floor. The teacher and his dozen students had heard too much, though they had not yet seen anything. They had heard a girl's piercing scream in the hallway. They had heard the pops, and more pops. By the time the gunman reached their room, many of the students were on the window ledge. There was grass below, not concrete, and even some shrubs. The old professor was at the door, which would not lock, pushing against it, when the gunman pushed from the other side. Some students jumped, others prepared to jump until Librescu could hold the door no longer and the gunman forced his way inside.

Matt Webster, a twenty-three-year-old engineering student from Smithfield, Virginia, was one of four students inside when the gunman appeared. "He was decked out like he was going to war," Webster recalled. "Black vest, extra ammunition clips, everything." Again, his look was blank, just a stare, no expression, as he started shooting. The first shot hit Librescu in the head, killing him. Webster ducked to the floor and tucked himself into a ball. He shut his eyes and listened as the gunman walked to the back of the classroom. Two other students were huddled by the wall. He shot a girl, and she cried out. Now the shooter was three feet away, pointing his gun right at Webster.

"I felt something hit my head, but I was still conscious," Webster said later. The bullet had grazed his hairline, then ricocheted through his upper right arm. He played dead. "I lay there and let him think he had done his job. I wasn't moving at all, hoping he wouldn't come back." The gunman left the room as suddenly as he had come in. When Webster opened his eyes, he saw blood everywhere. Some of it was his, though he didn't realize it until he noticed blood pouring out the sleeve of his sweatshirt. The girl nearby was unable to speak, only moaning. Blood seeped from her mouth.

By 9:45 a.m. the Virginia Tech police had received the first 911 call from inside Norris Hall. More calls started coming in to police and EMTs throughout the region, with reports of mass casualties. The first officers from the university and city police forces arrived in minutes to find a large crowd of students on the Drillfield, a vast expanse across from Norris. They ordered the students to leave the area immediately.

Tucker Armstrong, a freshman from Stephens City, Virginia, had been walking by Norris when he heard the shots and saw several students jumping out the second-floor windows. They were landing in bushes and struggling to get up. He saw the police arrive, fully armed, yelling at everyone to get inside. Matthew Murray, a freshman from

Herndon, Virginia, was watching as he huddled nearby in a second-floor doorway at McBride Hall. "People were running out of Norris and screaming. Streams of people were running out constantly. It was controlled, but you could tell everyone was panicked and very upset." An older man came out grabbing his bloody head. Then the jumpers. At least three people leaping out of second-story windows. One missed the grass and "hit the pavement especially hard. He landed kind of crunched up over toward his face and he didn't get up at all."

Jamal Albarghouti, a Palestinian graduate student in construction management from the West Bank, was nearby. He had been on his way to talk to an adviser about leadership skills when he heard the noise at Norris and instinctively ran toward it. With his silver Nokia N70 smartphone, he captured flitting video of the scene: shots firing, police scampering, wind blowing, terror. It only hinted at the horrific violence, but it would serve television as the primary video footage of what happened at Norris the rest of that day and night.

After storming the building, breaking the locks, the police ran up to the second floor and carefully entered each classroom, one by one. At some point, Seung Hui Cho apparently placed one of his guns at his temple and pulled the trigger. The scene was something these experienced officers had never before witnessed. As they entered each room, they asked students to hold out their hands, show that they had no weapons, and then led those who could walk down the stairs and outside. But there were so many bodies. Blood everywhere, pieces of flesh. The shooter himself, with a gun lying nearby, was almost unrecognizable, a face destroyed. And the innocent victims did not just have bullet wounds, the police would recount later, but were riddled with bullets, gushing blood. The scene was so emotionally overwhelming that many officers could not hold back tears even as they went about their business.

Matthew Lewis, the student EMT president, heard the distress call when he was at Roanoke Memorial Hospital, where he had taken the second victim of the West Ambler Johnston shooting. By the time he made it back to campus, a staging area for medical treatment and evacuations had been set up on Stanger Street, a block from Norris Hall. Emergency personnel were treating students with minor injuries, the jumpers and others who had been scuffed during the panic, but not shot. People were trickling out from Norris, but it was no longer chaos.

The first wave of wounded patients was carried into Montgomery Regional Hospital in Blacksburg shortly after ten—bloodied, mangled, some on the verge of death. Davis Stoeckle, a general surgeon, was on call that morning and worked the emergency room from beginning to end with a colleague, Holly Wheeling. They had been told to brace for the extraordinary number of victims and levels of trauma that they would face. They established a triage to focus first on the most gravely wounded.

One after another, the students came in.

Gunshot to the leg.

Bullet hole in the stomach.

Gunshot through the liver, part of a kidney, and colon.

As accustomed as he was to dealing with morbidity, Stoeckle felt himself thinking the scene was unreal. He had never encountered such a volume of patients, more gunshot victims in a few hours than the hospital had treated in nearly five years. As they worked, Stoeckle and Wheeling heard stories of bravery from the wounded: students pushing others into closets to protect them from the barrage of bullets and helping one another with makeshift tourniquets and bandages. In one case, Stoeckle concluded that one student might have saved his own life with quick medical action. Bleeding significantly from his right leg, this student had found an electrical cord in a classroom and wrapped it tightly around his wound, which kept him from bleeding to death until the rescue squad arrived and placed a tourniquet above the bleeding artery.

While the doctors took the wounded into surgery, the hospital filled with friends and relatives of students who were believed to be there. Some were, some had been taken elsewhere, and some, as it turned out, were already dead. The waiting parties were taken to a large, empty room in the back of the building, just drywall and concrete and folding chairs. They sat around in circles, talking, waiting for news. Food and water were brought in. There were no televisions there, so the only updates they could get were from new groups coming in.

Ross Berger arrived at noon and was there all day with more than twenty friends and family of Kristina Heeger, who had been shot during

French class. By mid-afternoon there were nearly two hundred people, Berger estimated, all doing the same thing. "We had people running out crying, running in crying. A group of people who got there an hour after I did sat around for two hours, and finally someone came in and read off the names of patients there, and their [child's] name was not on it, so they got up and asked, 'Where is he?' and were told, 'We have no idea.'" The news for Kristina was better. She was there, and she was stable, recovering from wounds to her lower abdomen.

The Inn at Virginia Tech was another assembly area for the concerned. Guards at the front door tried to limit admission to friends and families. As the day wore on, names of the dead and wounded trickled out. Parents cried out and clung to one another in grief. In the context of the horror, it was often a relief to hear that a loved one was at the hospital. It could have been worse. At quarter to six that evening, a woman in a long gray coat burst from an inner room, pushing her way past a grief counselor. "My baby!" she said, sobbing, cupping her face in her hands as she collapsed in the arms of a friend.

Here, as elsewhere, one of the rivers of conversation was about whether the university handled the day properly or should have shut down the entire campus after the first shootings at West Ambler Johnston. "I think they should have closed the whole thing. It's not worth it," said Hoda Bizri of Princeton, West Virginia, who was visiting her daughter, Siwar, a graduate student. The Bizris, like many others, were waiting for word about a friend who had been inside Norris and could not be reached. Nearby, Kristen Wickham was looking for news about her friend Caitlin Hammaren, a fellow New Yorker. Everyone was trying to reach Caitlin, with no luck. She should have called by now, Wickham thought, not knowing that her friend was among the dead. Hammaren's parents were trying to reach Blacksburg and could not get a plane, so they were making the long drive from upstate New York. Parents were making similar pilgrimages by car and plane from every corner of the country.

One of the early flights from the West Coast brought Nikki Giovanni, a renowned poet and Virginia Tech professor. At the end of her red-eye flight, Giovanni had heard about the shootings and the early reports that described the gunman in general terms. "When I heard the suspect was an Asian student, I had no doubt in my mind who did it," she said later. Cho had been in one of her classes, and his writing was so violent, so focused on death, that he had scared other students to the point where Giovanni had felt compelled to remove him from the class, sending him to a colleague for tutoring.

It was not until 9:06 that night—when Virginia State Police investigators knocked on the door at suite 2121 in Harper Hall—that Karan Grewal realized that the roommate he had last seen in boxers and T-shirt sixteen hours earlier was the cause of all the horror. The investigators interviewed Grewal and other roommates. No, they had not seen guns around the suite, but Cho was a strange guy. Wouldn't talk. Played the same songs over and over on his laptop. Didn't like to turn off the light in his room. Had a bike that he rode around campus late at night. Would not go out with them, except one rare time when they got him drinking at a party and he said he had an imaginary girlfriend who called him Spanky. Never saw him with a girl, though, or any friends whatsoever. Before spring break, he had seemed obsessed with a few women. He had been stalking them on his computer, and sometimes in person. The cops were called twice. Once, he was sent to counseling and said he might as well kill himself. He started shaving his head down to a fuzz cut. Wore contact lenses. Used something for his acne. Was working out at the campus gym. Recently had been getting up very early.

The investigators scoured Cho's room for evidence. The room looked like any college kid's, strewn with papers, food wrappers, cereal boxes. This is what they took away, according to a search warrant filed later by Virginia State Police special agent M. D. Austin:

> Chain from top left closet shelf
> Folding knife and combination lock
> Compaq computer serial # CND33100IL on desk
> Assorted documents, notepads, and writings from desk
> Combination lock
> Tool box
> Nine books, two notebooks, envelopes from top shelf
> Assorted books and pads from lower shelf
> Compact discs from desk

Items from top desktop drawer, mail, three notebooks, check
   credit card
Items from second drawer—Kodak digital camera, keys,
   Citibank statement
Two cases of compact discs from dresser top
Six sheets of green graph paper

Other officers walked the halls of Harper with photographs of Cho, asking students if they knew him. They were all rattled. Most did not recognize him; a few said they thought they had walked by him now and then. How lucky they were, thought Tom Duscheid, a management student from Pittsburgh. This is the residence hall where Cho lived, not Ambler Johnston. What if he had rampaged through here with his guns?

There were still many unanswered questions. Why did Cho go to West Ambler Johnston? Why did he choose Norris Hall for his rampage? Who was he looking for? How did he move around the campus unnoticed? Police questions. Questions of detail. They went to work on some of the little stuff, tracing Cho's movements. They found out that on February 9 he had stepped into a pawnshop directly across the street from the Tech campus, right on Main Street, JND Pawn Brokers, to make the first purchase of the guns he would use later. It was a Walther .22-caliber pistol, relatively inexpensive, commonly used for target shooting. From then until days before the shooting, he traveled to nearby stores to buy ammunition. Some at the Wal-Mart Supercenter, some at Dick's Sporting Goods over in Christianburg. On March 16, exactly a month before his killing spree, he went to Roanoke Firearms, a full-service gun dealership with more than 350 guns on display. He showed his driver's license, a checkbook with a matching address, and an immigration card. A surveillance camera captured him making the $571 purchase of a Glock 19 and a box of fifty cartridges.

Days later, a larger clue would come from NBC News and Cho himself. At 9:01 Monday morning, before going to Norris Hall, Cho sent an Express Mail package to NBC in New York that included photographs, video, and a note including these chilling words: "You had a hundred billion chances and ways to have avoided today."

When Ross Berger came home from the hospital Monday night, assured that his friend Kristina Heeger would survive, there was no more storage space for messages on his cell phone, and his computer was flooded with e-mails. Everyone was talking. Names were coming in. He knew four of the dead students. He turned on the television for the first time. Fox News was showing the shaky video footage taken by Jamal Albarghouti outside Norris Hall. A running count of gunshots was displayed alongside the shaky pictures. "And like that was the first thing I saw, and I went into my bathroom and puked," Berger said. But he came back and watched some more, inevitably, and the more he saw and heard, the more unsettled he became. So many conflicted feelings were banging around in his head. The country seemed to be harping on the police and the university administration and how they had handled, or mishandled, the unfolding tragedy. Berger and all his classmates, except one, were innocent, yet he felt as though they too were being tainted by the obsessive focus and the natural human desire to fix blame.

The guy to blame was dead, he thought. People didn't understand that 99.9 percent of the time this was a wonderful little place to be, that nothing really goes on. The cops here, what did they know about mass murder? They were used to dealing with some drunken kid, not a psycho. How can you stop something like that? Everyone felt horrible, Berger and his friends were still bawling, but they also still felt a deep pride in Virginia Tech. He thought about it all night, the killings, the conflict, and never found sleep.

Few who had endured the day could sleep that night. At his off-campus apartment on Patrick Henry Drive, Trey Perkins stayed up in the comfortable embrace of his parents. Don and Sheree Perkins had begun the four-hour car trip from Yorktown that afternoon as soon as Sheree could slip free from an elementary school field trip she had been leading. Trey had been one of the primary student voices all day, talking coolly and calmly about the horror that visited his German class. He had seen the worst that man can do to man, and now he was in a daze. It helped him to talk, to respond to questions, to go over the details in rote fashion, because when he spoke aloud, they seemed somewhat removed. When he was alone and silent, something deeper washed over him that made him shudder. It was a simple image that looped again and again in his mind's eye. The first moment, the classroom door opening, the gunman coming in.

(With help from R. B. Brenner, Michelle Boorstein, Chris L. Jenkins, Susan Levine, Jerry Markon, Nick Miroff, David Montgomery, Candace Rondeaux, Ian Shapira, Michael D. Shear, Sandhya Somaslekhar, Keith Alexander, Sari Horwitz, Carol D. Leonnig, Michael E. Ruane, Katherine Shaver, Jose Antonio Varga, William Wan, Alice Crites, and Julie Tate.)

News cycles had changed so much between 2001 and 2007 that I realized that we had to publish this narrative on Thursday, three days after the shootings, and not wait until Sunday, the traditional day that newspapers carry long narratives. Again, I wrote it in one day, setting an egg timer to go off every fifty minutes so I could walk around to exercise my hips three weeks after undergoing hip-replacement surgery.

Part II
─────────

POLITICAL LIVES

7

Dreams from His Mother

On weekday mornings as a teenager, Barry Obama left his grand-parents' apartment on the tenth floor of the twelve-story high-rise at 1617 South Beretania, a mile and a half above Waikiki Beach, and walked up Punahou Street in the shadows of capacious banyan trees and date palms lining the gradual incline on his way to school. Before crossing the overpass above the H1 Freeway, where traffic zoomed east to bodysurfing beaches or west to the airport and Pearl Harbor, he passed Kapiolani Medical Center, walking below the hospital room where he was born on August 4, 1961. Two blocks farther along, at the intersection with Wilder, he could look left toward the small apartment on Poki where he had spent a few years with his little sister, Maya, and mother, Ann, back when she was getting her master's degree at the University of Hawaii before she left again for Indonesia. Soon enough he was at the lower edge of Punahou School, the gracefully sloping private campus where he studied some and played basketball more.

An adolescent life told in five blocks, confined and compact, but far, far away. Apart from other unprecedented aspects of his rise, it is a geographical truth that no politician in American history has traveled farther than Barack Obama to be within reach of the White House. He was born and spent most of his formative years on Oahu, in dis-tance the most removed population center on the planet, some 2,390 miles from California, farther from a major landmass than anywhere but Easter Island. In the westward impulse of American settlement, his birthplace was the last frontier, an outpost with its own time zone, the fiftieth of the United States, admitted to the union only two years before he came along.

No man is an island, but those who come from islands are inevitably shaped by the experience. For Obama, the experience was all contradiction and contrast.

As the son of a white woman and a black man, he grew up as a multiracial kid, a *hapa*, "half-and-half" in the local lexicon, in one of the most multiracial places in the world, with no majority group and an array of minorities. There were native Hawaiians, Japanese, Filipinos, Samoans, Okinawans, Chinese, and Portuguese, along with Anglos, commonly known as *haole* (pronounced "howl-lay") and a smaller population of blacks, traditionally centered at the U.S. military installations. But diversity does not automatically translate into social comfort, Hawaii had its own difficult history of racial and cultural stratification, and young Obama struggled to find his place even in that many-hued milieu.

He had to leave the island to find himself as a black man, eventually rooting in Chicago, the antipode of remote and exotic Honolulu, deep in the fold of the mainland, and there set out on the path that led toward politics and national power. Yet life circles back in strange ways, and in essence it is the promise of the place he left behind—the notion if not the reality of Hawaii, what some call the spirit of aloha, the transracial if not postracial message—that has made his rise possible. The ideal of a color-blind place, much like the gentle idealism of his internationalist mother, always seemed somewhat unrealistic to the young Obama, who stood guard against family naïveté from an early age, when he became, in his sister's words, "the most reliable and stable male force" in the family. Yet the simple fact is that he would not exist as a human being, let alone as a politician, without his mother's sensibility, naïve or adventurous or both.

There are two main threads weaving through the cloth of Barack Obama's life. The first is Hawaii and the second is Chicago. Each involves more than geography.

Hawaii is about the forces that shaped him, and Chicago is about how he reshaped himself. Chicago is about the critical choices he made as an adult: how he learned to survive in the rough-and-tumble of law and politics, how he figured out the secrets of power in a world defined by it, and how he resolved his inner conflicts and refined the subtle, coolly ambitious persona on view in the 2008 presidential election. Hawaii comes first. It is what lies beneath, what makes Chicago possible and understandable.

Hawaii involves the struggles of a teenage hapa at Punahou School who wanted nothing more than to be a professional basketball player. It is about his extraordinary mother, Stanley Ann Dunham, deeply loving if frequently physically absent. While politicians burnish their histories by laying claim to early years of community work and lives of public service, she was the real deal, devoting her career, unsung and underpaid, to helping poor women make their way in the modern world. It is about his mysterious father, Barack Hussein Obama, an imperious if alluring voice gone distant and missing. It is about his grandparents, Madelyn and Stan Dunham, Toot and Gramps, the older white couple with whom he lived for most of his teenage years—she practical and determined, he impulsive, hokey, well-intentioned, and, by his grandson's

Obama at ironing board

Alex Brandon, AP

account, burdened with the desperate lost hopes of a Willy Loman–style salesman. It is about a family's incessant migration away from the heartland, from the Great Plains to the West Coast to Hawaii.

And that was not far enough for the daughter, who followed the Pacific farther to Indonesia, and traveled the world until, at the too-early age of fifty-two, she made her way back to Honolulu, taking an apartment next to her parents' place in the high-rise on the corner of Beretania and Punahou, to die there of cancer in 1995.

In the same year, her son made his debut on the national stage with a book about himself that searched for the missing, the void—his dad, Kenya, Africa—and paid less attention to the people and things that had shaped his life, especially his mother.

Of all the relationships in Obama's life, none was deeper, more complex, and more important than that with his mother. They lived under the same roof for perhaps only twelve years, and were frequently apart during his adolescence, but her lessons and judgments were always with him. In some sense, because they were only eighteen years apart, they grew up together, each following a singular path toward maturity.

Who was his mother? The shorthand version of the Obama story has a woman from Kansas marrying a man from Kenya, but while Stanley Ann Dunham was born in Wichita in the fall of 1942, it is a stretch to call her a Jayhawk. After leaving Kansas when she was a youngster, she and her parents lived in Berkeley, California, for two years, Ponca City, Oklahoma, for two years, and Wichita Falls, Texas, for three years before they ventured to Seattle. A year later, they arrived in time for her to enter ninth grade at the new high school on Mercer Island, a hilly slab of land in Lake Washington that was popping with tract developments during the westward boom of the postwar fifties. Mercer was an island, but not much more isolated than Staten Island, on the other side of the country. It was situated on the way out of Seattle toward Bellevue, and connected by what was then called the floating bridge.

The population boom, along with a nomadic propensity, brought the Dunhams to Mercer Island. Stan was in the furniture trade, a salesman always looking for the next best deal, and the middle-class suburbs of Seattle offered fertile territory with all the houses going up that needed new living room and dining room sets. He took a job in a furniture store in Seattle. Madelyn, who brought home a paycheck most of her life, found a job in a banking real estate escrow office, and they settled into a two-bedroom place in a quiet corner of the Shore-wood Apartments nestled near the lakeshore in view of the Cascade Mountains. Many islanders lived there temporarily as they waited for new houses to be finished nearby. The Dunhams never looked for another home, and filled their high-ceilinged apartment with the tasteful Danish modern furniture of that era.

Stanley Ann was an only child, and in those days she dealt head-on with her uncommon first name. No sense trying to hide it, even though she hated it. My name is Stanley, she would say. My father wanted a boy, and that's that. Her mother softened it, calling her Stanny or Stanny Ann, but at school she was Stanley, straight up. "She owned the name," recalled Susan Botkin (now Blake), one of her first pals on Mercer Island. "Only once or twice was she teased. She had a sharp tongue, a deep wit, and she could kill. We all called her Stanley."

In a high school culture of brawn and beauty, Stanley was one of the brains. Often struggling with her weight, and wearing braces her junior year, she had the normal teenage anxieties, according to her friends, though she seemed less concerned with superficial appearances than many of her peers. Her protective armor included a prolific vo-cabulary, free from the trite and clichéd, a quick take on people and events, and biting sarcasm. Her friend John W. Hunt said those traits allowed Stanley to become accepted by the predominantly male intel-lectual crowd, even though she had a soft voice. "She wasn't a shouter, but sat and thought awhile before she put forth her ideas. She was one of the most intelligent girls in our class, but unusual in that she thought things through more than anyone else," Hunt said. "She was very cogent in discussions. She spoke very clearly and succinctly and said what she meant, and had a lot to back it up with. That's what brought her into our circle. Our circle loved to discuss and argue things."

Stanley would not use her wit to bully people, her classmates re-called, but rather to slice up prejudice or pomposity around her. Her signature expression of disdain was an exaggerated rolling of her big brown eyes. The eye roll could be seen in class, but people also noticed it when she was with her father, who enjoyed getting a rise out of his daughter and was prone to saying corny things that embarrassed her.

Susan Botkin thought back to late afternoons when she and Stanley would go downtown to the Seattle library and hitch a ride home with Stan and Madelyn. "We would climb into the car and immediately he would start into his routine." In the backseat, the daughter would be rolling her eyes, while in the front, Madelyn—"a porcelain doll kind of woman, with pale, wonderful skin, red hair, carefully coiffed, and lacquered nails"—would try to temper her husband with occasional interjections of "Now, Stan . . ." Another high school friend, Maxine Box, remembered that they enjoyed getting rides in the old man's white convertible, and that he was always ready and willing to drive them anywhere, wanting to be the life of the party. "Stanley would gladly take the transportation from him," Box said, but would "just as soon that he go away. They had locked horns a lot of times." The mother, she sensed, was "a buffer between Stan and Stanley."

It is a reflection of Stanley's individuality that she did not obtain a driver's license when she turned sixteen and never drove in high school. In fact, as much of a fearless world traveler as she later became, she never got a license and did not drive her entire life. She walked to and from the high school, up toward the northern end of the island, often stopping at Box's house on the way home because her own parents were still at work. John Hunt was not her boyfriend in the Mercer Island crowd—no one remembers her having one—but he often stopped by her apartment on weekend nights to pick her up and take her home. "I had a car and she didn't," he said. "The pretext was I was her date, but we didn't really date. She was just desperate to get out of the house. She wanted us to get her out of there. I got the feeling she debated a lot with her folks. I think her dad liked that, liked the repartee, and her mother was like, 'Don't argue.' He was definitely a salesman. He had that outgoing personality. He was a shake-your-hand, bring-you-in, see-what-was-happening kind of guy. The big grin was there. He would have loved to pump us."

But Stanley wanted none of that, and instead she and her friends would escape across the bridge into Seattle, where they could hang out at a small espresso café near the University of Washington. Anything, said Hunt, to "get away from the suburban view. We would go to this café and talk and talk and talk"—about world events, French cinema, the meaning of life, the existence of God. They were young dilettantes, he said. Chip Wall, another member of the intellectual circle, thought

Stanley stood out among the girls as the one with the sensibility closest to his. She wore pleated skirts and sweater sets like the others, but
would make fun of the current fad or fashion. "Her reaction to a lot of
that was, 'Oh, God.' We were looking for fakes and phonies and real
stuff in the world," Wall said. "We were in a search for truth."

Their curiosity was encouraged by the teachers at Mercer Island
High, especially two men, Jim Wichterman and Val Foubert, who
taught Advanced Humanities courses open to the top twenty-five
students. The assigned reading included not only Plato and Aristotle,
Kierkegaard and Sartre, but also late-1950s critiques of societal con-
ventions like *The Organization Man* by William H. Whyte, *The Lonely
Crowd* by David Riesman, and *The Hidden Persuaders* by Vance Pack-
ard, along with the political theories of Hegel, Mill, and Marx. *The
Communist Manifesto* was on the reading list. That last drew protests
from some parents, prompting what Wichterman later called "Mothers
Marches" on the school, a phrase that conjures up a larger backlash
than really occurred but conveys some of the tension of the times.
"They would come up in ones and twos and threes and berate the
teacher or complain to the principal," recalled Hunt.

Wichterman and Foubert, noted Chip Wall, were "instrumental in
getting us to think, and anybody who tries to do that, particularly in
high school, has trouble. Make my kid a thinker, but make sure he
thinks like I do." In tracking the Obama story during the 2008 election, some conservative Web sites seized on the high school curriculum
of his mother as evidence of an early leftist indoctrination. Wall, who
has spent his life challenging dogma from any ideology, and whose
take on the world often veers from the politically correct, answered this
interpretation with a two-word dismissal, "Oh, crap."

Stanley was decidedly liberal. She challenged the existence of God
and championed Adlai Stevenson. But while some of her friends turned
toward cynicism, she did not. "She was intrigued by what was happening in the world and embraced change," recalled Susan Botkin.
"During our senior year, the doomsday clock seemed as close as it had
ever been to boom. And the thought [of nuclear annihilation] affected
people in our class. There was a sense of malaise that permeated the
group. Why bother? The boom is going to happen. But Stanley was
better able to laugh it off, to look beyond it. Come out of that bomb
shelter and do something."

Their senior class graduated in June 1960, at the dawn of the six-ties. A few days after commencement, Stanley left for Honolulu with her parents. Decades later she told her son that she had wanted to go from Seattle to Chicago to begin her undergraduate education at the University of Chicago, where she had been accepted, but that her father would not let her be that far from them, since she was barely seventeen. Her friends from Mercer Island recalled that, like many of them, she intended to stay in Seattle and go to "U-Dub," the University of Wash-ington, but that again her father insisted that she was too young even for that and had to accompany them to Hawaii.

That was nearly a half century ago. Time compresses, and the high school classmates of Stanley Ann Dunham now had an unusual van-tage point from which to witness the presidential campaign of her son. "You see so much of her in his face," Maxine Box said of Barack Obama and his mother. "And he has his grandfather's long chin." In watching Obama speak and answer questions, Chip Wall could "instantly go back and recognize the person" he knew decades ago. Stanley is there, he said, in the workings of the son's mind, "especially in his wry sense of speech pattern." The fact that her son was black was surprising but not out of character; she was attracted to the different and untouched by racial prejudice. The hardest thing for them to grasp was that Barack Obama Jr. came into being only a little more than a year after Stan-ley left Mercer Island. She seemed like such an unlikely candidate for teenage motherhood, not just because of her scholarly ways and lack of boyfriends, but because she seemed to have zero interest in babies. Susan Botkin had two little brothers and was always babysitting, she recalled, but "Stanley never even babysat. She would come over to the house and just stand back and her eyes would blink and her head would spin like, 'Oh, my God, what's going on here?'"

In the fall of 1960, as Botkin worried about whether she had the proper clothes to go through sorority rush at U-Dub, where they pinched the young women to make sure they were wearing girdles, and nylons were part of the uniform, she received her first letter from her friend in Hawaii. Stanley was enjoying newfound freedoms. She had ditched her first name and was now going by Ann. And no more nylons and perfect outfits either. "I'm wearing shorts and muu-muus to class," she wrote. In the next letter, she said that she was dating an African student she had met in Russian class. Botkin was more interested in the fact that her friend was studying Russian than in whom she was dating. But soon enough came a card revealing that Ann was in love, and then another that said she was married and expecting a baby in the summer.

The first African student at the University of Hawaii, Barack Hussein Obama, reached Honolulu eleven months before Stanley Ann Dunham and her parents got there from Seattle. He was on the first airlift of Kenyan students to study at U.S. universities as part of a program organized by the Kenyan nationalist Tom Mboya, and funded primarily by hundreds of American supporters. At the time, there were no colleges in Kenya, which was in the last throes of British colonialism. His arrival in Honolulu was announced in an article in a local newspaper, the *Advertiser,* under the headline "Young Men from Kenya, Jordan and Iran Here to Study at U.H." The story noted that the university had been attracting more foreign students in recent years, but that the three latest "come from areas that are very foreign to the man on the street in Honolulu. But by the same token, Hawaii to them was an exotic, tropical world."

Obama told the journalist Shurei Hirozawa that he grew up on the shores of Lake Victoria in Kenya, East Africa, and was a member of the Luo tribe. He said he had worked as an office clerk in Nairobi for several years to save money for college and settled on the University of Hawaii "when he read in an American magazine about its racial tolerance." Other accounts have said that he went to Hawaii because it was the only American university to offer him a scholarship, but that appears unlikely based on this contemporaneous report, Obama told Hirozawa that he only had enough money to stay in Hawaii for two semesters unless he applied for a scholarship. He said he would study business administration and wanted to return to Kenya to help with its transition from its tribal customs to a modern economy. He was concerned, he said, about his generation's disorientation as Kenyans rejected old ways yet struggled uneasily with Westernization.

Taking a room at the Charles Atherton branch of the YMCA, not far from campus, Obama quickly adapted to the rhythms of student life. One of his frequent hangouts was the snack bar in an old army barracks–style building near his business classes. It was there that he met the Abercrombie brothers, first Neil and then Hal, who had escaped the darkness of Buffalo to attend graduate school in Honolulu, and their friends Peter Gilpin, Chet Gorman, and Pake Zane. They were antiestablishment intellectuals, experimenters, outsiders, somewhere between beatniks and hippies, and they loved to talk and drink coffee and beer. They were immediately taken by the one and only African student in their midst.

"He was very black, probably the blackest person I've ever met," recalled Pake Zane, a Chinese Hawaiian who now runs an antiques shop a few miles from the university. "Handsome in his own way. But the most impressive thing was his voice. His voice and his inflection—he had this Oxford accent. You heard a little Kenyan English, but more this British accent with this really deep, mellow voice that just resounded. If he said something in the room and the room was not real noisy, everybody stopped and turned around. I mean he just had this wonderful, wonderful voice. He was charismatic as a speaker."

It was not just the voice, said Neil Abercrombie, who went on to become a congressman from Honolulu, but Obama's entire outsized persona—the lanky six-foot-one frame, the dark horn-rimmed glasses, the booming laugh, the pipe, and an "incredibly vital personality. He was brilliant and opinionated and avuncular and opinionated. Always opinionated. If you didn't know him, you might be put off by him. He never hesitated to tell you what he thought, whether the moment was politic or not. Even to the point sometimes where he might seem a bit discourteous. But his view was, well, if you're not smart enough to know what you're talking about and you're talking about it, then you don't deserve much in the way of mercy. He enjoyed the company of people who were equally as opinionated as he was."

An interesting note about the snack-bar crowd is that, even decades later, they would all pronounce the first name of their Kenyan friend "Bear-ick," with the accent on the first syllable. That is how he referred to himself, they all said. In Hawaii at least, they never heard him call himself "Buh-*rock*," with the accent on the second syllable, the pronunciation his son would adopt in his adult life. Perhaps it was a minor accommodation to Westernization.

In late November, a few months into Obama's first semester, the Honolulu paper wrote another story about him, this time focusing on his positive conclusions about racial attitudes on the island. "No one seems to be conscious of color," he said. But there were stereotypes to shatter on both sides—his of Hawaii and Hawaii's of Africa. "When I first came here, I expected to find a lot of Hawaiians all dressed in native clothing and I expected native dancing and that sort of thing, but I was surprised to find such a mixture of races," he acknowledged. When asked if people questioned him about Kenya, he laughed and said, "Oh, yes. People are very interested in the Mau Mau rebellion [a long-standing uprising against the British] and they ask about race relations in Kenya. I tell them they've improved since the rebellion but are not perfect. They also ask if Kenya is ready for self-government. Some others ask me such questions as how many wives each man has back home, what we eat, how I dress at home, how we live, whether we have cars."

He did not answer those questions in the story. Nor, on one matter, was he forthcoming with his friends at the university. Neither newspaper readers nor his fellow students knew that he had left a son and pregnant wife back in Kenya.

The events in Africa intrigued Obama's fellow students, and were inevitably part of the movable discussion, which often went from the university snack bar over to the Stardust Lounge or George's Inn, where beer pitchers went for two bucks, and then on to Peter Gilpin's apartment nearby. As they listened to Sonny Terry and Brownie McGhee on the hi-fi, Obama pontificated on Kenya and nationalism and colonialism and his fears about what might happen. "He was very concerned that tribalism would trump nationalism," said Neil Abercrombie. "And that people like himself would not be properly recognized, would not be fully utilized, and there would be discrimination and prejudice. Jomo Kenyatta [Kenya's first postcolonial leader] was a Kikuyu, and Barack and Mboya were Luo, and Kikuyu were going to run things. We'd get into it that deeply."

Obama founded and served as the first president of UH's International Students Association, and became a popular speaker in larger forums, appearing at church gatherings, at the Y, and at the NAACP office to offer his interpretation of the changes sweeping the African continent. In 1960 alone, fourteen new African nations would emerge from colonialism, and in most cases liberation did not come without violence. Stories of rampant rape and killing scared the wits out of white people, complicating their perspective on the independence movement. The *Honolulu Star-Bulletin* ran an editorial early in 1960 about

"Terror in the Congo" whose central theme was about how much the nation had been damaged by Belgian colonial rule. But now, the editorial added:

> *the Congolese—inflamed with the spirit of independence—want to expel the only culture they possess. What's worse, many apparently intend to do it brutally. Belgian women are stricken with fear. Many of the Belgians are giving up their homes and moving their families to safety. . . . Many predict that after the independence day there will be riot and rapine.*

The editorial caught Obama's attention, and he typed out a long letter of reply. "I note your concern with the state of affairs in the Congo now and the 'fear' which you say has been instilled in the white colonial minority who reside there, but I wonder whether this sort of fear does not occur everywhere where a country is throwing off the yoke of colonialism?" he asked. "May it not be that these former colonials are returning to Belgium because the time for exploitation, special prerogatives and privilege is over?" Obama said he was writing as someone who had been to the Congo and "had seen with my own eyes how the Africans there were whipped and put to jail for such petty offenses as walking on the wrong side of the street." But what bothered him most, he said, was "to hear people say that the Congolese have turned into savages."

Only a few months later, late in the summer of 1960, at the start of his second year and the beginning of her first, Obama and Stanley Ann Dunham met in a Beginning Russian class. He was twenty-five; she was not yet eighteen. She called him "Bear-ick" too. He called her Anna. Decades later, Ann would tell her son a story about their first date that he then depicted in his memoir, *Dreams from My Father.*

> *He asked me to meet him in front of the university library at one. I got there and he hadn't arrived, but I figured I'd give him a few minutes. It was a nice day, so I laid out on one of the benches, and before I knew it I had fallen asleep. An hour later he showed up with a couple of friends. I woke up and three of them were standing over me and I heard him saying, serious as can be . . . "You see, gentlemen, I told you she was a fine girl, and that she would wait for me."*

Recounting the scene long after the fact, knowing how the relationship would end, the son was at his most lyrical.

My mother was that girl with the movie of beautiful black people in her head, flattered by my father's attention, confused and alone, trying to break out of the grip of her own parents' lives. The innocence she carried that day, waiting for my father, had been tinged with misconceptions, her own needs, but it was a guileless need, one without self-consciousness, and perhaps that's how any love begins.

This was the prelude to conception, the beginning of the second Barack Obama, the hapa, and in the narrative he creates about his mother, here, as always after, he writes with the sensibility not so much of a son as an acute if sympathetic psychologist, approaching condescension but not quite crossing over that line.

During his time in Hawaii, Obama seemed adept at walling off various aspects of his life. He eventually told Ann about a former marriage back in Kenya, but claimed that he was divorced, which she would only discover years later was a lie. While the scene in the book included two friends who were with him when he arrived late for a first date with Ann, few members of the snack-bar crowd remember the Obama-Dunham relationship. Hal Abercrombie said he never saw them together. Pake Zane, who left the island for a spell in 1961, could not recall Ann from those days, but had precise memories of Obama. Neil Abercrombie did remember her appearing at some of the weekend gatherings. Obama was such a strong personality, he said, that he could see how the young woman was awed and overwhelmed by him. "She was a girl, and what I mean by that is she was only seventeen or eighteen, just out of high school. And he brought her at different times. She mostly observed because she was a kid. Everybody there were pretty high-powered grad-student types and the women were older. She never participated much in the discussions but she was obviously interested in Barack."

Before the end of her first semester, Ann learned she was pregnant. The jolt that most parents might feel at such news from a teenage daughter was intensified in this case for the Dunhams by the fact that the father was Obama. Madelyn Dunham (who died on the eve of the election), in 2008, steadfastly declined requests for interviews, but a few years earlier she did talk to the *Chicago Tribune*'s David

Mendell, who was researching his biography *Obama: From Promise to Power*. Dunham, known for her practicality and skepticism in a family of dreamers, told Mendell that Stanley Ann had always been stubborn and nonconformist, and often did startling things, but none more stubborn or surprising than her relationship with Obama. When Mendell pressed her about Obama, she said that she did not trust the stories the Kenyan told. Prodding further, the interviewer noted that Obama had "a great deal of charm" and that his father had been a medicine man. "She raised her eyebrows and nodded to herself," Mendell wrote of Madelyn. " 'He was . . . ,' she said with a long pause, 'strange.' She lingered on the *a* to emphasize 'straaaaaange.' "

On February 2, 1961, against Madelyn's hopes, and also against the desires of Obama's father back in Kenya, Ann and Obama hopped a plane to Maui and got married. No guests, not even families, were there. Barack Hussein Obama Jr. was born six months later in Honolulu. Ann, the earnest student, had dropped out of school to take care of him. Her husband finished his degree in three years, graduating in June 1962 as a Phi Beta Kappa straight-A student. Then, before the month was out, he took off, leaving behind his still-teenage wife and namesake infant child, and did not return for ten years, and then only briefly. A story in the *Star-Bulletin* on the day he left, June 22, said that he planned a several-weeks grand tour of mainland universities before he arrived at Harvard to study economics on a graduate faculty fellowship. He gave the newspaper his farewell remarks on the state of race relations in Hawaii, saying that he found it "rather strange . . . even rather amusing, to see Caucasians discriminated against here." But he also said the world could learn something from Hawaii. "Here in the government and elsewhere, all races work together toward the development of Hawaii. At home in Kenya, the Caucasians do not want to work as equals."

The story did not mention that he was married and had a young son. Many years later, Barack Jr., then in high school, found a clipping of the article in a family stash of birth certificates and old vaccination forms. Why wasn't his name there, or his mother's? He wondered, he later wrote, "whether the omission caused a fight between my parents."

On his way east, Obama stopped in San Francisco, and went to dinner at the Blue Fox restaurant in the financial district with Hal Abercrombie, who had moved there with his wife, Shirley. Abercrombie would never forget the dinner; he thought it showed the worst side of his old friend, a combination of anger and arrogance that frightened him. Shirley was a blonde with a high, bouffant hairdo, and when she showed up at the side of Hal and Barack, the maître d' took them to the most obscure table in the restaurant. Obama interpreted this as a racial slight. When the waiter arrived, Obama tore into him, shouting that he was an important person on his way to Harvard and would not tolerate such treatment. "He took it out on the waiter, not the maître d'," Abercrombie recalled. "He was berating the guy and condescending every time the waiter came to our table. There was a superiority and an arrogance about it that I didn't like."

In the family lore, the story goes that Obama was accepted into graduate school at the New School in New York and also at Harvard, and that if he had chosen the New School, there would have been enough scholarship money for his wife and son to come along, but that he opted for Harvard because of the world-class academic credentials a Crimson degree would bring. But there is an unresolved part of the story. Did Ann try to follow him to Cambridge? Her friends from Mercer Island were left with that impression. Susan Botkin, Maxine Box, and John W. Hunt all remember Ann showing up in Seattle late that summer with little Barry, as the son was called.

"She was on her way from her mother's house to Boston to be with her husband," Botkin recalled. "[She said] he had transferred to grad school and she was going to join him. And I was intrigued with who she was and what she was doing. Stanley was an intense person . . . but I remember that afternoon, sitting in my mother's living room, drinking ice tea and eating sugar cookies. She had her baby and was talking about her husband, and what life held in store for her. She seemed so confident and self-assured and relaxed. She was leaving the next day to fly on to Boston." But as Botkin and others later remembered it, something happened in Cambridge, and Stanley Ann returned to Seattle. They saw her a few more times, and thought that she even tried to enroll in classes at the University of Washington, before she packed up and returned to Hawaii.

The memory reel in Barry Obama's brain started to record five years later. He was a hyperaware boy with much to think about. His mother had returned to school at the University of Hawaii and had received a degree in what her family considered an unlikely major—math. She had divorced Barack Obama Sr., who had finished his graduate work at Harvard and was back in Kenya, now living with a third woman. Ann had moved on, soon to wed another international student, Lolo Soetoro, and follow him back to his home country, Indonesia, bringing Barry along. Her brief first marriage was in the past, Seattle in the remote distance, and Kansas farther still. The last remnants of the heartland lingered only in a few figures of speech. She said "Mun-dee," "Toos-dee," and "Wins-dee" as days of the week. She called her son Bar (pronounced "Bear," as in "Bear-ick"). If he was unresponsive, she might complain that he was "as slow as a herd of turtles in a cloud of peanut butter." Sharing a secret would be "Just between you and me and the lamppost."

It was at this point, when Barry was six and his mother twenty-five, that he developed a way of looking at her that essentially would last until her death three decades later. His take on his mother—both the ways he wanted to be like her and how he reacted against her—shaped him permanently and is central to understanding his political persona today, the contrast of an embracing, inclusive sensibility accompanied by an inner toughness and wariness. Starting at an early age, he noticed how his mother was curious and open, eager to find the best in people and situations, intent on softening the edges of the difficult world for her hapa son. There were many times when this made him think she was naïve, sometimes heartbreakingly so, and that he had to be the realist in the family. To some degree, especially as he tried to explain himself later in *Dreams from My Father,* he seemed to use his mother as a foil, setting her up as the quintessential well-intentioned white liberal idealist as a contrast to his own coming of age as a modern black man.

Whether this perception reflected objective reality is open to question. In her dealings later as a community worker and anthropologist in Indonesia and around the world, Ann showed a keen appreciation of the power structure and how to work with it or around it, and her doctoral thesis and other writings revealed a complex understanding of people and their motivations, free of dreamy idealism or wishful thinking. But she certainly tried to present the world in the most hopeful, unthreatening light to her children, first Barry and then his little sister, Maya, the daughter Ann bore with Lolo Soetoro. As Maya explained recently, looking back on the way she and her brother were raised:

"[She wanted to] make sure that nothing ever became acrimonious and that everything was pretty and everything was sacred and every-thing was properly maintained and respected—all the cultural artifacts and ways of being and living and thinking. We didn't need to make choices. We didn't need to discard anything. We could just have it all and keep it all. It was this sense of bounty and beauty."

The son's notion of his loving mother's naïveté began in Indone-sia, when they arrived in the capital city of Jakarta in 1967, joining Soetoro, who had returned to his home country several months ear-lier. The place was a fantasia of the unfamiliar and grotesque to young Barry, with the exotic scent of danger. Monkeys, chickens, and even crocodiles in the backyard. A land of floods, exorcisms, cockfights. Lolo was off working for Union Oil, Ann taught English at the U.S. embassy, and Barry was overwhelmed in this strange new world. He recalled those days in his memoir with more acuity than he could pos-sibly have had as a six-year-old, but the words reflected his perceptions nonetheless.

> *Sometimes, when my mother came home from work, I would tell her the things I had seen or heard, and she would stroke my forehead, listening intently, trying her best to explain what she could. I always appreciated the attention—her voice, the touch of her hand, defined all that was secure. But her knowledge of floods and exorcisms and cockfights left much to be desired. Everything was as new to her as it was to me, and I would leave such conversations feeling that my questions had only given her unnecessary cause for concern.*

His mother could teach him history, math, reading, social studies—and she did, waking him at four each morning to give him special tu-toring, pouring her knowledge into his agile brain. But it was left to his stepfather to orient him in the cruel ways of the world. Soetoro taught him how to fight and defend himself, how not to give money to beg-gars, how to deal strictly with servants, how to interact with the world on its own unforgiving terms, not defining everything as good or bad but merely as it is. " 'Your mother has a soft heart,' he told me after she tried to take the blame for knocking a radio off the dresser," Obama, in his memoir, quoted Soetoro instructing him one day. " 'That's good in a woman, but you will be a man someday, and a man needs to have more sense.' " Men, Soetoro explained, take advantage of weakness in other men. "They're like countries that way."

All of this, as Obama later interpreted it, related to the exercise of power, hidden and real. It was power that forced Soetoro to return to Indonesia in the first place. He had been summoned back to his country from Hawaii in 1966 and sent to work in New Guinea for a year because the ruling regime, after a widespread bloody purge of Communists and leftists—what came to be known as the Year of Living Dangerously—was leery of students who had gone abroad and wanted them back and under control. To his mother, power was ugly, Obama determined. "It fixed in her mind like a curse." But to his stepfather, power was reality—and he "made his peace" with it.

Which response to the world had a deeper effect on the person Barry Obama would become? Without doubt it was his mother's. Soetoro, described later by his daughter, Maya, as a sweet and quiet man, resigned himself to his situation and did not grow or change. He became a nondescript oilman, befriending slick operators from Texas and Louisiana who probably regarded him with racial condescension. He went to their parties and played golf at the country club and became Western and anonymous, slipping away as far as possible from the dangers of the purge and the freedom of his student days. Ann certainly had more options, but the one she eventually chose was unusual. She decided to deepen her connection to this alien land and to confront power in her own way, by devoting herself to understanding the people at the core of Indonesian culture, artisans and craftsmen, and working to help them survive.

Here was an early paradox that helped shape Obama's life, one he would confront again and again as he matured and remade himself. A certain strain of realism can lead to inaction. A certain form of naïveté can lead to action.

By the time Maya was born in 1970, Ann's second marriage was coming apart. This time there was no sudden and jarring disappearance. The relationship lingered off and on for another ten years, and Lolo remained part of Maya's life in a way that Barack Obama failed to do for Barry. As Maya analyzed her parents' relationship decades later, she concluded that she came along just as her mother was starting to find herself. "She started feeling competent, perhaps. She acquired numerous languages after that. Not just Indonesian, but her professional language and her feminist language. And I think she really got a voice. So it's perfectly natural that she started to demand more of those who were near her, including my father. And suddenly his sweetness wasn't enough to satisfy her needs."

Dreams from My Father is as imprecise as it is insightful about Obama's early life. He offered unusually perceptive and subtle observations of himself and the people around him. Yet, as he readily acknowledged, he rearranged the chronology for his own literary purposes and presented a cast of characters made up of composites and pseudonyms. This was to protect their privacy, he said. Only a select few were not granted that protection, for the obvious reason that he could not blur their identities—his relatives. And so it is that of all the people in the book, the one who took it on the chin the most was his maternal grandfather, Stan Dunham. It is obvious from the memoir, and from interviews with many people who knew the family in Hawaii, that Stan Dunham loved his grandson and did everything he could to support him physically and emotionally.

But in the memoir, Gramps comes straight out of the plays of Arthur Miller or Eugene O'Neill, a once-proud soul lost in self-delusion, struggling against the days. When Barry was ten years old, his mother made the difficult decision to send him back to Honolulu to live with her parents so that he could get better schooling. He had been accepted into the prestigious Punahou School, and Madelyn and Stan had moved from a large house on Kamehameha Avenue to the apartment on Beretania only five blocks from the school. Gramps now seemed as colorful and odd as those monkeys in the backyard in Jakarta. He cleaned his teeth with the red cellophane string from his cigarette packs. He told off-color jokes to waitresses. A copy of Dale Carnegie's *How to Win Friends and Influence People* was always near at hand—and only those who lived with him knew the vast distance between his public bonhomie and his private despair. The most powerful scene in the memoir, as devastating as it was lovingly rendered, described how Stan, by then out of the furniture industry and trying his hand as a John Hancock Mutual Life Insurance salesman, prepared on a Sunday night for the week ahead.

Every Sunday night, I would watch him grow more and more irritable as he gathered his briefcase and set up a TV tray in front of his chair, following the lead of every possible distraction, until finally he would chase us out of the living room and try to schedule appointments with prospective clients over the phone. Sometimes I would tiptoe into the kitchen for a soda, and I could hear the desperation creeping out of his voice, the stretch of silence that followed when the people on the other end explained why Thursday wasn't good and Tuesday not much better, and then Gramps's heavy sigh after he had hung up the phone, his hands fumbling through the files in his lap like those of a cardplayer who's deep in the hole.

Sooner or later, someone on the other end would relent, and Gramps would pack up his business and walk down the hall to his grandson's room to tell stories and jokes and conjure up dreams.

If his calls had gone especially well that night, he might discuss with me some scheme he still harbored—the book of poems he had started to write, the sketch that would soon bloom into a painting, the floor plans for his ideal house, complete with push-button conveniences and terraced landscaping. . . . Then, somewhere in the middle of his presentation, we would both notice Toot standing in the hall outside my room, her head tilted in accusation.

And one of their familiar little arguments would begin, often with Gramps saying, "I'm not hollering, Jesus H. Christ," and Toot retreating to her room for a read and a smoke. She "smoked like a chimney, two packs a day," according to her granddaughter, Maya.

By the time Barry returned to Hawaii, Toot had become the stable financial source in the family, well known in the local lending community. In the library of the Honolulu *Advertiser,* no clippings mention Stan Dunham, but Madelyn Dunham crops up frequently in the business pages. A few months before Barry arrived from Indonesia, his grandmother had been promoted to vice president at the Bank of Hawaii along with Dorothy K. Yamamoto—the first two female vice presidents in the bank's history. She had been a trailblazer throughout her career, starting in the escrow department in 1960 and by 1962 becoming the only female escrow manager in Hawaii. Like many presidential aspirants before him, and perhaps most like Bill Clinton, Obama grew up surrounded by strong women, the male figures either weak or absent. Once, during the heat of the primary campaign between Obama and Hillary Clinton, a claim came from Bill Clinton that he "understood" Obama. As different as their backgrounds and families were, it was no doubt this strong female–weak male similarity that he had in mind.

It was during Barry's first year at Punahou School that his long-lost father stepped briefly into his life, and just as quickly disappeared again. He came for the month of December, and his mother returned from Indonesia, arriving beforehand to prepare Barry for the visit. She taught him more about Kenya and stories of the Luo people, but all of that knowledge dissolved at the first sight of the old man. He seemed far skinnier than Barry had imagined him, and more fragile, with his spectacles and blue blazer and ascot and yellowish eyes. It was not an easy month, and what stuck in the boy's memory were the basketball that his dad gave him as a present and two dramatic events: When his father ordered him, in front of his mother and grandparents, to turn off the TV and study instead of watching *How the Grinch Stole Christmas;* and when his father came to Miss Mabel Hefty's fifth-grade class at Punahou's Castle Hall to talk about Kenya. The first moment angered Barry, the second made him proud. But nothing much lingered after his father was gone.

That visit to Honolulu was bracketed by two trips that Barack's old snack-bar friends from the University of Hawaii made to see him in Kenya. Late in 1968, Neil Abercrombie and Pake Zane traveled through Nairobi on a yearlong backpacking trip around the world and stayed with Obama for several days before they made their way on to the port city of Mombasa and across to India. No mention was made of Ann or the boy, but it was clear to Abercrombie that his old friend's life was not turning out as he had planned. "He seemed very frustrated and his worst fears in his mind were coming true—that he was being underutilized," Abercrombie said. "Everybody's virtue is his vice, and his brilliance and his assertiveness was obviously working against him as well." Five years later, in 1973, Pake Zane returned on another trip around the world.

"This time when I met Barack [*Bear*-ick, he said] he was a shell of what he was prior to that," Zane recalled. "Even from what he was in 1968. He was using a walking stick and he was very upset. He told us he had been in another automobile accident but he thought it had been an assassination attempt. He said he was found by the side of the road and pronounced dead by the attending medical people but that he was only saved because by chance one of his brothers drove by, and he was a doctor. He said his brother stopped by, took his pulse, realized there was life in the body, and immediately took him to the hospital and he survived. I know his injuries were real. I saw them. Whether the rest of it was real—maybe true, maybe not. He was drinking very heavily and he was very depressed and as you might imagine had an amount of rage. He felt totally vulnerable."

By the time of that second visit to Kenya, Barry's circumstances had changed somewhat. His mother, separated from Lolo, was back in Hawaii with little Maya. Barry joined them to share an apartment at Poki and Wilder, even closer to Punahou School. Ann was now fully into the artisan culture of Indonesia, and beginning her master's degree work in anthropology. They had no money beyond her graduate school grants. Maya's earliest memories go back to those years. Thirty-five years later, she could remember a filing cabinet and a rocking chair, and how she and her big brother would sit in the rocking chair and keep rocking harder until it flipped over, which is what they wanted it to do. There was a television across from the rocker, and she would purposely stand in front of it during basketball games to irritate him. There were picnics up at Puu Ualakaa State Park with Kentucky Fried Chicken and Toot's homemade baked beans and coleslaw and potato salad with the skins still on. And there was Big Sandwich night, when Gramps would haul out all the meats and cheeses and vegetables.

Three years of that, and then Ann had to go back to Indonesia to conduct her fieldwork, and Barry had absolutely no interest in returning to that strange place, so he stayed behind, again, with his grandparents. Ann and Maya moved to Jogjakarta, the ancestral home of the Soetoro family, which had been part of the royal court. They lived there inside the ancient palace walls with Lolo's aging mother. It was a far different place than Jakarta, more traditional, less chaotic, Javanese dancers and open markets everywhere, overflowing with batiks and shadow puppets, street vendors selling their wares in three-legged carts. Ann would teach Maya in the early mornings, just as she had done with Barry, then leave her behind with the grandmother and servants and head off to do her fieldwork with batik makers and potters and blacksmiths.

Keith and Tony Peterson were rummaging through the discount bin at a bookstore in Boulder one afternoon and came across a copy of *Dreams from My Father* several years after it was first published. "We've got to buy this," Keith said to his brother. "Look who wrote it. Barry Obama." Their friend from Punahou School. They both bought copies and raced through the memoir, absorbed by the story, especially by the sections on their high school years. They did not recognize any of the names, since they were all pseudonyms, but they recognized the smells and sounds and sensibility of the chapters and the feelings Obama expressed as he came of age as a black teenager. This was their story too. They wondered why Obama focused so much on a friend he called Ray, who in fact was Keith Kakugawa. Kakugawa was black and Japanese, and the Petersons did not even think of him as black. Yet in the book, Obama used him as the voice of black anger and angst, the provocateur of hip, vulgar, get-real dialogues.

But what interested the Petersons more was Obama's interior dialogue with himself, his sense of dislocation at the private school, a feeling that no matter what he did he was defined and confined by the expectations and definitions of white people. Keith Peterson had felt the same way, without being fully able to articulate his unease. "Now keep in mind I am reading this before [Obama] came on the national scene," he said later. "So I am reading this still person to person, not person to candidate, and it meant a lot more for that reason. It was a connection. It was amazing as I read this book, so many decades later, at last I was feeling a certain amount of closure. Having felt so isolated for so long. I wasn't alone. I spent a good portion of my life thinking I had experienced something few others had. It was surprisingly satisfying to know I wasn't crazy. I was not the only one struggling with some of these issues."

But his brother Tony, who reached Punahou first, said he did have regular discussions with Obama about many issues, including race. Tony was a senior when Obama was a freshman. The Petersons lived miles away, out in Pearl City, having grown up in a military family that was first based at Schofield Barracks. While Obama walked only five blocks to school, Tony had to ride city buses for an hour and a half each morning to get there. As he remembered it, he was one of a handful of African Americans at Punahou then, a group that also included

Obama, Lewis Anthony, Rik Smith, and Angie Jones. For some odd reason, Punahou ran on a five-day week but a six-day schedule, the days lettered A through F. Every week on F day, whatever day of the week that was, Peterson, Smith, and Obama would meet on the steps outside Cook Hall for what, with tongue in cheek, they called the Ethnic Corner. Obama and Smith were biracial, one black and white, the other black and Indian. Both of Peterson's parents were black, but he felt his unease because he was an academically inclined young man who people thought "sounded white."

"Barry had no personal reference for his blackness. All three of us were dealing with it in different ways," Peterson recalled. "How do we explore these things? That is one thing we talked about. We talked about time. We talked about our classes. We talked about girls. We talked specifically about whether girls would date us because we were black. We talked about social issues. . . . But our little chats were not agonizing. They were just sort of fun. We were helping each other find out who we were. We talked about what we were going to be. I was going to be a lawyer. Rik was going to be a lawyer. And Barry was going to be a basketball player."

Obama's interest in basketball had come a long way since his absent father showed up that one time in Honolulu and gave him his first ball. Now it was his obsession. He was always dribbling, always playing, either on the outdoor courts at Punahou or down at the playground on King Street across the street from the Baskin-Robbins ice cream parlor where he worked part-time. He was a flashy passer with good moves to the basket but an uneven and unorthodox jump shot, pulling the ball back behind his head so far that it almost disappeared behind him. "It was impossible to block, but people made fun of it," recalled one of his pals, Greg Ramos. Basketball dominated his time so much that his mother worried about him. In ninth grade, at least, he was the naïve one, believing he could make a life in the game.

In Tony Peterson's senior yearbook, Obama wrote: "Tony, man, I sure am glad I got to know you before you left. All those Ethnic Corner trips to the snack bar and playing ball made the year a lot more enjoyable, even though the snack bar trips cost me a fortune. Anyway, great knowing you and I hope we keep in touch. Good luck in everything you do, and get that law degree. Some day when I am a pro basketballer, and I want to sue my team for more money, I'll call on you."

Barry's mother, who had a wry sense of humor, once joked to friends that she was a pale-skinned Kansan who married a Kenyan and an Indonesian so that she could have brown children who would not have to worry about sunburn. Her understanding of race was far deeper than that joke; she was always sensitive to issues of identity and made a point of inculcating her children in the cultures of their fathers. Still, there were some problems that she could not resolve for them. Maya later said that her mother's overriding desire that her children not suffer perhaps got in the way. "She didn't want us to suffer with respect to identity. She wanted us to think of it as a gift that we were multilayered and multidimensional and multiracial. This meant that she was perhaps unprepared when we did struggle with issues of identity. She was not really able to help us grapple with that in any nuanced way. Maybe it would make her feel like she hadn't succeeded in surrounding us with enough love. I remember Mom wanting it *not* to be an issue."

In an apparent effort to show a lifelong plot to power, some 2008 election opponents pushed a story about Barack Obama in which he predicted in kindergarten that one day he would be president. The conspiracy certainly seemed to go off the rails by the time he reached high school. Unlike Bill Clinton, who was the most political animal at Hot Springs High in Arkansas—organizing the marching band like it was his own political machine, giving speeches at the local Rotary, maneuvering his way into a senate seat for the American Legion–sponsored Boys Nation—Obama stayed away from student leadership roles at Punahou and gave his friends no clues that a few decades later he would emerge as a national political figure. "When I look back, one of the things that stood out was that he didn't stand out," said Keith Peterson, who was a year younger than Obama. "There was absolutely nothing that made me think this is the road he would take." His friends remember him as being kind and protective, a prolific reader, keenly aware of the world around him, able to talk about foreign affairs in a way that none of the rest of them could, and yet they did not think of him as politically or academically ambitious. In a school of high achievers, he coasted as a B student. He dabbled a little bit in the arts, singing in the chorus for a few years and writing poetry for the literary magazine *Ka Wai Ola*.

The group he ran with was white, black, brown, and eclectic—Greg Orme, Mark Bendix, Bobby Titcomb, the Ramos brothers—Joe

Hansen, Tom Topolinski, Kenj Salz, and others. They were not identified with any of the traditional social sets at the private school. Punahou broke down into sets of rich girls from the Outrigger Canoe Club,
and the football players, and the math guys, and the drama crew, and
the volleyball guys, but Obama's friends did not fall into any of those
niches. "There were some basketball players in there, but it was kind
of eclectic," recalled Mike Ramos, also a hapa, his mother Anglo and
his father Filipino. "Was there a leader? Did we defer to Barry? I don't
think so. It was a very egalitarian kind of thing, also come as you are. I
don't know that there was a lot of 'we can't party with that guy.' And
I think that what was good was that we enjoyed each other's company
and people valued the friendship and maybe we couldn't quite describe
it but we knew that hanging out with these guys was important, and
was really fun."

They bodysurfed at Sandy Beach Park on the south shore, played
basketball day and night, went camping in the hills above the school,
snuck into parties at the university and out at Schofield Barracks, listened to Stevie Wonder, Fleetwood Mac, Miles Davis, and Grover
Washington at the Ramoses' place across from the school or up in
Barry's room at his grandparents' apartment. ("You listen to Grover? I
listen to Grover," were the words Mike Ramos remembered three decades later as the ones Barry uttered as a means of introducing himself
during a conversation at a party.)

And they smoked dope. His use of drugs is right there in the
memoir, with no attempt to make him look better than he was. He
acknowledged smoking marijuana and using cocaine but stopped short
of heroin. Some have suggested that he exaggerated his drug use in
the book to hype the idea that he was on the brink of becoming a
junkie, since dysfunction and dissolution always sell in memoirs. But
his friends quickly dismissed that notion. "I wouldn't call it an exaggeration," said Greg Ramos. Keith Peterson said, "Did I ever party
with Barack? Yes, I did. Do I remember specifically? If I did, then I
didn't party with him. Part of the nature of getting high is you don't
remember it thirty minutes later. Punahou was a wealthy school with
a lot of kids with disposable income. The drinking age in Hawaii then
was eighteen, so a lot of seniors could buy it legally, which means the
parent dynamic was not big. And the other partying materials were
prevalent, being in Hawaii. There was a lot of partying that went on.

And Barack has been very open about that. Coming from Hawaii, that would have been so easy to expose. If he hadn't written about it, it would have been a disaster."

If basketball was his obsession during those years, it also served as a means for Obama to work out some of his frustrations about race. In the book and elsewhere, he has emphasized that he played a "black" brand of ball, freelancing his way on the court, looking to drive to the hoop rather than wait around for a pick and an open shot. His signature move was a double-pump in the lane. This did not serve him well on the Punahou varsity team. His coach, Chris McLachlin, was a stickler for precisely where each player was supposed to be on the court and once at practice ordered his team to pass the ball at least five times before anyone took a shot. This was not Obama's style, and he had several disagreements with the coach. He never won the arguments, but the team did well enough anyway. Adhering to Coach McLachlin's organized offense, the Buffanblu won the state championship, defeating Moanalua 60–28. Obama came off the bench to score two points. So much for the dream of becoming a rich NBA star. It is true that Michael Jordan was once cut from his jayvee squad, but Barry was no Michael. He would have to find another court on which to shine.

His mother, who could exhibit her famous rolling of the eyes at her son's basketball jones, became concerned at the end of his senior year what the other court might be. She was back home from Indonesia then, and concerned that he had not even sent in his college applications. In their tensest confrontation in the memoir, he eggs her on by saying it was no big deal and he might goof off and stay in Hawaii and go to school part-time because life was just one big crapshoot anyway.

Ann exploded. She had rebelled herself once, at his very age, reacting against her own parents, and perhaps against luck and fate, by ignoring their advice and getting pregnant and marrying a man she did not know the way she thought she did. But now she was telling her son to shape up, that he could do anything he wanted if he put in the effort. "Remember what that's like? Effort? Damn it, Bar, you can't just sit around like some good-time Charlie, waiting for luck to see you through."

Sixteen years later, Barry was no more, replaced by Barack, who had not only left the island for two years at Occidental College, but then gone on to two Ivy League schools, Columbia undergrad and Harvard Law, and written a book about his life. He was into his Chicago phase, reshaping himself for his political future, but now was drawn back to Hawaii to say goodbye to his mother. Too late, as it turned out. She died on November 7, 1995, before he could get there.

Ann had returned to Honolulu early that year, a few months before *Dreams from My Father* was published. She was weakened from a cancer that had been misdiagnosed in Indonesia as indigestion. American doctors first thought it was ovarian cancer, but an examination at the Memorial Sloan-Kettering Cancer Center in New York determined that it was uterine cancer that had spread to the ovaries. Stan had died a few years earlier, and Madelyn still lived in the apartment on Beretania. Ann took an apartment on the same floor, and underwent chemotherapy treatments while keeping up with her work as best she could. "She took it in stride," said Alice Dewey, chairman of the University of Hawaii anthropology department, where Ann had done her doctoral dissertation. "She never complained. Never said, 'Why me?'"

Ann's career had reached full bloom in recent years. Her dissertation, published in 1992, was a masterwork of anthropological insight, delineating in a thousand pages the intricate world of peasant metalworking industries in Indonesia, especially traditional blacksmithing, tracing the evolution of the crafts from Dutch colonialism through the regime of General Suharto, the Indonesian military strongman. Her deepest work had been done in Kajar, a blacksmithing village near Jogjakarta. In clear, precise language, she described the geography, sociology, architecture, agriculture, diet, class structure, politics, business, and craftsmanship of the village, rendering an arcane subject in vivid, human terms. It was a long time coming, work that had begun in 1979, but Dewey said it was worth the wait—each chapter as she turned it in was a polished jewel.

Her anthropology in Indonesia was only part of Ann's focus. She had also worked in Lahore, New Delhi, and New York, helping to develop microfinancing networks that provided credit to women artisans in rural communities around the world. This was something she had begun in Jakarta in the early 1980s for the Ford Foundation, when she helped refine the Bank Rakyat Indonesia, a special bank set up to provide loans to farmers and other rural entrepreneurs in the fields she knew best, textiles and metalwork. David McCauley, who worked with her then, said she had earned a worldwide reputation in the development community. She had a global perspective from the ground up, he said, that she passed along to her children, Barack and Maya.

Maya was in New York, about to start graduate school at New York University, when her mother got sick. She and her brother were equally slow in realizing that the disease was advancing so rapidly. Maya had seen her during that visit to Sloan-Kettering, and "she didn't look well. She was in a wheelchair . . . but I guess I thought that was the treatment. I knew that someday she would die but it never occurred to me that it would be in November. I think children are capable of stretching out the boundaries of denial." School always came first with Ann, and she had urged Maya to stay at NYU until the December break.

But by November her condition had worsened. She was put on morphine to ease the pain and moved from her apartment to the Straub Clinic. One night she called Maya and said she was scared. "And my last words to her where she was able to respond were that I was coming. I arrived on the seventh. My grandmother was there and had been there for some time so I sent her home and talked to Mom and touched her and hugged her and she was not able to respond. I read her a story. A book of Creole folk tales that I had with me about renewal and rebirth, and I said it was okay with me if she decided to go ahead, that I couldn't really bear to see her like that. And she died. It was about eleven that night."

Barack came out the next day. He had just finished a book about his missing father, but now it was more clear to him than ever that his mother had been the most significant force in shaping his life. Even when they were apart, she constantly wrote him letters softly urging him to believe in himself and to see the best in everyone else.

A small memorial service was held at the Japanese Garden in the rear of the East-West Center conference building on the University of Hawaii campus. Photographs of her life were mounted on the board: Stanley Ann in Kansas and Seattle, Ann in Hawaii and Indonesia. Barack and Maya "talked story," a Hawaiian phrase that means exactly what it sounds like, remembering their uncommon mother. They remembered her spirit, her exuberance and generosity, a worldliness that was somehow also very fresh and naïve, maybe deliberately naïve, sweet and unadulterated. And her deep laugh, her familiar little midwestern sayings, the way she loved to collect batiks and wear vibrant colors and talk and talk and talk. Only about twenty people made it to the service. When it was over, they formed a caravan and drove to the south shore, past Hanauma Bay, stopping just before they reached Sandy Beach, Barry's favorite old haunt for bodysurfing. It was a lookout point with a parking lot, and down below, over the rail and at the water's edge, a stone outcropping jutted over the ocean in the shape of a massive ironing board. This is where Ann wanted them to toss her ashes. She felt connected to Hawaii, its geography, its sense of aloha, the fact that it made her two children possible, but she loved to travel, and wanted her ashes to float across the ocean. Barack and Maya stood together, scattering the remains. The others tossed flower petals into the water.

Suddenly a massive wave broke over the ironing board and engulfed them all. A sign up at the parking lot had warned visitors of the dangers of being washed out to sea. "But we felt steady," Maya said. "And it was this very slippery place and the wave came out of nowhere and it was as though she was saying goodbye."

Barack Obama left Hawaii soon after and returned to his Chicago life.

8

January 20, 2009

Here was history at its most sweeping yet intimate. In taking the oath of office as the first African American president in the nation's 233 years of existence, one man had reached a singular achievement. At five minutes after noon, Barack Hussein Obama was transformed—inevitably, no matter what happens during his administration—from an individual, a regular guy, a politician, to an icon and a symbol for the ages.

An essential rhetorical theme of his presidential campaign was that his candidacy was less about him than it was about the coming together of the people of the United States of America, as he ritually called it in his rolling cadence. We are the change we are waiting for, he would proclaim, repeating the mantra so often that he left himself open to sardonic mocking. Yet that idea, more than anything he said or did during the hours that he stepped into history, became the dominant sensibility of an extraordinary day.

With the inauguration of President Obama, witnessed by the largest crowd ever to assemble in Washington, let alone for a swearing-in ceremony, this of course was about him. But more than that, it was about everyone out there in the audience that stretched from the west side of the U.S. Capitol all the way past the Washington Monument. Every person there came with an individual story, a set of memories and meanings and reference points for a moment that many thought would never happen in their lifetime.

This created a compelling juxtaposition of the man, the moment, and the audience. The massive throngs exuded a palpable sense of euphoria over what was happening right now versus what had occurred in the past, while Obama, in his inaugural address, focused mostly on the difficult trials to come. Drawing more on the metaphors of George Washington than of Abraham Lincoln, he evoked a figurative winter of hardship that the nation must and will endure, harking back to the uncertain revolutionary winter of 1776. The crowds, meantime, seemed ready and willing to stand for as many hours as it took in the literal winter, in the whipping cold of a January day, to celebrate the meaning of the moment and not concentrate so explicitly on the tasks ahead.

Obama's message was somber, serious, and forceful, with several graceful rhetorical riffs but no attempt at lyrical exaltation. It was as though he understood that the crowd would have enough hope and joy on its own, without need of more from him. He was talking past the moment, with no need for votes, more with a sense of preparation. "We must pick ourselves up, dust ourselves off, and begin again," he said at one point, but his celebrants already seemed picked up about as straight and high as they could get.

On a weekend train down from New Jersey, an old black man wearing presidential cuff links, stooped with arthritis but in good voice, kept saying to the people in his car, "There are all these stories. Everyone has a story. We all have stories." And so they did. They were not stories about Barack Obama and his own unlikely saga, no more than his own speech was. The word "me" was utterly missing from his address, and there was only one glancing reference to his black father and none to any other relatives. So it was not his story alone that preoccupied people on this day, but the connection of his reality to their own. Emotional bits of their personal histories washed over them as they watched the forty-seven-year-old son of a white mother from Kansas and a father from Kenya place his hand on Lincoln's old Bible and begin to speak: "I, Barack Hussein Obama . . ."

Patricia Lother and her childhood friend Naomi McDowell Bryant said they started crying, eyes closed, rocking in prayer, as soon as Obama opened his mouth. They were women in theirs seventies now, one living in New York City, the other in suburban Virginia, who had grown up together in Aiken, South Carolina, during the era of Jim Crow segregation. Lother carried underneath her winter bundling a folded piece of paper that held photocopies of her great-grandmother, her grandfather, and her mother. From slavery through segregation to this moment on a lone page, which she clutched close, whispering to their memories as if she could tell her ancestors about what to them might have seemed like an unimaginable event.

Lillian Winrow, after taking a cross-country trip to Washington with her husband and two children from Sacramento, was overwhelmed by thoughts of her late father, Obed Rhodes, who grew up in Alabama, in Tuskegee and Mobile, and kept a single artifact of his early life as a reminder to his children of what used to be. It was another small piece of paper, crammed with small, almost illegible writing, inscrutable phrases, that represented the poll tax imposed on voters as a means of discouraging African Americans from participating in American democracy. Winrow had never dreamed of coming to an inaugural before, had never felt connected to the official history of her country, and yet here she stood, looking up at a giant screen of Obama becoming president, a scrap of paper in her pocket linking past to present in a way that nothing else could.

The first thought that flitted through the mind of Julie Springwater when Obama became president was also of her father, she said, though for a far different reason and from the other side of America's difficult racial history. Springwater, a white fifty-two-year-old civic activist from Providence, thought of the long-ago day in her Pittsburgh childhood when, after playing in the nearby woods with a band of young boys, she walked into her house and called her father, the social worker Harry Foreman, a "nigger." She was too young to realize what she was saying, Springwater recalled, but not too young to feel her father's wrath: *Never, ever, ever* say that word again, he told her. That memory did not reflect the sheer exhilaration she felt because of Obama's inauguration, but it was nonetheless her first unbidden thought. "That moment made an impression on me that I've talked about ever since," she said, framed by her young daughters, Mia and Sachie, adopted Cambodians who had helped form a BOG, Barack Obama Group, at the Gordon School in East Providence.

The very mention of that racial slur seemed somewhat incongruous in this setting, but Springwater was not the only white American willing to confront an ugly legacy as if this were an opportunity for cleansing along with everything else. Ed Baxter, who runs a center for homeless children in San Antonio with his wife, Lenna, said the reality of President Obama made him think back to a moment when he was ten years old, living at the Whitaker State Orphanage in Pryor, Oklahoma, and traveled with the orphanage's boxing team to fight an all-black squad from a nearby city. Baxter was accustomed to boxing against Native Americans. He had seen people with red skin, but not black. When he asked his coach what tribe they were, the answer was that one awful word. Baxter, now sixty-four, never forgot it, and it came back to him again today. "There was a lot of prejudice then," Baxter said. "We were taught prejudice."

Mark Smith, a black tractor-trailer driver who organized a busload of postal workers to come down from northern New Jersey, was another in the crowd who thought of his father as Obama took the oath of office. His dad, Russell Smith, a retired army sergeant major who fought in Korea and Vietnam, lied about his age back in the late 1940s and enlisted at age sixteen so that he could "escape from the oppressive racism of Mississippi," his son said. Russell Smith, mostly confined to the Armed Forces Retirement Home on North Capitol Street, could not make the inauguration himself, so Mark planned to skip the parade and visit briefly with his father before heading back north.

Smith's bus had rolled into the capital in the predawn darkness, joining the masses that were congregating in the vicinity of the Mall. "Let us in!" a crowd began chanting outside one of the gates leading to the parade route along Pennsylvania Avenue shortly after seven that morning, expressing a can't-wait mood that had been evident already for many hours, long before sunrise. Metro trains overflowed at four, parking lots at many outer stations were filled by five. Thousands upon thousands of early arrivers moved as friendly tribes toward their places of witness, the way illuminated by the slivered moon, the high-tech glistening of JumboTrons stationed along the vastness of the Mall, and there in the far distance, the bright white lighting of the U.S. Capitol, facing west.

Hours before the action, in a sense, and yet the assemblage in itself was its own piece of unmatched history, not just the largest but most diverse as well. In the morning chill around eight, an hour before the standing-room sections for the swearing-in were opened, thick lines stretched back three blocks from the security gates, and grew longer by the minute. At the same time, the grass and dirt fields on the western end of the Mall, where no tickets were required, filled like a vast sea of full-color humanity. Parkas, sleeping bags, blankets, American flags, Obama hats, Obama sweatshirts. People of every race, background, occupation, and geography, with tens of thousands more heading their way, an army of citizens marching quietly along the perimeter of the federal area, people for as far as the eye could see west down H Street, with a jog at Vermont Avenue and then west again along I Street, circumnavigating for eventual positions between the Lincoln Memorial and the Washington Monument.

The crowds kept coming as the president-to-be went through his traditional inaugural morning stations of the cross. Obama, in black suit and red tie, and his wife, Michelle, in brilliant yellowy gold, emerged from Blair House at quarter to nine for church services at St. John's Church, the little Episcopal chapel off Lafayette Square. Just over an hour later they arrived at the White House for coffee and a chat with the departing residents, a ritual that has come to symbolize the calm, peaceful transfer of power from one president to the next. Two more hours flitted past, and Barack Obama was president.

Betsy Tomlinson, a fifty-nine-year-old lawyer from Doylestown, Pennsylvania, had been wrapped in a sleeping bag since seven, stationed with friends directly in front of a JumboTron near the Washington Monument. Everything had been festive, "cold but happy" for more than five hours. And then Obama appeared, Tomlinson said, and the mood began to change. She thought he looked "so royal, so presidential, in charge," and serious. And as he started to speak, she sensed a shift in disposition coming over her and the crowd around her. "It was like, time to get serious," she said. "The mood change was noticeable, though not in a bad way. Just, there is a lot of work to do. Let's get to work. It was sort of a reality check."

9

Where Clinton's Coming From

Hot Springs, Arkansas

Hope gets you nowhere in the Bill Clinton story. As a small town in Arkansas and the birthplace of a potential president, the name carries with it an unavoidable poetry, but its importance beyond that falls into the realm of myth. No one named Bill Clinton was born in Hope. The boy brought into the world there on August 19, 1946, was called Billy Blythe. He became Bill Clinton years later in Hot Springs, only an hour up the road but an altogether different place, a city of secrets and vapors and ancient corruption and yet somehow purely American idealism. Hot Springs gets you somewhere.

Hot Springs is a place where when you ask county historian Inez Cline if she has any information on someone, the spunky grandmother heads to her file cabinet and says, "Let's see, why don't we look under 'Gangsters'?"

Hot Springs is a place where Dick Hildreth, the leather-faced masseur at the Arlington Hotel bathhouse, describes his intention to vote for Clinton in the idiom of an old gambler who once gave rubdowns to Lucky Luciano, Meyer Lansky, and the Capone boys from Chicago. "Yeah," he says, "I think I'll make a play on Billy this year."

Hot Springs is a place where Melinda Baran, the mayor, a contemporary of Clinton, says that "every family in town has a skeleton rattling around in the closet," and then goes on to describe how her grandfather was a member of the political machine that made the city safe for gamblers and mobsters in the 1930s and how he accumulated a wide swatch of valuable hillside property despite his modest clerk's salary.

Hot Springs is a place that inspired an elegant memoir titled *The Bookmaker's Daughter* by Shirley Abbott, who was exactly that—the daughter of a bookie who would leave for the office every morning saying, with only the slightest hint of irony, that he was off to make an honest buck. It is a place, Abbott writes, that

> *deconstructs and demolishes the American dream of virtue and hard work crowned by success, as well as all platitudes and cant about the democratic process and small-town American life. After an upbringing here, New York City politics, or Watergate, or even the savings and loan scandal, could hardly come as a surprise.*

The governor of Arkansas and Democratic nominee for president had his upbringing here. He arrived in town at age five in 1952 with his mother, Virginia, and her new husband, Roger Clinton—a little family with secrets of its own. He left at age seventeen in the fall of 1964 to study at Georgetown University—a bright and worldly young man on his way to a career that three decades later would prompt his proud hometown to hang "Boyhood Home of Bill Clinton" banners across Central Avenue.

Listening to Clinton on the trail this year, one might never know that Hot Springs was his boyhood home. At the Democratic convention in New York, he closed his acceptance speech with the words "I still believe in a place called Hope." Hot Springs went unmentioned. It sometimes seems to be the great black hole of his campaign's anecdotal history. The only time it comes up is in a context Clinton would just as soon forget: when questions are raised about whether he got special treatment from the Hot Springs draft board.

Even Clinton's mother, who still lives here, feels sensitive about the dominant role that benign and symbolically wholesome Hope has played in the Clinton story at Hot Springs's expense. She sighed with relief this summer when her son showed up at his fifties-theme forty-sixth birthday bash in Little Rock wearing his old navy-blue Hot Springs High letter sweater. "Make sure you take note of that sweater," she said as Bill and wife Hillary promenaded through the party throng. "Hot Springs people are feeling kind of left out."

The valley with the world-famous mineral springs in the Ouachita Mountains has always been a separate place from the rest of Arkansas: part restorative mecca, part safe haven, diverse, cosmopolitan, open to all the competing impulses and contradictions of human beings. Two hundred years ago the territory was neutral ground for the Caddo, Osage, Quapaw, and Natchez Indians who first came here to be healed by sweat baths in the natural hot water—and that atmosphere of tolerance persisted.

By the time the first Clinton arrived from the small Arkansas town of Dardanelle in 1919, sin had been flourishing in Hot Springs for a half century. Central Avenue was lined with ornate bathhouses on one side and betting parlors on the other. Gambling was illegal but open, as was prostitution, and in fact both enterprises funded the local government, such as it was. On the twenty-seventh of each month, officers would round up the prostitutes and march them over to the courthouse, where, in the words of an old judge, "every young blade in town was there to look them over." The prostitutes would pay five bucks, their madams twenty, and then go back to business. The gambling entrepreneurs made their payoffs in quieter fashion. It was said they had to bribe a string of thirteen judges, cops, and public officials.

There were four Clinton brothers in town between the two world wars: Roger, who would later become Bill's stepfather; Robert, who moved to Texas; Roy, a feed merchant who owned an antiques store; and Raymond, who rose to prominence as a civic leader and Buick dealer. Raymond was a sharp-eyed financier who at times challenged the status quo but knew how to accommodate it when that better suited his purposes. He had been well aware of the gangster presence in town since the days when he worked as a salesclerk as a young man.

"I was working in a drugstore back in the early twenties when Al Capone used to come down, walk down the street with his hat . . . turning his hat down . . . and he would have two men behind and two in front and two on each side," the now-deceased Clinton recalled for an oral history project in 1980. "You couldn't miss him . . . and I stood out lots of nights in front of the drugstore watching him walking down the street because just above me was the Southern Club, and that's where they hung out when gambling was going on."

Capone and all the other notorious mobsters of that generation made frequent visits to the spa in provincial Arkansas. They felt protected in the valley of hot waters. Federal agents and Chicago detectives would trail them down to Hot Springs, but for the most part there was an uneasy truce here. It was a common sight at the bathhouses for cops and criminals to be resting side by side on massage tables getting rubdowns, chatting amiably. Raymond Clinton appreciated one aspect of the gangland presence after he got his Buick dealership. "I did a lot of business with them," he said. "They bought a lot of cars."

The city boss from 1926 to the end of World War II was a colorful little dictator named Leo P. McLaughlin, who would take daily tours of his town in a buggy pulled by his show horses, Scotch and Soda. His political machine was the envy of the big-city boys back East. His theory of politics, as described by his partner in power, Judge Verne Ledgerwood, was: You rub my back and I'll rub yours. His version of integrity was summarized in what he once said about his police chief: "He was honest. He did exactly what we told him to do."

Raymond Clinton got on the wrong side of Leo P., and vice versa, in the aftermath of a fire that leveled four downtown stores in the late 1930s. Clinton complained that the fire raged out of control only because all the fire trucks were unavailable. The firefighters were cruising around town at the time with political banners promoting McLaughlin's candidate for governor. One of the mayor's cronies heard Clinton's complaint, and here is how the scene went from that point, according to Clinton's tape-recorded recollection:

"The next morning he called me and said, 'Raymond, this is Leo.' I said, 'All right.' He said, 'I heard what you said about me yesterday and I want you to know that I am in politics and you are in the automobile business and I'm going to break you and run you out of Hot Springs.' And I said, 'Well, you SOB, crack your whip.' And that was the beginning of what you might say was our political battle."

McLaughlin told the gamblers to stop buying Buicks and bullied Clinton in minor ways, but he never ran him out of town. In 1946, at about the same time that Billy Blythe was born down in Hope, Raymond Clinton and several of his buddies who had just returned from the war plotted McLaughlin's overthrow. They formed what was known as the GI Movement and ran veterans for all city and county offices on an antigambling reform ticket. The GIs won, and their first act was to strip McLaughlin's name off the new airport. Shirley Abbott, the author whose father was a bookmaker, still remembers that year and Clinton's role in the reform movement. "I remember my dad would go around the house muttering about 'that damn Raymond Clinton,' " she says.

But the reformers turned out to be a mixed lot. They included prosecutor Sid McMath, who went on to become the governor of Arkansas, and Q. Byrum Hurst, who went on to become Jimmy Hoffa's lawyer. In the end, as with many reformers, it turned out they were mainly interested in power. As Raymond Clinton himself said of McLaughlin: "He could've been a great man and I still say they would've built a monument to him when the boys came back had he said, 'Boys, I've had enough of it, you all want it, I'll help you.' But he didn't do that. He was too greedy."

McLaughlin was indicted twice on corruption charges, but never convicted. And gambling soon returned to Hot Springs. This time the big man in town was an international mobster, Owney Madden, who moved to Arkansas as part of a probation deal with East Coast prosecutors. Raymond Clinton sold Madden his cars. The first was a black Buick convertible with a khaki top.

"Mr. Madden wanted to call me Ray, and he said, 'Ray, can I give you a check?' I said, 'Sure.' I knew he had to be worth that kind of money," Clinton recalled. "So he wrote the check out—he had a hard time doing it—and when he handed it to me I looked at it and I said—uh, he told me to call him Owney—I said, 'Owney, this check is no good.' He said, 'Jesus, Ray, I just put twenty Gs in, it had better be good.' So after a bit I showed him what was wrong. He didn't put the amount and he didn't sign it."

People say Roger Clinton knew how to have a good time—his friends called him "Dude"—but he was never much with money. His brother Raymond looked after him in a sense, and kept him employed in his auto business. In 1933 Roger married the widow Murphy, Ina Mae, who had two young sons, George and Roy. Roy Murphy remembers him as "a great stepfather" who would take the boys fishing and camping and who never showed signs of being the violent drunkard who later tormented his second wife and her son Billy. When Raymond expanded his business in 1946 and opened a Buick dealership in the small town of Hope, he sent Roger down to run the shop. Roger did not want to move there, so he commuted, coming back to his wife and stepchildren on weekends. His marriage swiftly deteriorated, and in 1948 Ina Mae divorced him. The divorce papers in the Garland County Courthouse in Hot Springs indicate that heavy drinking played a role in the divorce. At least once, Roger hit his wife in the head with a shoe, giving her a black eye and a bloody scalp.

Two years later, on June 19, 1950, Roger married Virginia Cassidy Blythe, a young nurse who had lost her first husband, William Jefferson Blythe, in a car accident in 1946 three months before her son Billy was born. The new Clinton family split time between Hope and Hot Springs until 1952, when they moved up to Hot Springs for good. Roger steered clear of his ex-wife and the Murphy boys; for much of the next decade Ina Mae fought with little success to get Roger to pay $135 a month in child support.

Roger Clinton did not adopt Billy, according to court papers, but in a sense Billy adopted him. He started calling himself Billy Clinton from the moment he began school in Hot Springs. They lived in a big house on Park Avenue that was owned by Raymond Clinton. Roger ran the parts department at the Buick agency. Virginia was a nurse-anesthetist. Billy was her special kid—big, talkative, inquisitive, earnest beyond his years. Even before he reached his teens, she later recalled, he seemed to be taking care of her.

For every shadow of darkness in Hot Springs, there was a corresponding ray of light, and Billy Clinton seemed to live in that light. The same springs that drew the gamblers to town also brought a rich mix of tourists and new residents from all over the country and Europe, giving the city an international flair that excited young Clinton to the possibilities of the outside world. "This is just a little thing, but for example I remember once I was playing a New Year's Eve dance at the Arlington Hotel, our little band, and there were all these Jewish kids from New York who asked me to play 'Hava Nagila,' " Clinton, a saxophonist, recalled in an interview. "So I said, 'Hum a few bars for me.' And I played it by ear for them. I will never forget that."

The cosmopolitan nature of the town also attracted an excellent corps of teachers to Hot Springs High, the elite school in Garland County. While many schools in Arkansas were so backward they offered no foreign languages and gave students credit for parking cars at football games, Hot Springs High offered Latin—which Clinton studied for four years—all the higher mathematics courses, and sophisticated world events classes where Clinton examined the early stages of the Vietnam War and President Kennedy's initiatives in Latin America. "The whole culture surrounding the high school was of a very strong middle class. Education was extremely important," said Bob Haness, one of Clinton's classmates. "We were the Chosen Ones. We were the ones who were going to do better than our parents did. We never skipped school and never thought about skipping school. It was a small town but a very liberal town in a sense. We always felt different from the other people in Arkansas, who were hicky and redneck."

Shirley Abbott attended Hot Springs High a decade before Clinton, and remembers how open and intellectual the school seemed even then in comparison with the rest of Arkansas, and how its idealism stood in such sharp contrast with the cynicism of the gambling milieu. Although the state forbade the teaching of evolution at the time, Abbott recalled a biology teacher who ignored the ban and spent a semester on the subject, comparing the seven days of Genesis to seven geologic eras. When Billy Clinton came along, he was like a vessel for all the knowledge the teachers of Hot Springs could pour. "The teachers all loved Billy," said classmate Peggy Parker Janske. "That kind of gagged everybody, that he was the teachers' pet, but he was such a nice guy nobody could dislike him."

Virginia was an interesting combination of the competing forces of her new town. She was devoted to learning and self-improvement, and from an early age pushed her son to excel, often boasting that he would be president someday. She had an exotic side to her as well, driving around town in Buick convertibles, dyeing a white streak in her hair, building a sunken bathtub in her house. She worked nights as a nurse and often went to the Oaklawn racetrack in the afternoons, placing her two-dollar bets.

Roger Clinton's drinking grew worse year by year. On March 1, 1959, according to divorce papers at the Garland County Courthouse, he took Virginia to a dance and beat her. "My husband became quite drunk and kicked me and struck me," she said. Later that month he "threw me to the floor and began to stomp me, pulled my shoe off and hit me on the head several times." She separated from him then and filed for divorce, but he promised to quit drinking and they reconciled. Two years later Virginia again was humiliated in public. "We went to a party given by Mrs. Perry for Christmas 1961," she said in a divorce deposition. "My husband was so intoxicated I was unable to get him home. I was finally able to get my oldest son, Billy, to help me with the car and we were finally able to get him home." Bill tried to protect his mother. On dates, he would call home every hour to make sure she was okay.

On May 15, 1962, Virginia divorced Roger Clinton. Less than a month later, Bill went to the county courthouse and officially had his name changed from William Blythe to William Jefferson Clinton. The reason for the name change, the court document states, was: "No pleasant associations connected with the name Blythe as he never did know his father and he has always been known by his friends and in school records as William Jefferson Clinton." Less than two months later, Virginia remarried Roger, largely out of pity, she later said, and against her son's advice. They stayed married until his death, which occurred while Bill was away at Georgetown.

The gambling culture was hotter than ever during Bill Clinton's high school years. It embarrassed him, he said. He told his mother that he hated to see so many lives wasted by the false lure of quick money. And it was becoming a national embarrassment as well. Attorney General Robert F. Kennedy cited the town as a haven of gangland corruption and sent an army of agents to Arkansas to try to clean up the place. It was not until 1967, when a reform Republican, Winthrop Rockefeller, took over the governorship, that the last slot machines were hauled off to a dump and ground to dust by bulldozers.

In some ways, Hot Springs has changed considerably over the past twenty-five years. It hit bottom and is now enjoying a renaissance. The bathhouses, which turned seedy and closed, are reopening one by one. Grand old Hot Springs High was abandoned for a newer facility, but the academic talk of the town these days is a statewide math and science high school opening here next fall, a product of Governor Clinton's education agenda. The Southern Club, the main gambling parlor, is now a wax museum. Family entertainment centers have taken the place of nightclubs such as the Vapors, the place where Clinton's mother would go to see Vegas-style acts. An old man described by neighbors as a grouchy hermit now inhabits the Park Avenue house where the Clinton family lived for a decade. Clinton's mother now goes by the name Virginia Kelley. She lives out on Lake Hamilton with her fourth husband.

If Hope takes you nowhere in understanding Bill Clinton, Hot Springs tells much about his past, present, and future. Out of this town, this family, came someone who believed that the world could always be better, that people could start anew every day, that there were some things in the past just as well forgotten; someone with a full appreciation of the dark and light sides of human nature, with a divided soul: part earnest preacher, part fast-talking gambler, with an urge to reform, yet also to accommodate.

———

In writing about Bill Clinton in 1992, I spent most of my time in Arkansas, far from the presidential campaign trail, trying to figure out the places of his life and the forces that shaped him. It was only after spending weeks in each of his two hometowns that I came to a central understanding: Hope was largely a fiction and Hot Springs better explained him.

10

The Great Escape

On a bright and crisp early October noon, the "best men for the world's fight" assembled at the foot of West Forty-sixth Street in Manhattan for a most curious passage. There, at pier 86 on the Hudson River waterfront along what once was known as luxury liner row, Bill Clinton, who had graduated months earlier from Georgetown University, embarked on a great adventure, certainly, yet one that found him advancing, retreating, escaping, and searching all at once, sailing away from the fiery tumult of 1968 America in an opulent vessel from a bygone age bound for the sheltering, silent libraries of medieval England.

He arrived wearing a gray suit and was seen off by his college girlfriend, Denise Hyland, who boarded the liner with him and stood on the deck for a few minutes. When she looked into his eyes one last time to bid him bon voyage, she was struck by his expression of awe—a sense of "Oh, my God, I'm the luckiest guy in the world!" The anxiety he felt about his uncertain draft status gave way to the thrill of the moment. Here he was, the first from any branch of his family to graduate from college, now standing amid the academic gold medalists of his generation, headed overseas for the first time, carrying not a rifle but a sack of books and a saxophone case, graced with a mark of prestige that would brighten his résumé forever, retracing the path to Oxford and worldly sophistication that Senator Fulbright, his Arkansas mentor, had followed nearly half a century earlier as a Rhodes Scholar.

The SS *United States,* with her razor-sharp bow and two massive funnels, was an impressive sight as she edged down the river out past the Statue of Liberty to the broad ocean beyond. She was known as "the Big U," an affectionate nickname for the biggest, sleekest American luxury liner plying the North Atlantic, a quadruple-screw turbine steamship that since her maiden voyage in 1952 had proudly retained the Blue Riband as the world's fastest liner, averaging more than thirty-two knots and surpassing forty knots in occasional bursts of record speed. Fast and elegant she was, but also obsolete, destined for dry dock within a year. The group voyage to England by sea had been a cherished Rhodes tradition, a rite of bonding, a decompression chamber of sorts from the New World to the Old, but it seemed out of date if not vulgar by now, when airplanes could reach the same destination in hours rather than days, and the world moved to a more urgent rhythm. The great ship and the elite young men sailed off together facing the same paradox. They were molded to succeed in a way of life that was vanishing.

There were dozens of other students sailing the Big U to England that month, including a sizable number of undergraduate women in junior year abroad programs whose presence greatly enlivened the trip. But as the voyage got under way, the first-year Rhodes scholars spent much of their time among themselves, erasing and redrawing the invisible but palpable lines of highbrow versus middlebrow, Ivy League versus land grant, cool versus uncool. A historian among them once said of the American Rhodes scholars that they go through several stages of self-realization. First, hearing the accomplishments of the others, they wonder, How did I get here? After spending five days together on the boat, the question becomes, How did they get here?

This might seem a hard crowd to intimidate. When "How Gentle Is the Rain" played over the sound system in the restaurant bar and Paul Parish of Mississippi blurted out assuredly, "Anybody know what this song is based on?" it seemed that the answer—a Bach cantata— arrived from thirty voices at once. But beneath their surface composure many of the young men were struggling with a measure of self-doubt. George Butte, an English major from the University of Arizona, the son of Phoenix schoolteachers, looked around the group of intellectuals and "felt like an outsider amid the mandarins." Darryl Gless from the University of Nebraska suddenly assessed himself as "something of a provincial hick." The women on board seemed equally imposing to him. "A woman would say she was from Vassar or Barnard and I'd say, 'Where's that?' and they'd look at me as if I were teasing them."

Butte and Gless might not have realized that many of the fellows they considered mandarins were sizing up the competition and feeling deficient themselves. Robert Reich of Dartmouth, who made everyone else's list of the most impressive figures in the brood, was "overwhelmed by the intellectual firepower and felt grossly inadequate" during the first round of mingling aboard ship. The others, to Reich, "seemed ready to launch their careers in the direction of ambassadors or presidents or university professors." He felt that "a great mistake had been made by the selection committee in picking me." Reich's Dartmouth friend John Isaacson, a college debate champion, felt as unsure of himself as anyone, though he was certain that he intimidated some of the others. "At that age you don't really know about somebody, so you just try to talk your way through."

Clinton was different. While others looked for one or two compatriots, he ignored the hierarchy that was developing and looked for friendships everywhere. He had an ability to walk into any conversation on the deck and immediately place himself at the center of it. Some of his fellow scholars took to him quickly. Darryl Gless thought that Clinton was "down to earth and altogether lacking in pretense. Aside from the self-deprecating humor, he was also an extraordinary listener. Others were good at self-presentation with a script to impress you with." Others found Clinton a bit manipulative. Daniel Singer's first impression was that Clinton "sought out everybody that he thought was informative or valuable and debriefed them. He picked brains." Douglas Eakeley of Yale classified him as "a classic Southern glad-handing politician." Was he open about his political aspirations? Rick Stearns of Stanford certainly found him to be. "I remember meeting Clinton and him telling me within forty-five minutes that he planned to go back to Arkansas to be governor or senator and would like to be a national leader someday." Then and always, these contradictions coexisted in Clinton—considerate and calculating, easygoing and ambitious, mediator and predator.

The first day at sea was smooth and sunny. George Butte, virtually penniless but for the Rhodes stipend, in a burst of optimism rented a deck chair for the full five days. Bob Reich basked in the afternoon warmth, his feelings of inadequacy melting along with larger burdens. The assassinations of King and Bobby Kennedy, the Vietnam War, the draft, the raging cities—they were sailing away from all that. "What a relief!" Reich sighed. After four years of college activism, he was feeling "a little burnt out," and now, as they left America, he felt as though a weight were being lifted from his shoulders.

Reich was a formidable character, with his piercing blue eyes, his curly black hair, his quizzical, hectoring nature—"What are you saying there?" he would ask, never at a loss for words himself. He was a physical runt, only four-foot-ten, his growth stunted by Fairbanks disease, a rare genetic illness in which the hip joints fail to grow fully. Yet he was an overpowering theatrical presence. Tom Williamson, from Harvard, discovered of Reich that "you put his size aside within minutes of meeting him." At Dartmouth, Reich had acted as though he were a peer to the administrators and sometimes as if he were their boss. John Sloan Dickey, the college president, relied on him for advice on how to accommodate the contentious forces of youth, from antiwar radicals to black power advocates pushing for their own studies program and union. Reich ended his college days by being selected from the multitudes for a *Time* cover story on the class of 1969, placed on the cutting edge of a class of 630,000 seniors that the magazine said included a fair share of draft dodgers and pot smokers but also "the most conscience-stricken, moralistic, and perhaps, the most promising graduates in U.S. academic history."

At the time, Reich not only seemed more imposing than the six-foot-three Clinton, he also more clearly personified the agitated, rebellious mood of his comfortably born generation. Clinton brought with him the values of lower-middle-class Arkansas, not yet ready to reject an established order that he and his kinfolk were striving to become part of, not so eager to denounce American materialism when his family had never enjoyed much of it. Reich, who came out of the wealth and conservatism of suburban Westchester County, New York, fretted that his generation was being seduced by status and the accumulation of goods. He was rebelling against "status quo-ism," he informed *Time,* and was promoting a new humanist ethic that allowed for self-initiative and creativity. "Destruction is the choice when creation is impossible," he said, as a means of explaining the violence seeping into protest movements in 1968.

By the second morning aboard the Big U, a North Atlantic storm pushing twenty-foot swells sent Reich back to his cabin, where he remained thereafter, immobilized by seasickness, "vomiting quietly and wondering how my forefathers made it across." The *United States* was a rough-riding ship, designed with speed in mind at a time when the government thought it might be needed for troop transport. It rode light, fast, and high in the water, rather like a duck, rolling with the waves, undulating rather than chopping, its stern yawing. Often penned indoors by the nasty ocean wind, the scholars and their friends set up camp in the bar and drank, smoked, and talked the days and nights away. It was in mid-ocean aboard the Big U, his stepfather dead and the memories of his abusive bouts of drunken rage buried with him, that Bill Clinton broke his long vow of alcoholic abstinence. Someone offered him a drink, and rather than automatically declining, he said to himself, It's wrong for me to be scared of this, and he accepted. No longer "terrified of indulgence," he became an occasional beer and wine drinker.

Clinton excused himself from the bar scene once and knocked on Reich's cabin door holding a tray of crackers and a ginger ale. "I thought you might be needing these—heard you weren't feeling well," he said. As the story was told and retold and embroidered over the years, it seemed that Clinton devoted hours to nursing Reich back to health, forgoing all pleasure for the sake of a sequestered friend. In fact, Reich had several concerned visitors, and his wretched condition was one of the regular topics of discussion in the lounge, along with the draft, the war, the Democratic convention in Chicago that August, and the attractiveness of various young women aboard the ship.

Most conversations returned to each young man's draft status and how long he expected to last at Oxford before the fateful induction notice arrived. "A lot of us whose futures were uncertain were going to Oxford by the grace of God and weren't sure how long we would stay over," Doug Eakeley said later. Hannah Achtenberg, a Smith College graduate on her way to St. Anne's to study economics, spent hours chatting with the Rhodes crew in the ship lounge. She thought that "all the boys were scared stiff because of the draft. Some didn't know whether they would last a month. Some were tortured about whether they should have left at all. Some were wondering whether they should ever go back. Everyone was trying to figure out how to manage the dilemma." One scholar, Frank Aller from Washington, intimated that his inclination was to resist rather than accept induction.

Aller was at the center of the draft discussions along with Strobe Talbott, who perhaps more than any other member of his Rhodes class captured the crosscurrents of the moment. Talbott was the cautious, correct, accomplished son of a liberal Republican investment banker from Cleveland, a straight arrow who, following in the tradition of his grandfather and father, was registered at birth for admission to Yale, and who would later become such an Old Blue that he would sing "The Whiffenpoof Song" in the shower. Talbott had been trained at elite private schools for leadership by the establishment and was now unsettled because of the Vietnam War. At Yale he was Mr. Inside, close to campus officials and chairman of the *Yale Daily News,* at a time when the inside was in chaos, rebelling against itself. Disheveled and earnest in a prep school way, he was in the conservative wing of the antiwar movement and could never be a revolutionary. Unlike Reich, who painted his world with broad brushstrokes, Talbott was precise and incremental. John Isaacson compared them by saying that "Reich saw nothing but forests, one forest after another, while Talbott saw every single tree in the forest."

But Talbott was to Yale what Reich was to Dartmouth, a link to the administration and a student leader. He and his best friend at Yale, Derek Shearer, the son of the journalist Lloyd Shearer, met every month with Yale's president, Kingman Brewster, to talk about student social issues, including their proposal to make the institution coeducational. They also spent hours talking to Brewster about the war. Yale was one of the intellectual battlegrounds of the time. At Shearer's invitation, James Reston of the *New York Times* visited the campus and, after having lunch with Talbott, wrote a column saying that the Washington establishment was in trouble if it had lost the trust of responsible young men like Talbott. At Yale's 1968 commencement, Talbott led a petition drive signed by four hundred of the one thousand seniors declaring that their opposition was so strong that they would not accept conscription into the military. In a Class Day speech, he said that his class faced a paradox of facing induction into a war it opposed. Few members of his class had experience with the military, he said, but "all of us, the entire class of 1968, are in a sense already veterans of the war in Vietnam. We are certainly veterans of that dimension of the war which has brought such frustration and intellectual if not literal violence into our country, into our homes and into our lives."

Now Vietnam reached them even in the darkest recesses of the Big U. When Talbott and his friends ducked inside the ship's cinema to watch a movie, they found themselves confronted by John Wayne starring in the Vietnam glory film *The Green Berets*.

There was another aspect to the voyage that seemed even more incongruous—in retrospect, deliciously so. Also aboard the luxury liner, making his own escape of sorts to Europe, was Bobby Baker, the ultimate Washington wheeler-dealer, a longtime LBJ crony who had been convicted in a splashy 1967 corruption trial of income-tax evasion, theft, and conspiracy to defraud the federal government. Baker knew that he was bound for prison sooner or later, whenever his defense lawyer, Edward Bennett Williams, emptied his ample briefcase of appeals. In the meantime he would continue living the high life. Baker's set of first-class cabins lodged a traveling entourage that included some slick-haired sharpies in sharkskin suits and a few platinum-blond escorts. "The whole scene was bizarre. Here were the bright academics slipping across the Atlantic to flee thoughts of the draft and Vietnam and *The Green Berets* is playing in the boat theater, and Baker and his boys are in the bar every time we go in there, trying to instruct us on the ways of the world," recalled John Isaacson. "The whole crowd of us were appalled. They were racist and jingoistic and stupid. Here we were heading off as idealists and they persuasively convinced us that there was something sleazy and corrupt in the government."

If the Rhodes boys were appalled by Baker, he was enthralled by them. Near the end of the voyage, Baker emerged at the center of a reception held in their honor. Rick Stearns, already active in the reform wing of the Democratic Party, refused to attend "as a matter of principle." But Bill Clinton was there, standing at Baker's side, soaking in tales of power and intrigue. Robert Gene Baker of South Carolina had worked on Capitol Hill since he was a young page. When Lyndon Johnson became Senate majority leader, he tapped Baker for his staff

Brooke Shearer

Strobe Talbott, Bill Clinton, Frank Aller

and relied on him thereafter as a vote counter, schmoozer, gossip, and bill collector. The other senators called him "Lyndon Jr." or "Little Lyndon." Clinton, a connoisseur of practical politics, loved to hear Baker's stories about Johnson and the Senate and the way things really worked. It was while watching his performance with Bobby Baker that Strobe Talbott first understood Clinton's "raw political talent."

They reached Europe on the fifth day, first making a short stop early in the morning at Le Havre, across the English Channel in France. Bob Reich stayed on deck, looking out at the port with a sense of awe, thinking, This is actually France! He had never been overseas before. "I remember hearing people shout at each other in French. It seemed remarkable." Ten of his fellow travelers skipped off the ship and roamed the dock, absorbing the foreign sounds and smells, but soon grew afraid that the Big U would leave without them. Hannah Achtenberg, who had become a little sister to the Rhodes crew, later remembered how they linked arms and started running wildly back to the boat together. As they clambered across the wharf, arm in arm, Strobe Talbott cried out, "What a motley group of Christian gentlemen!"

Late that afternoon they steamed past the Isle of Wight and landed at Southampton, on the south English coast. The passengers lined the deck as the ship eased up to the pier. Darryl Gless stood next to Clinton at the rail. They looked down and saw a slender man in big glasses, wearing a bowler hat and a long black raincoat, and holding an umbrella. "Look at him!" Clinton said, and they both laughed. He seemed to fit the upper-crust stereotype so perfectly that Clinton thought he might be an entertainer in period costume. In fact he was Sir Edgar Williams, who had served as chief of intelligence for British field marshal Bernard Montgomery during World War II. Sir Edgar, the warden of Rhodes House, was a man of tradition who drank sherry every afternoon and quite enjoyed his annual trek to Southampton to meet the boat from America and escort the Yanks to their colleges at Oxford.

He rounded up the class of 1968 and directed them to a waiting bus for the ride north to Oxford. It was a strange, disorienting ride through the dark English countryside that chilly October night. The boys on the bus could see little but slanting rain pounding against the windows. When the bus reached Oxford, it deposited the scholars in clumps at each of the colleges to which they had been assigned. Four of them—Doug Eakeley of Yale, Reich and Isaacson of Dartmouth, and Bill Clinton of Georgetown—were dropped off at University College on High Street, a curving thoroughfare lined with the dark stone fronts of several medieval Oxford colleges.

At the front gate they were met by Douglas Millin, the college porter who was every bit as much an English character as Sir Edgar. Where the warden came out of the officer corps, the porter was the veteran enlisted man—crusty, foulmouthed, cynical, all-knowing, protective of his turf, scornful of superiors. He took one look at the quartet and muttered, "They told me I was getting four Yanks and here they send me three and a half!" Then, turning directly to Reich, he bellowed, "You're the goddamn bloody shortest freaking American I've ever seen in my life! I didn't know it was possible for America to produce someone that freakin' small." He insulted each of the Americans in turn and intimidated them so thoroughly that they rarely dared to venture too far into his cloistered world thereafter. All of them but one, that is. To Bill Clinton, this ornery porter was just another skeptical voter to swing his way.

11

"Nice Tie"

Once, in 1981, when Bill Clinton was out of government briefly, having been defeated as governor of Arkansas after only one two-year term, he appeared as a guest lecturer at a political literature course at the University of Arkansas in Fayetteville. He analyzed some of the more complex and compelling political characters in literature, including Willie Stark, the corrupt Southern governor in Robert Penn Warren's *All the King's Men*. He also discussed several biographies that had helped shape his perspective, including ones of Lincoln, Hitler, and Churchill. In all political leaders, Clinton told the class, there was a struggle between darkness and light. He mentioned the darkness of insecurity, depression, and family disorder. In great leaders, he said, the light overcame the darkness, but it was always a struggle.

This observation is obvious, yet it stuck with me throughout my study of Clinton. I tend to be forgiving, interested in finding light as well as darkness: The struggle between those two forces is what fascinates me, the humanity in any person, especially one who appears to have the makings of an underdog. It was not difficult to find the darker corners of Clinton's life. He could be deceptive, and he came from a family in which lying and philandering were routine, two traits that he apparently had not overcome. As he grew older, the more tension he felt between idealism and ambition, the more he gave in to ambition, sometimes at the expense of friends and causes that he had once believed in. I could also see his sources of light. He was a fatherless son who came out of the depths of provincial southwestern Arkansas and never seemed ashamed of his roots. Many people who have dismissed him as a phony are far more invented creatures and less connected to their pasts than he has always been. I was struck by the friends he made over the years, many of them people I greatly admired, such as Taylor Branch, the chronicler of the civil rights era, or others who were lovable and utterly without guile, such as his Hot Springs childhood pal David Leopoulos and Georgetown roommate Tom Campbell. He seemed to have multiple personalities, some redeeming. The forces of light often prevailed when he dealt with African Americans and other minorities. When he was a young law professor at the University of Arkansas, he tutored the first wave of black students at the law school, who before he arrived had felt alienated, without mentors. It was his intense interest in their lives, many of them said later, that made it possible for them to survive and get their law degrees. They called him "Wonder Boy."

Clinton's ability to empathize with others, his desire to become a peacemaker and bring diverse groups together, always struck me as the better part of his character. It was, to me, the first necessary ingredient of any good leader, and something that most American politicians seemed to lack. I also came to think of his indomitable nature as a mostly positive trait; his refusal to give up and his ability to find a way out of whatever predicament he found himself in, usually a mess of his own making, in some sense represented to me man's eternal struggle to persist in spite of his imperfections. It was often tempting to try to separate the good from the bad in Clinton, to say that the part of him that was indecisive, too eager to please, and prone to deception was more revealing of the inner man than the part of him that was tireless, intelligent, empathetic, and self-deprecating. But they could not be separated. They came as part of the same package.

Some of it can be explained by my bias for the underdog, but I usually find Clinton least impressive when he is riding high. The symbolic expression of that arrogance came when he was in Africa and received word that the Paula Jones case had been dismissed, and the cameras that evening found him up in his lighted hotel room, champing on an unlit cigar, pounding joyously on a drum. When I see him like that, only one thought enters my mind: Trouble is on the way. The endless cycle of Bill Clinton's life is loss and recovery. When he is down, he will find his way back, and when he is up, he will find a way to screw up again. Clinton was riding high for most of 1996, after the Republicans had shut down the government and handed him back his presidency, and done him the further favor of running old Bob Dole against him, allowing him to frame the election as a choice between the twenty-first and nineteenth centuries.

I covered that election for the *Post* and submitted numerous requests to Press Secretary Mike McCurry for interviews with the president. Clinton had not talked to me since my book *First in His Class* came out. I knew that many of his friends and associates regarded it as accurate, but that he had hated the half of it that was critical of him. Dick Morris, who had talked to me extensively for the biography and was then running the reelection campaign, told me that Clinton would never deal with me for two reasons: First, I knew him too well, and it made him uncomfortable; and second, the few portions of the biography that examined his sex life upset the first lady so much that she had turned "frosty" on the president for several weeks and had refused to talk to him or sleep in the same bedroom with him in the White House residence.

This struck me as peculiar. What I wrote about Clinton's sexual behavior was so mild compared with the stories that Arkansas state troopers had told the *Los Angeles Times* and the *American Spectator,* and Mrs. Clinton had been dealing with her husband's waywardness for more than two decades—why would my book trigger such a fierce reaction? The answer, as it came back to me from White House aides, was revealing then, and had echoes in Hillary's response to the Lewinsky scandal two years later. When it came to Clinton and sex, she knew but she didn't want to know. Unless confronted directly by evidence that she accepted and could not ignore, she redirected her attention and her anger at their shared enemies. She believed what I wrote, especially since some of it came not from their adversaries but from Betsey Wright, Clinton's former chief of staff in Arkansas. She did not consider me part of a right-wing conspiracy, though she was starting to develop a theory that the *Washington Post* was somehow out to get her and the president.

Clinton, in a winning mood, gave interviews to all the major news organizations during the week before his triumphant train ride to Chicago in August 1996, where he would accept his party's nomination for a second term. The *Post* was granted an interview, and three reporters were to take part in it: John Harris, the White House correspondent; Dan Balz, the chief political correspondent; and me, the Clinton biographer. I was writing a piece examining how he had come back from the depths of 1994. A few hours before the scheduled appointment at the White House, as I was sitting at my desk preparing questions, the phone rang and it was McCurry on the line. Was I really planning to participate in the interview? he asked. Yes, of course, he already knew that. "Well," he said, "it would be better if you didn't come. If you're there, it might blow up the interview." McCurry never said it directly, but the implication was that Clinton had learned I was coming and had indicated to his staff that he did not like it. I told my editors on the national staff, and we decided that this was not worth taking a principled stand over; Balz and Harris could go without me.

The truth is I had no intention of asking Clinton uncomfortable questions about his private life, and in fact never was particularly interested in doing so. In any case, when the *Post* delegation entered the Oval Office that afternoon, Clinton noticed that it consisted only of Harris and Balz. "Where's David?" he asked, with the wistful tone of someone missing a long-lost friend. "I haven't seen him in a long time."

The next month, I put in another request for an interview with Clinton, this one for a *Washington Post Magazine* story I was preparing on Dole and Clinton, "The Old Man and the Kid." I traveled with the White House press corps following the president on a campaign swing from Chicago to the Grand Canyon to Las Vegas and up to Washington State, where the Clintons and the Gores launched another of their bus trips. On the second day, McCurry told me that Clinton and Hillary had spotted me in the crowd a few times and wondered aloud why I was there. On the third day, he informed me that the Clinton entourage was unhappy with a story from the campaign trail I had written describing Clinton on a roll as a man with a voracious appetite, wanting more crowds, more speeches, more hands to shake, more programs to promise, more of everything. Harold Ickes, the deputy chief of staff, complained that I was using "appetite" as a code word for "sex." Not really, but an interestingly defensive perspective.

Near the end of the trip, McCurry came up to me with promising news: I would finally get the Clinton interview. There would be a long flight back to Washington, D.C., interrupted only by a brief stop in South Dakota, and for the second leg of that journey, he said, they would take me off the press plane and put me in the back of Air Force One. "It's going to be a Maraniss moment," he said, smiling wryly. So I traipsed off the press plane in Sioux Falls and found a seat with the small press pool that accompanies the president in the partitioned jumbo jet. Thirty minutes into the flight, McCurry came back and found me. "Follow me," he said, leading me to an empty quarter in the midsection of the plane that looked like a small classroom. "Look, the president's tired," McCurry said. "He's not going to talk to you. He's not in the mood to entertain your questions about the condition of his soul. What you are interested in has nothing to do with this campaign. He's got an election to win."

We landed in Washington late that night, and on the tarmac at Andrews Air Force Base, as I was hauling my suitcase to the terminal, McCurry came over to me one last time. "After the election," he said. "You'll get the very first interview after the election. Promise." Then he explained that his boss was as difficult for him to deal with as he was for me, and he turned his baseball cap around with the bill facing backward, Junior Griffey style, and ran across the runway to Marine One for a chopper ride through the darkness to the White House.

I did not get the first Clinton interview after the election. That went to David Brinkley of ABC News, who had eased the way for his scoop by thoroughly trashing the president as a phony a few days earlier. After that, McCurry stopped answering my faxes, and I persuaded my wife to move out to Green Bay, Wisconsin, with me for the winter so that I could begin research on my biography of Vince Lombardi, whom I did not have to worry about avoiding me, since he was dead.

There is a coda to my dealings with Clinton. In May 1997, the president and I found ourselves on the same dais at a luncheon meeting of the American Society of Newspaper Editors. He was the guest speaker; I was among the award winners. Clinton was on crutches, hobbling from his late-night scramble down golfer Greg Norman's stairs. He entered the room from the other side and did not have to go past my seat on his way to the podium. But after the speech, he had to come by me to shake hands with people in the audience. As he approached me, my mind raced. So much that I knew, so many questions to ask. But of course I could think of nothing to say.

"Long time," I muttered.

"Hi, David," he said. "Congratulations on the award. Nice tie."

And then he was gone, hobbling on. My wife and father were in the audience, and I whispered down to them, "He said, 'Nice tie.' " Clinton worked the rope line, and when he reached my family, he stopped and chatted with them for a few minutes. Classic Clinton, I thought. He won't talk to me but he'll wow my wife and father. Later, I heard that my dad's first words to him were, "Nice tie, Mr. President."

The following summer, in New York, I was talking to George Stephanopoulos, who had left the White House and was struggling to finish his bittersweet memoir of his Clinton years. We talked about what a brilliant, exhausting, frustrating, amazing, exasperating, contradictory person Clinton was, and then he asked me whether Clinton had ever talked to me about my biography. Not really, I said. We had only met once after that, and his only words were, "Nice tie."

Well, said Stephanopoulos, you know what he meant by "nice tie" in that context?

Not really.

It meant "Fuck you," he explained.

I was heartened to realize that my father, the old progressive, had unwittingly responded in kind.

12

Al Gore's Sting

Here, for the young investigative reporter, was a rare moment of drama ready to unfold. Within the next few hours, if all went as planned, he expected to ensnare a public official in the very act of corruption. He would overhear and tape-record a local councilman asking for a bribe, then watch as his paper's photographers took pictures of the illicit transaction. It promised to be a major scoop, top of the front page guaranteed, the kind of story that inspires a proud newspaper to display a copyright notice under the byline. And it would be his byline, capitalized in boldface:

. . . BY ALBERT GORE JR. . . .

The date was January 19, 1974, a midwinter morning so unseasonably warm that people strolled around downtown Nashville in shirtsleeves. Gore, in his fourth year as a reporter at the *Tennessean,* sat crouched in his little yellow Volkswagen, his profile a shock of black hair with fashionably long and stringy sideburns. He was parked just out of view of Haddox Pharmacy, a community drugstore owned by druggist Morris Haddox, a prominent black member of the Metro Council. Stationed nearby were officers from the Tennessee Bureau of Criminal Investigation, also there to monitor what was about to go down. The reporter and the state investigators were working together on a classic sting operation. Days earlier, a local developer had alleged to Gore that Haddox was hitting him up for a bribe to approve a zoning variance. Now that developer agreed to walk into the pharmacy, wired with a microphone hidden beneath his shirt, and see if he could get Haddox to solicit the money again. This time it would be heard by Gore and the officers, who also had recording equipment in their car.

So excited was Gore by the prospect of the story, so certain were he and his editors that they were righting a wrong, that they participated as virtual adjunct members of the prosecution team, offering crucial assistance in every aspect of the case. Rather than pursue the story on their own, they went to the district attorney general and established a joint enterprise. The newspaper provided the cash (three hundred-dollar bills) that passed from the developer to Haddox later that day. Gore, with help from his wife, Tipper, transcribed the audiotapes and spent hours going over them with the district attorney general. He and three *Tennessean* photographers testified before the grand jury, and the paper held the story for three weeks, until Haddox was indicted. All for what seemed likely to be the young reporter's moment of triumph. A moment that never came.

The newsroom that Al Gore had entered in 1971 as a novice reporter covering night cops and obits was typical of that era, redolent of a time now gone forever, with cluttered rows of steel desks jammed together, the floors stained with ancient grease and littered with cigarette butts, desk drawers hiding whiskey and hard-boiled eggs, gruff editors barking orders to copyboys, reporters hunched over their desks banging out stories on manual typewriters and triplicate copy paper, some hidden behind fire-hazard stacks of newspapers, press releases, and long-forgotten notes. Newspapers were less homogenized then, each defined by its idiosyncratic politics and history. The *Tennessean* had a muckraking history, a sense of mission that was evident when David Halberstam worked there in the late 1950s and covered the early civil rights movement. "We all believed that the paper was of great value, that the paper really mattered," Halberstam said. "It had a moral legitimacy. Going against the conventional grain in Tennessee."

John Seigenthaler, the editor, who had once been the paper's star investigative reporter before his stint at the Kennedy Justice Department, was now carrying forward that tradition while shaping the newsroom subculture in his own image. The place was a nonstop scene of practical jokes. The journalistic hazing of Al Gore, in which newsroom prankster Jerry Thompson called in a fake obit for a Swedish gynecologist from Carthage named Trebla Erog (Gore fell for it, and turned in the obit copy before realizing that it was his own name spelled backward), was a variation of the obit trick played on every new writer. When Carter Eskew, whose uncle was city editor, came to the *Tennessean* as a summer intern, sitting at a desk near Gore, he was ordered to write an obit about a man named Wekse who died of a rattlesnake bite. A second call came an hour later with news that the sheriff who had found the dead man had also died of a rattlesnake bite. Eskew's heart started pumping with the thrill of a certain front-page story—until he realized what Wekse spelled backward.

Gore the journalist was earnest and persistent in gathering facts, spending hours in the library studying clips, and hours more in document rooms at state and county offices, which he seemed to enjoy more than going out to interview people. He was slow and plodding as a writer, sometimes forcing exasperated editors to rip copy from his typewriter a paragraph at a time. While other reporters went home or over to the Brass Rail for a few drinks after turning in their copy, he would stick around, planting himself in a seat next to the night editor, waiting to see if there were any questions. At first he told his editors that he would write about anything but politics. "I didn't want anything to do with it," he said later. "I also didn't want to swim in the whirlpool that was left by the election wake of 1970 [when Albert Gore Sr. was defeated for reelection to the U.S. Senate]. That was a bitter race, and there were people who played pivotal roles in that election I would have had to interview, on both sides, for and against my father. And I didn't want to perfect the craft of reporting while simultaneously trying to navigate in such turbulent waters. But the main reason was I just didn't want anything to do with it."

If there was disagreement among his peers at the *Tennessean* about Gore's future, it was about how long he would be able to resist politics. Few of them believed that he would remain in their profession forever. Six of his newsroom friends, including the political reporters, spent one night drafting a plan for Gore to be president, replete with timetables of when he had to run for the House and Senate. They had him winning the Oval Office in the year 2008. One member of the cabal was Frank Sutherland, who sat across from Gore and became his closest friend at the paper. Decades later, when Gore was running for president, Sutherland, then editor of the *Tennessean*, said they had miscalculated when they plotted his political rise. "We didn't have the vice presidency in our plan," he said. As much as they teased Gore about it, he never seemed to think the 2008 plan was funny.

Seigenthaler, perhaps alone in this belief, had become convinced that his young charge would make journalism his career. But soon enough, the editor thought, he would lose Gore to a national newspaper or network. The *Tennessean* would be his training ground. In December 1972, just after President Nixon's reelection, Seigenthaler sent Gore to New York for a seminar on investigative reporting. A dozen reporters sat around a room critiquing one another's stories, swapping tricks of the trade, and discussing Topic A: Is investigative journalism dead? "The argument," Gore recalled later, "was that this was a medium that inherently requires so much complexity in the number of facts and the arrangement of facts that, in the age of television, people are not going to follow it. And Exhibit A was the work done to that point by Woodward and Bernstein on Watergate. It was ironic that at that time there were serious investigative reporters thinking this was a dying art."

Gore's request that he not cover politics dissolved soon enough, and he found himself attending night meetings of the Metro Council. Sometimes, when their sessions droned on late into the night, he was the only reporter there. He sat at a table in the middle of the room, surrounded by politicians arrayed in front of him on a U-shaped podium. The power he wielded in that situation made him feel giddy. When he picked up his pen and started writing, every council member suddenly wanted to talk. When he put his pen down, they would shut up. Something else started burning inside him: a sense that he could do what they were doing better than they were doing it. This reawakening did not lead Gore to befriend the local pols he was covering, but rather seemed to increase the tension between them. Some of the officials began to think of him as a self-righteous political heir posturing as a journalist, trying to have it both ways. The prickly relations became most intense in November 1973, when Gore tailed a pack of junketeering councilmen to a convention in Puerto Rico, and mocked their trip in a front-page story, only to be found munching at their snacks table.

The next year Gore began picking up anecdotes from business sources about possible abuses of the zoning system. The city had a policy of councilmanic courtesy that allowed individual members to grant zoning variances within their districts. Gore started accumulating data on when and how these decisions were being made, and thought he saw a pattern of corruption. One day, he barged into his editor's office. "He came in with a stack of papers eighteen inches high," Seigenthaler recalled. "And he put them on the coffee table and began to break them down. I put my hand on them and said, 'Al, is there any way you could cut this short?' And he said, 'No, damn it! There's no way to cut this short!' He sort of scolded me a little bit, which took some guts, and so I went over and sat down, laughing to myself, 'You smart young prick.' " Gore spent an hour showing him the documents. Seigenthaler realized that there was a big story and gave Gore the go-ahead to drop everything else and dig deeper.

While covering the police beat earlier, Gore had helped break some stories about how police were abusing prostitutes and shaking them down for sexual favors. His key source was the foreman of a standing grand jury, a local developer named Gilbert Cohen. Now, as Gore was investigating the zoning system, Cohen came to him with a complaint that he was being shaken down by a councilman. "You're kidding!" Gore said. It fit his suspicions perfectly.

Cohen told him the story. He and his business partners needed a variance to close an alley, he said, but Morris Haddox was holding it up, yanking it from the council agenda and implying that it would take money to change his mind. Gore took the story back to Seigenthaler, who was not only an editor but a power broker in the Democratic establishment, a man who held virtual veto power over the party slate of candidates. One of his friends in the party, Thomas Shriver, was the local prosecutor and a close friend of Gore's sister, Nancy. "It's a small town, or it was then," Gore explained later. He and Seigenthaler talked to Shriver, who agreed to work with the newspaper to see if Haddox could be caught in the act of soliciting and receiving a bribe. Gore brokered the contact between Shriver and Cohen. The sting operation was set.

Cohen entered the pharmacy on January 19, wired for sound, with Gore in his yellow Volkswagen and the Tennessee Bureau of

Investigation agents in their unmarked cars listening nearby. Haddox was working at the back counter. The developer and the pharmacist talked for nearly two hours. Their discussion had a comic interruption once, when local promoter Abe Stein came in and joined the conversation, passing the time of day. Eventually, according to the tape recording, Stein left and Haddox got down to business, saying to Cohen, "It will take a grand to get it done."

Cohen left the drugstore, drove downtown, and called Haddox, saying he should meet him to pick up a down payment on the grand. He instructed Haddox to drive to the corner of Seventh Avenue and Union Street, where Cohen would be waiting. The location was selected because it was a prime spot for a stakeout. Three *Tennessean* photographers were perched above the corner, looking out from the offices of the newspaper's law firm. Also watching were Gore, Seigenthaler, and the TBI agents. Siggy, as Seigenthaler was known, munched ferociously on an apple.

As Haddox's Lincoln Continental approached the intersection and slowed to a stop, Cohen stepped from the sidewalk outside the Downtowner Motor Inn. He was wired for sound again, and the conversation was recorded by the TBI agents.

"Okay, you don't have to count it for me, Gibby," Haddox said.

"Okay. Well, there's three hundred here. That's all I got. Okay?" responded Cohen.

"All right," said Haddox. "I'll take care of it."

But none of that proved to be enough in court. Gore, after spending hours going over the tapes with assistant prosecutor Robert H. Schwartz, took the stand to testify about what he had seen and heard, providing a play-by-play explanation of the tape recordings. But Judge Allen Cornelius ruled that the tapes were of debatable accuracy and not admissible evidence. Haddox insisted that he had been forewarned that Cohen might be out to get him, and that he had no intention of keeping the bribe, but intended to report it to authorities. He just never got around to it before the indictment broke, he claimed. The first jury was deadlocked along racial lines and dissolved in a mistrial. At the second trial, Haddox's attorney, William C. Wilson, in his final argument, railed against entrapment, which he called "the meanest, vilest, sneakiest method of law enforcement." The jury voted to acquit Haddox after deliberating for four hours, determining that it was uncertain he intended to keep the money as a bribe and that the news-paper and prosecutors might have conspired to entrap him. Gore was outside the courtroom when he heard the verdict. He sat stunned on a bench, slumped down, head in hands.

The drama had profoundly different effects on its two central characters. Haddox was wiped out in the next election, then slowly worked his way back in local politics and returned to office two decades later. As a Democrat in a city where Gore, the erstwhile investigative reporter, went on to become the party's favorite son, Haddox felt some obligation to forget the past. When Air Force Two landed at Nashville one night during the 1996 campaign, Haddox stood in the receiving line and greeted the vice president with a two-armed embrace. Four years later, a "Gore for President" sign could be seen in the storefront of the pharmacy. In the privacy of his store, standing behind the back counter in a traditional white frock, Haddox still harbored a touch of bitterness about the reporter and the newspaper that pursued him. "They never admitted that they might have gone too far," he said in a whisper.

Gore's life was also changed by the case. "It was an outcome that amazed me," he said decades later. The verdict, in fact, helped put him back on the political track. When the trial ended, struck by the "unusual power of some words and phrases thrown around in the courtroom," he decided that there was more for him to learn, and he enrolled in Vanderbilt Law School. He soon begged off the investigative reporting beat and began writing editorials for the paper, then ran for office and began the long climb toward the White House, where as vice president he watched his political patron, Bill Clinton, face an impeachment vote after being caught in a sex-and-lies scandal that relied on tape recordings and a variation of an investigative sting. Through it all, Gore never entertained a second thought about the way he pursued Haddox. "I thought a crime was being committed," he said. "I thought it was a big story. I thought I had an exclusive. And two out of three ain't bad."

13

Jackson and King

This is an Easter season story about Martin Luther King Jr. and Jesse Louis Jackson, two of the best-known public figures of modern America. King was shot twenty years ago at 6:02 on the evening of April 4, 1968, as he stood on the balcony outside his room at the Lorraine Motel in Memphis. When he died, at age thirty-nine, he was a great and troubled man in a troubled country. Now he is a legend. Jackson was there when King was shot. He was twenty-six, the youngest of several disciples who were looking up to their leader, literally and figuratively, as they waited for him in the parking lot eight feet below. They were all going to dinner.

Hours after King died, Jackson flew back to Chicago, a city in flames, and the next day he spoke at a memorial session of the Chicago City Council. "I come here with a heavy heart because on my chest is the stain of blood from Dr. King's head," Jackson said. "He went through, literally, a crucifixion. I was there. And I'll be there for the resurrection."

It is said that history moves in twenty-year cycles. Twenty years are up, and Jackson is running for president. Did King die so that Jackson might someday rise? Is this the event that Jackson long ago prophesied? Jackson's speeches this year are rich with metaphors of the cross. He describes the suffering of the civil rights era—King's death—as the crucifixion; black enfranchisement represented the rolling back of the stone; and now, with Jackson's stunning political success this year, comes the resurrection. It is remarkable to think that Jackson first uttered the phrases he uses today the day after King died, when Jackson was so young, unknown and untested.

Biblical stories are rarely simple, and neither is this one. The relationship between King and Jackson is not divine. It is shrouded in myth, exaggeration, confusion, controversy, resentment. The two men knew each other for only three years—from the voting rights march in Selma, Alabama, in 1965 to the sanitation workers' strike in Memphis in 1968—and they never were close. King, an outwardly self-effacing person who stressed teamwork among his aides in the Southern Christian Leadership Conference, thought that young Jackson, director of his Chicago office, was too boastful, self-promoting, and independent.

Some of the people closest to King—his widow and several former top aides—hold that assessment even now; to them, the day King died explains their feelings.

They have had a hard time forgetting what Jackson said and did, or claimed to do, that day: how he said he was the last one King talked to before he was shot; how he told the press that he held the dying King in his arms; how he left so quickly for Chicago, saying that he felt ill; how he dominated the television interviews that day and the next day; how he kept wearing the turtleneck sweater that he said had King's blood on it; how even before King's funeral he was talking with advisers about the best way to take King's place as leader of the civil rights movement.

Most of those details are in dispute. There is no evidence that Jackson cradled King in his arms and substantial testimony that he did not. Ralph Abernathy, King's closest friend and adviser, did that. Jackson's immediate reaction after the shooting, according to his close friend and fellow Chicagoan musician Ben Branch, who was standing in the parking lot with him, was not to run up to the balcony. "And Jesse, he ducked, and went around behind the swimming pool," Branch, now dead, told an oral history interviewer in August 1968, according to transcripts at the J. W. Brister Library at Memphis State University. Jackson eventually made it up to the balcony, and he might have come close enough to get some blood on his hands and shirt from the pool of blood on the floor. Whatever his reason for leaving for Chicago that night and missing an important SCLC meeting, it was not because he was sick. On the other hand, most testimony supports Jackson's recollection that he was one of the last people, if not the last person, whom King talked to before he was shot. And reports about his discussions in Chicago about assuming King's role seem to have been exaggerated.

But for some, these actions taken together formed a lasting image of Jackson as a vainglorious person willing to stretch the truth. Andrew Young, now mayor of Atlanta, then a young King aide, says he was always mystified by Jackson's account. Abernathy has tried to explain it by saying that Jackson had a burning need to be associated with King's glory. When Hosea Williams, King's field lieutenant, first heard Jackson claim that he cradled the dying King in his arms, he said it was only forty-five minutes after the assassination. Williams, enraged, tried to attack Jackson in front of the television cameras with the thought of wrestling him to the ground and making him retract what he was saying.

Sixteen years later, Williams decided to forgive Jackson and went to Coretta Scott King to see whether she would do the same. "I wanted to believe that Jesse had changed," Williams said. "I went to Mrs. King and tried to persuade her to support Jesse like I did in 1984. I said, 'I believe this is the new Jesse, not the overly ambitious young man we used to know.' She said, 'Hosea, Jesse Jackson has not changed one bit.' Now I'm not sure. She might have been right."

It is a grudge that will not go away, said the Reverend Billy Kyles of Memphis, who was on the balcony with King when he was shot and is the only witness whose statements partially support Jackson's version of events. "It hasn't healed. They won't let it heal," Kyles said. "But people have to understand that it wasn't just Jesse in this equation. The staff rivalry was intense, and it just blew apart after King died. There was tension between Mrs. King and the SCLC, between Hosea Williams and Andy Young, between Young and Jackson, between Abernathy and the younger ones. The whole thing was just so unfortunate."

Jackson's introduction to King and the national civil rights movement occurred in Selma, Alabama, in March 1965. He was a first-year student then at Chicago Theological Seminary, having graduated the previous spring from North Carolina A&T. On the night of what came to be known as Bloody Sunday, March 7, after six hundred civil rights marchers were attacked, beaten, and tear-gassed by mounted Alabama state troopers at Edmund Pettus Bridge, a call went out to clergy across the country to go to Selma to support the cause. Jackson organized a caravan of twenty-one students from the seminary. He was the only black among them. Andrew Young was one of King's aides then, and his first memory of Jackson in Selma is of a guy whom nobody knew standing on the steps of Brown Chapel giving orders. Abernathy remembers Jackson doing errands and asking him for a job on the SCLC staff.

In any case, Jackson never marched in Selma. He arrived there after Bloody Sunday and left long before the march to Montgomery resumed two weeks later. Jackson and two friends left for Chicago on March 11. Sick with the flu, they hit their beds when they got home. On the way back, they talked about the need to organize the movement in Chicago.

The next year King went to Chicago, pushing the civil rights battle to the north with what was called his "War on Slums." Jackson by then was on the SCLC staff, organizing the Chicago chapter of a ministerial alliance, Operation Breadbasket, that was designed to pressure white businesses to provide more jobs and opportunities in the black community. During King's months in Chicago, which produced more headlines than results, Jackson was on the outer rim of SCLC power and sometimes frustrated King by speaking for him or placing him in unexpected situations.

King left Chicago without victory—there were to be no substantial changes in housing conditions—but Jackson and Operation Breadbasket endured and prospered, winning more jobs from soft-drink firms and food chains. Partly by choice, partly because he was so far from the SCLC headquarters in Atlanta, Jackson built his own empire in Chicago, and as its dimensions grew so did King's concern. At one point King assigned William Rutherford, a black Chicago businessman, to straighten out several problems, including Jackson. "Jesse Jackson's so independent," King told Rutherford. "I either want him in SCLC or out."

On March 30, 1968, after his first march in Memphis on behalf of the striking garbage workers ended in a violent confrontation, King met with his staff at Ebenezer Baptist Church in Atlanta. He said that he needed the full support of everyone. They had to stop arguing and get behind him. After chewing them out, King headed for the door. Jackson tried to follow him. "If you are so interested in doing your own thing that you can't do what the organization is structured to do, go ahead," King told him. "If you want to carve out your own niche in society, go ahead, but for God's sake don't bother me."

Five days later, April 4, Jackson was part of the team in Memphis. They had rooms at the Lorraine Motel. Jackson spent part of the afternoon at a meeting in room 306, where King and Abernathy were staying. In the early evening, Billy Kyles arrived, ready to take King to dinner at his house. Kyles's wife, Gwen, had prepared a soul food dinner for King and his entourage. In the parking lot below, other people invited to the dinner were gathering. Solomon Jones, a driver for the night, was there with his Cadillac. Jim Bevel and Jim Orange were standing behind the car. Andrew Young was nearby, along with Chauncey Eskridge, an SCLC lawyer. Hosea Williams was on the first floor, working the key into his room.

King and Kyles stepped out on the balcony and started chatting

King's assassination

with the people below. Jackson and Ben Branch, the Chicago musician, were approaching from another room where Branch's Operation Breadbasket band had been rehearsing.

"Our leader!" Jackson shouted up to King.

King exchanged greetings with everyone. He asked Jackson, who was dressed in a turtleneck sweater, brown leather coat, and rolled-up blue jeans, whether he would wear a suit and tie to dinner, like the others. Jackson joked that he thought the only requirement for eating was an appetite.

Jackson introduced King to Branch, his bandleader. "Yeah, that's my man," King said. "Look, tonight. I want you to play that 'Precious Lord' like you never played it before. . . . Especially for me I want you to play it real pretty."

According to some witnesses, King was shot right after he said that. Jackson says it happened after he talked to King about his appetite. But most of those who were there say there was one further conversation, that Solomon Jones, the driver, told King that it was getting chilly and that King should get his coat. "Okay, Jonesy," might have been Martin Luther King's last words.

Kyles was the only other person on the balcony when the shot exploded at King's neck, throwing him into the air and down to the balcony floor and severing his spinal cord. Kyles had been walking away from King at that moment, toward the stairwell. Abernathy was inside the room. Within seconds, he was on the balcony, cradling King in his arms. A Justice Department official who had been traveling with King came with a towel. Andy Young and several others rushed up to the balcony. When an officer asked where the shot came from, they pointed across the street, toward a rooming house.

That scene was captured for posterity by a *Life* magazine photo. Jackson is not visible in the picture as one of the people pointing. Ben Branch and Hosea Williams remember Jackson telling them not to talk to the press. Then they both saw him giving interviews. He was quoted on one news report as having been on the balcony when King was shot. Later that night, after King died, Abernathy held an emergency meeting. Jackson was not there. "To my amazement, early the following morning, there sits Jesse Jackson on the *Today* show in Chicago, with that bloody shirt," Williams recalled. Jackson kept the shirt on all day. He wore it to the memorial session of the Chicago City Council, where he made the crucifixion speech.

On Saturday morning, two days after King's death, Jackson held his weekly rally of Operation Breadbasket. The rallies before then had attracted a few hundred people. This time, five thousand people showed up. And they kept coming back week after week. Jesse Jackson had reached a new level.

That is most of what there is to the story of Jackson and King, except for the question of lineage and legacy. History moves in twenty-year cycles, and twenty years after King's death Jesse Jackson was running for president. He could never live up to King, but he could be the transition to whatever was coming next. "If King was Moses, then Jesse is Joshua," said Billy Kyles. "We can't say Jesse is Moses again. Black people can't keep starting over. To say Jesse is the new Martin is not right. He stands on Martin's shoulders. Whoever comes after Jesse will stand on his shoulders."

This story was written on Easter Sunday 1988, twenty years before Barack Obama was elected president. Jackson was running for president and Obama was a complete unknown then, doing organizing work in Chicago, still a few years away from his first claim to fame as president of the Harvard Law Review.

14

The World According to Edwin Edwards

The judge said he would expel anyone who laughed or cheered, for this was a court of law, not theater, but the trial of Louisiana's governor had reached its final act, the lead character was onstage, and what he was doing up there seemed like theater to the overflow audience in room 468 of the federal building. It was a production of "The World According to Edwin Edwards."

In the world according to Edwin Edwards, governor of Louisiana, there are different kinds of oaths. That is crucial to understand, since the performance was in a judicial setting—the fraud and bribery trial of Edwards and seven associates—where oaths are taken every day. There is, for example, the paralyzing oath.

On Wednesday, when U.S. Attorney John Volz asked Edwards a question, the governor answered with the hedge, "I'm not going to take a paralyzing oath on it."

"What, Governor, is a paralyzing oath?" Volz asked.

"Oh, that's when if you lie under oath, you get paralyzed," said Edwards.

Delving into the governor's world for a moment, Volz inquired as to whether a paralyzing oath was what Edwards had taken that morning on the witness stand.

"Oh, no," said the governor. "This is a far more serious oath. My soul in eternity rests on the validity of my testimony here today. And that's far more serious than any malady that can be visited upon me on this earth."

Since the world according to Edwin Edwards is primarily a political one, and has been since he first won a seat on the Crowley, Louisiana, city council, it is also essential to grasp the governor's concept of politics. Last Tuesday, Edwards explained what it meant to do one's job as a state senator.

Joe Sevario was his idea of a good state senator. Sevario represented the Gonzalez area between Baton Rouge and New Orleans, where Edwards and two associates wanted to develop a hospital complex. "Joe came to me and said he and some other politicians would have to say they were against it for their constituents, but they really were not against it," Edwards explained. " 'We'll oppose it,' Joe said to me. 'But we won't say much about it.' Joe was doing his job as senator."

Exchanging pleasantries is also important in the world according to Edwin Edwards, as the governor made clear when he testified about his dealings with the Gamble brothers, Kit and Kevin, a pair of nursing home operators in the Shreveport area. After the Gamble brothers got a special exemption to construct three nursing homes despite a state moratorium, word went out that one of the brothers was bragging about how he had bribed state officials.

"When I heard rumors of the bribe, I called Kit Gamble," Edwards testified. "We exchanged pleasantries. Then I said, 'I hear you're going around saying you paid off the governor.' He said it wasn't true. We exchanged more pleasantries. And I hung up."

When exchanging pleasantries with people like the Gamble brothers, in the world according to Edwin Edwards, it is sometimes necessary to remind them to tell the truth. After asking Kit Gamble about the bribe, for instance, Edwards later talked to Kevin Gamble about it. They were on a receiving line in Shreveport. Kevin said he did not know about any payoffs either. "Well, whatever you do, if anyone asks you about our conversation just now, tell the truth," Edwards told him.

Volz asked Edwards why he felt compelled to remind a Gamble brother to tell the truth. "Well," explained the governor, "the fact is that at grand jury investigations, it is standard policy of prosecutors to ask people, 'What did the governor tell you?' So this way they could say I told them to tell the truth."

Edwards is considered a grand jury expert. He has been investigated by eleven of them since 1973.

The truth is an interesting concept in the world according to Edwin Edwards. At a news conference in September 1984, Edwards said he received a fee for his role in the development of a hospital in East Baton Rouge. In fact, Edwards received more than a fee: He was 50 percent owner in a concealed arrangement with two associates.

"Why didn't you tell people you had a part ownership?" prosecutor Volz asked the governor.

"It was in part a fee," said Edwards, who then acknowledged it was more than a fee.

"But that is not the whole truth," said Volz.

"It is partially true," Edwards said.

"And it was partially false," said Volz.

"If something is only partially true, it must be partially false," conceded Edwards.

Logic of such clarity is commonplace in the world according to Edwin Edwards. When Volz asked him why he forgot to list something on a financial disclosure document, the governor replied, "But I didn't forget, because that implies a conscious effort to remember."

The matter that Edwards made no conscious effort to remember was the money he made as a partner in four hospital plans. The financial disclosure statement he filed after winning the gubernatorial election in 1983 did not list his role in the hospitals or the money he made from them. The financial disclosure statement was prepared for Edwards by a consultant named Tom Jones.

"When he finished it, I leafed through it, kind of like I do with my income taxes," Edwards testified. "I leafed through it and gave it back to him. No, first I noticed that he had listed the wrong address on one of the corporations. I had that fixed, then I gave it back to Mr. Jones."

"You noticed a wrong address but you didn't notice that nearly two million dollars had been left off?" Volz asked incredulously.

"Well, it wasn't two million dollars yet," Edwards responded, correctly. "I had made seven hundred and sixteen thousand dollars at that point."

"So a little less than a million, then," said Volz.

"Two hundred and eighty-four thousand less," said Edwards.

"Your memory gets better when it's more than a million, then?" said Volz.

"A natural human reaction," said Edwards.

Millions come and millions go. Edwards testified that he made ten million dollars in the four years between his gubernatorial terms, only two million of that from the hospital enterprises that got him in trouble. He kept a lot of the money in cash for his trips to the gaming tables of Nevada, where he lost $10,000 to $50,000 a year playing under the aliases of Ed Neff and T. Wong.

There is a kind of thrill to going by an alias in the world according to Edwin Edwards. "I guess it kind of makes you feel good to walk up to a crap table, get some chips, and give them a false name," the governor testified. "It's kind of a braggadocio, a kind of security, a kind of anonymity. One time I stood behind the computer printout at Harrah's and, boom, out came my aliases, my credit on the trip, what I had spent, what I had left. It was kind of a good feeling."

But just because Edwards made ten million dollars in four years and gambled a lot of it away does not mean that he lost his populist touch. The little people play a very big role in the world according to Edwin Edwards. He felt especially proud of the hospitals he was involved in, he testified, because they would improve medical services for the poor and needy and bring more jobs to the state, jobs for "the plumbers, the bricklayers, the electricians." Those have always been his people, he said. In the 1983 gubernatorial election against Republican David Treen, Democrat Edwards noted, he represented "the average man, the working man, the needy, the minorities, the unemployed," whereas Treen was "the business candidate."

Free enterprise is good for the average man in the world according to Edwin Edwards. "There's a nightmare out there," he testified when explaining the red tape and bureaucracy one encounters trying to get hospitals built. The state and federal rules for hospitals, he said, are "restrictive and silly."

"So silly that you made almost two million dollars from them," said Volz, ever the straight man. "That was silly?"

"No," said the governor. "No, that was smart."

15

Back Home in Indiana

Dan Coats, the hardworking Republican congressman from Fort Wayne, emerged from a brown van and walked to the front door of the suburban high school. It was a Saturday morning and Coats was there for the fourth of five town meetings he was holding to take the pulse of Indiana's Fourth Congressional District during the Columbus Day recess. As Coats entered the school, he noticed a chair in the middle of the hallway with a handmade sign taped to it. His name was stenciled on the sign, with an arrow pointing toward an eight-hundred-seat lecture hall. His name was spelled wrong.

Coats and his aide went where the arrow pointed, the click of their heels echoing through the locker-lined corridor. Finally they reached the lecture hall, opened the door, and gazed inside. To their left was a bank of theater seats. Empty. Directly in front of them was row after row of tables and seats. Empty.

It was five minutes before nine. The town meeting was to begin at nine. Last January, Coats recalled, his town meetings had attracted two hundred, four hundred, five hundred people. He walked to an old graffiti-scratched desk at the front of the hall, sat down, and waited. Ten minutes passed. It was *very* lonely. After fifteen minutes, a figure appeared in the doorway—another aide. Eventually another figure appeared. It was the janitor.

The janitor's keys jangled loudly in the empty room as he strolled up to the desk.

"Well," said the janitor.

"Well," said the congressman.

"Well," said the janitor.

"You got any questions you want to ask me?" said the congressman.

"Nope. Not really," said the janitor. "I'm pretty content."

The town meeting thus adjourned, Coats and his assistants went to breakfast.

Two days earlier, seventy miles to the south, Sparky "Old Money Bags" Walsh and two clerks were talking, eating, and smoking their way through lunch at a table in the back of the county treasurer's office. In came Philip R. Sharp, the energetic Democratic congressman from Muncie, making his way through the courthouse on a handshaking tour.

"Hey, Phil," said Walsh, the county treasurer, who got his nickname years ago, long before the recent incident in which he was picked up by Muncie police on suspicion of shoplifting camera equipment. "Whaddaya think of this guy Watts? Jeez, Watts and Butz, you put 'em in a paper bag and shake it and see what comes out, huh, Phil? And now we got Wallace too. This guy Wallace is talkin' as crazy as Watts and Butz."

Sharp had spent enough time schmoozing with the courthouse gang over the years to catch the drift of Sparky's chatter. Watts, surely, was James G. Watt, the outgoing interior secretary. And Butz had to be fellow Hoosier and former agriculture secretary Earl L. Butz, whose racist joke had bounced him from an earlier federal cabinet. But who was Wallace? It couldn't be George C. Wallace, the Alabama governor, who hadn't been heard from lately. Sharp decided it must be the Wallace who the day before had stepped down from the chairmanship of the Indiana Public Service Commission. "I see in the papers Wallace resigned from the PSC," the fifth-term congressman said earnestly to the old, white-haired treasurer, who had cotton balls stuffed in one ear, and teeth that looked like a parched row of feed corn. "What did *he* say?"

Sparky jabbed a white plastic spoon into a Styrofoam cup of egg salad and took a drag from his filter cigarette. "Nah, Phil, not that Wallace," he said, his tone implying that Sharp, a former political science professor, still had a few things to learn. "I mean that damn football coach over there at Ball State. You know what he said, Phil? He said the Indiana State game wasn't that important. Hah! They keep losin' to Indiana State and he keeps sayin' it ain't important."

Sharp and Coats, members of the House Energy and Commerce Committee, were back home in Indiana. It was, as always, a long, long trip from here to there, from the catered lunches of Capitol Hill to Sparky Walsh's egg salad, from the bustling marble corridors of the Rayburn House Office Building to the abandoned lecture hall of New Haven High School, from Independence Avenue in Washington to the Jefferson, Jackson, and Washington streets of Muncie, Columbia City, and Shelbyville, from the drop-dead-serious committee deliberations about national energy, communications, and health care to the provincial backbiting and good humor of small-town politics and sports.

"It's hard to figure out exactly what the real relationship is between what happens in Washington, what we do and say on the committee, and what the people care about back home," Sharp said as he journeyed down Route 9 from his district office in Muncie to a town meeting in Shelbyville. "But every time I come back here I am struck again—and humbled—by how different the two worlds are."

When most of the 435 House members fled Washington for what is called the Columbus Day District Work Period, a reporter went home with Sharp and Coats to explore the relationship between these two very different worlds that all congressmen must straddle. The mission began for both of them as an effort to find out what the people of eastern Indiana were saying about the major consumer issues that the Energy and Commerce Committee is dealing with this fall, such as natural gas deregulation and telephone pricing. Swiftly, and perhaps inevitably, it devolved into something more chaotic, unpredictable, and ego-deflating—almost metaphysical. The words and issues of the Hill usually did not obtain in the flatlands seven hundred miles to the west.

For Sharp, chairman of the Fossil and Synthetic Fuels Subcommittee, where billion-dollar decisions loom and $150-an-hour lobbyists hover, the morning of October 13 began at seven in the morning at Miller Cafeteria on Main Street in Richmond, "the City of Roses" along the Indiana-Ohio border. Sharp was there to speak to the Gateway Kiwanis Club. Among the faithful at the breakfast gathering were the local Republican prosecutor, who was busy with a scandal in the license plate office run in patronage-rich Indiana by the county Republican Party, and Coach Etchison, the living legend who had just retired as football coach at Richmond High after sending nine of his boys to the pros. Before Sharp was introduced, it became clear to him that his presence was something of a political mistake.

The reason was the fellow Democrat sitting next to him, Frank Waltermann, who was running for mayor and had a good chance of breaking the Republican Party's decades-long grip on city hall. Waltermann had been the scheduled speaker for that morning, but Sharp's staff, by making it known that the congressman would be in town, unwittingly bumped him. In odd years in Indiana, few aspects of politics are more important than municipal elections, certainly not the utterings of a congressman whose job isn't on the line for another twelve months. Sharp apologized to Waltermann, gave the short version of his speech on the exceedingly complicated subject of natural gas pricing, and offered to take any questions.

"I'd like to ask a general, philosophical question," said a gentleman in the back of the windowless room. "Does Congress work?"

Sharp began his answer by talking about the budget process and then realized that a philosophical question deserved a philosophical answer. "I still think that with all its problems Congress is very representative," he said. "The fact is that the disabilities of Congress reflect the disabilities of the American people."

From Richmond, Sharp drove thirty miles up Route 35 to Southside High School in Muncie, a working-class city of 76,000 where he had lived when he was an associate professor of government at Ball State University. Sharp had sought and lost the Muncie area's congressional seat in 1970 and 1972 before finally making it in the Democrats' 1974 post-Watergate sweep, displacing incumbent Republican David Dennis, who had been one of President Nixon's staunchest defenders on the House Judiciary Committee. He thus became one of only two Democrats to represent Muncie in Congress in modern times. The other was Randall "Front Porch" Harmon, who served from 1959 to 1961 and got his nickname by renting his front porch to the federal government for use as his district office.

In the auditorium of Southside, Sharp was introduced to the high school seniors by civics teacher Andy Phipps, who once ran for the state legislature on a ticket with Sharp and made a name for himself in central Indiana with his radio gospel show. Sharp spent about two minutes telling the students what he did in Congress and on the Energy and Commerce Committee and then asked for questions. A long minute passed before the first question was asked. "Hey, yeah," a student near the front of the room said. "I want to know, what's it like inside the White House? You know, what was it like when you first stepped into the White House?"

Sharp handled this deftly, saying the White House wasn't as large as you might think, nowhere near as large as palaces in Europe. But soon far more penetrating questions came nonstop. How did you vote on sending troops to Lebanon? Are the troops there provoking the hostilities? (A few days earlier, on October 23, 299 servicemen, including 220 U.S. marines, had been killed in a terrorist bombing of their military barracks in Beirut.) How would you compare it to Vietnam? What did Congress do about the South Korean jetliner? Could the Soviets have had a justifiable reason for shooting it down? What do you think about the use of drugs in school?

The congressman turned the last question around by asking students to raise their hands if they thought more than 50 percent of them had tried marijuana. Three-fourths of them raised their hands. Then he asked how many thought there was a serious drinking problem at the school. Even more raised their hands. Only fifteen or so raised their hands when Sharp asked whether they thought marijuana should be legalized, and one of those fifteen was soon expelled from the auditorium for making too much noise. Sharp was in the middle of a sentence when the bell rang. The room was virtually empty before he could finish his thought.

From the high school Sharp traveled across town to the courthouse, where he encountered Old Money Bags Walsh on the first floor and William Ora Shroyer on the second. Shroyer was running for a Muncie council seat on the Democratic ticket, and he had a problem he wanted to talk to Sharp about. It seems he had spent most of his campaign money on a handbill that told residents which lever to pull to vote for him. The problem was the handbill told them the wrong lever. Sharp told him not to worry, that the Democratic precinct chairmen could take care of it by getting the number right on the voting cards they would hand out on election day.

That problem apparently resolved, Sharp drove over to the Senior Citizens Council Center at the corner of Fifth and South Walnut, where he found about thirty elderly Muncie residents playing bingo in the basement. Two seniors told him the government should nationalize the oil companies. Three others urged him to make sure their telephone bills didn't go up. One asked him whether it was still raining outside. And a woman asked him why congressmen keep taking vacations.

"You mean foreign travel?" Sharp asked.

"Yeah, you know, vacations," she said. "As far as I get is from Hackley Street to here in the morning and back to Hackley Street at night."

After spending the next hour at his district office, next to the Muncie Psychiatric Clinic, Sharp drove south to Shelbyville in Shelby County, a predominantly Republican area that had been added to his district by the Republican legislature two years ago. His first stop was the Shelbyville Holiday Inn, where he unloaded his traveling gear and received a call from Michigan representative John D. Dingell, the chairman of the Energy and Commerce Committee, who wanted to meet with Sharp as soon as he returned to Washington to plot strategy on natural gas legislation. But now Sharp had other matters to attend to, such as a gathering of Shelbyville Democrats at the Victorian home of policeman Mike Shaw. A local newspaper was there, but the reporter confided that Sharp's presence would be a story only if he endorsed the Democratic candidate for mayor, Bill Cole. Sharp did just that, although he had only met Cole minutes earlier. "A lot of you know Bill better than I do," he began his endorsement speech. The newspaperman was relieved. Finally, he got a story out of the mayor's race. "We tried to get the candidates to debate, but they refused to," he said. "They told us they didn't have anything to debate about."

Standing next to the would-be mayor was Charles Moore, an engineer who worked for General Motors in Indianapolis and was running for council, his first political effort. Moore said he loved Shelbyville, especially the Varmints Club in town ("What do we do at the Varmints Club? Mostly drink beer and lie."), but he wasn't entirely sure he loved the town enough to devote his life to it. "You know, I was over at the Varmints Club the other night and this fella who had been on the council way back said people call you up in the middle of the night with their problems," Moore said to Duane Coy, a fellow council candidate. "Is that the way it is, Duane? In the middle of the night?"

"Yup," said Coy. "In the middle of the night, they call you. Mostly 'bout dogs."

The next morning, at ten thirty, on the second floor of the old Post Office building in downtown Fort Wayne, Representative Coats met the press to talk about natural gas. For many weeks he had been taking it from both sides on the issue. The big oil companies, under the ruse of a grassroots campaign, had flooded his office with thousands of postcards urging him to vote to decontrol the industry. At the same time, the Citizens Action Council, a local offshoot of the Citizen-Labor Energy Coalition, had been going door to door in his district collecting money to lobby Congress to roll back and freeze natural gas prices. Coats is against total decontrol, because 70 percent of the natural gas supplied to his district is classified as cheap "old gas." If it were decontrolled, it would cost his constituents millions of dollars. As a free-market conservative, he is also against a rollback and price freeze. "Both sides have got the facts wrong," Coats said, in a statement that made local television that night but not the next day's newspapers.

After the news conference, Coats went to a nearby worker rehabilitation center in danger of losing federal funds, and then to a senior citizens nutrition center in the basement of a Baptist church. He ate a macaroni and hamburger lunch, helped the ten elderly luncheon regulars sing "Happy Birthday" to a woman named Opal, and listened to the stories of a delightful old man who said he had corresponded with Herbert Hoover.

"I wrote you a letter once," someone told Coats.

"Well, thank you for writing," he responded. "What did you write about?"

"I can't remember now."

From the church, Coats returned to his office and met with a lobbyist for United Telephone of Indiana, who urged him to oppose Energy and Commerce legislation (sponsored by Tennessee congressman Al Gore) eliminating long-distance access fees for local telephone users. Next came his senior citizens advisory council. They talked for a while about telephones and natural gas, but soon the conversation drifted to nutrition and the carcinogenic dangers of various foods. Ben Decker, a retired microbiologist at Purdue who serves on the Republican congressman's council even though he is a liberal Democrat, told Coats to stop eating pepper and toast but to keep eating potatoes and carrots.

"What about rutabaga?" asked Coats.

That night, Coats traveled twenty-five miles to Columbia City for the third of his five town meetings. Twenty people were waiting for him in the basement of the Methodist church on Washington Street, including two rambunctious toddlers who screeched fire truck and airplane noises most of the night and knocked down the blackboard behind Coats as he was speaking. They seemed less troublesome than two old codgers in the audience who kept complaining about taxes, progress, and Communists.

"Ya know, 'bout eighty percent of the country is run by Communists right now," said G. M. Hauck. "The only way to stop 'em is to hang 'em two by two from the telephone poles. Hell, right now old Castro could come right up through the central USA and no one could stop him. I betcha all the tea in China he could." Compared with the screaming kids and G. M. Hauck, the audience at Coats's next town meeting the following morning in New Haven was somewhat of a relief. That's where, not counting the janitor, there was no audience.

I spent the year 1983 trying to explain Congress through the workings of the House Energy and Commerce Committee, a high-powered panel that dealt with most of the major domestic issues of that era, from acid rain to auto pollution standards to health insurance to natural gas regulation. The committee was chaired by Democrat John Dingell of Michigan, and included such heavyweight legislators as Henry Waxman of California, Tim Wirth of Colorado, Al Gore of Tennessee, Ed Markey of Massachusetts, Mike Synar of Oklahoma, Bill Richardson of New Mexico, and Phil Sharp and Dan Coats of Indiana. Ten months into following the committee in Washington, I decided to go home with Sharp and Coats. It was the only story in the occasional series I wrote over the course of that year that did not appear on the front page of the Post. *It was also my favorite.*

16

City of Presidents

Cuba City, Wisconsin

Who knows, given the closeness of the election in the swing state of Wisconsin, it might all come down to what happened here in the City of Presidents. First, a few months ago, President George W. Bush blew right on by, his bus rumbling down Main Street at forty miles an hour without stopping, done and gone in a wave and a blink. Then, last Tuesday evening, right at supper time and before the big lightning storm, here came John Kerry, zigzagging his Believe in America bus caravan several miles off route on the road from Beloit to Dubuque just so he could stop at the place Bush slighted.

Reg Weber, one of three brothers who run a sausage factory on the edge of town, was waiting for Bush that day in May when he breezed past and was there again this time when Kerry bounded off his bus to work the rope line, a gesture that seemed to make all the difference. "By God, he's my man now," Weber said of Kerry. "All he had to do was stop and he got my vote. He recognizes the little people."

You might ask why Cuba City, with its population of 2,174 and its remote location near Wisconsin's southwest corner, is getting any personal attention at all in this presidential election. Good question, but first let us deal with other imponderables. For starters, why is Cuba City called Cuba City? Turns out its original name was Yuba, but there was another Yuba in Wisconsin, so some town father a hundred years ago or more started going through the alphabet: Auba, Buba, and stopped at Cuba. It might have been Guba or Ruba or Tuba. Nothing to do with Hemingway or cigars.

And how in the world did Cuba City become the City of Presidents? Even better question. No president has ever come from Wisconsin, let alone from this little sausage and dairy town. But back during the bicentennial in 1976, the elementary school principal had a dream that morphed into a reality beyond his expectations. Joe Goeman's dream was to have a Parade of Presidents on Main Street. From George Washington onward, the lampposts running through town would have red-white-and-blue shields of the presidents, with their silhouettes, terms in office, and home states. The shields have been upgraded twice over the years, and now glisten in invulnerable vinyl, but the dream did not stop there. Then came flag posts in front of every shop and house along Main Street, with dozens of American flags "flying twenty-four–seven," as the proud chief of police, Kevin Atkinson, explained. Then the water tower was painted red-white-and-blue, declaring "City of Presidents" in lettering visible most of the way to the village of Hazel Green. Now all of Cuba City is in on the act. Turn into the parking lot near the Millard Fillmore shield (New York, 1850–1853) and there is the presidential caboose, all shiny red, with blue trim and white stars, the names of the presidents lining the top, and a bearded visage of President Ulysses Grant on the front. The general was not a native son, but at least he lived for a time nearby, across the Illinois border in Galena.

Once you've got yourself a City of Presidents, why not lure some real live presidents and would-be presidents? Goeman and other members of the City of Presidents commission, along with students in the Cuba City elementary school, all began writing Washington with invitations urging presidents to visit the city that honors them. Dreams are big in this modest corner of the universe. Baseball's Field of Dreams is only thirty miles away in a cornfield in Dyersville, Iowa. If you built it, they will come. Not only baseball immortals, but politicians as well.

It was May 7 when President Bush briefly came, and briefly saw, but didn't conquer. Word had reached Cuba City a few days earlier that the presidential caravan would pass through Cuba City on its way out of Dubuque and up through western Wisconsin. The city buzzed with anticipation. Schools were let out for the day, and kids were bused in all the way from Dickeyville. A thousand schoolchildren lined the sidewalks near the corner of Main and Clay. Two funerals were postponed so that they wouldn't get in the way. A huge cutout of President Bush was placed near the caboose. Chief Atkinson called in reinforcements from the Grant County sheriff's office and had the local fire department volunteers remove any possible hazards from Main Street. "We were all ready," Atkinson said. "And Bush didn't stop."

The Cuba City disappointment was big news in the tristate triangle from Dubuque to Galena and up to Platteville. When members of Kerry's advance team came to Dubuque in late July to plan a big rally downtown, they were told about Bush's Cuba City brush-off by Teri Goodmann, the key Kerry grassroots organizer in Dubuque, who knows just about everything that happens in the area. With that, the City of Presidents suddenly got on the Kerry map. They didn't want to make it an official stop, but memos in the Kerry camp made it clear that a jog to Cuba City would have a payoff.

Tuesday morning, Atkinson was dealing only with rumor. "Are they coming through?" townspeople would ask, and all he could say was that he was not sure. He had heard not a word from Kerry's advance team or the Secret Service. When he stopped for lunch at Nick's on Main Street with Dick Davis, the hardware store owner and mayor, he was still not certain. The Dubuque paper was saying that Kerry was only going to stop at an Amoco parking lot twelve miles away, in Shullsburg. Platteville radio had the same message: Shullsburg, yes, Cuba City, probably not.

At three that afternoon, the word arrived. Kerry was coming. Atkinson was sent to the parking lot between Owl Furniture and the presidential caboose to start preparing for a visit. He was met there by a young man in a blue shirt and dark shades. Secret Service. Joe Goeman showed up wearing his City of Presidents hat and T-shirt. A county sheriff K-9 team arrived with a dog called Najeh—named for a backup Packers running back, Najeh Davenport—who began sniffing around the caboose.

Into the parking lot bombed a white van with "Staff 1" on the windshield, carrying a four-person advance team led by Kerstin Smith, an events planner from Chicago. The parking lot was empty aside from the cops and Presidential Joe. Kerry was due in less than two hours. They had to make something out of nothing. The volunteer driver, Craig Miller, an electrician from Manitowoc, headed out into the neighborhood on foot to round up a crowd. He found men mowing lawns and kids playing in the street and older women sitting on their porches. "Come see John Kerry, the next president," Miller would say. "Is he really gonna stop or blow by like Bush?" they would ask.

Kerstin Smith persuaded the fire department to bring in a hook and ladder that children could sit atop next to the caboose. It is amazing how word can spread through a small town on a slow summer afternoon. Reg Weber came down from his sausage plant. Sam McGrew, the superintendent of schools, arrived in dress shirt and tie. Nearby was Quentin Bottoms, a handyman, in blue jeans and farmer cap, with a pocketknife that the Secret Service politely took for safekeeping. Mary Hoff, who writes a local recipe column, showed up in her white terry-cloth bathrobe. She had been on her way to water aerobics when she heard Kerry was coming. By five thirty the parking lot was full, four hundred strong, with another hundred people across the street. "Less than two minutes!" an advance man told the crowd, instructing them how to shout "Ker-Ree! Ker-Ree!"

These Cuba Citians were not big on shouting. They weren't going to get suckered again. But they were willing to wait. Mary Hoff went off to her water aerobics and was back in her bathrobe and still no Kerry. Finally, at 6:20 p.m., flashing lights could be seen down at the bottom of Main, and then the big blue bus and all the press buses behind, and the caravan circled around the block and pulled up right in front of the caboose, and Chief Atkinson was there, hand stretched out in greeting, and the door whooshed open and out bounded John Kerry, his bushy gray and black hair bobbing in the crowd—winning votes just by stopping in Cuba City, City of Presidents.

17

Just Jack and Jackie

As photographer Orlando Suero rode the bus down Fifth Avenue in New York on his way to work, he noticed a brief item in the paper about Senator John F. Kennedy's graceful young bride, Jacqueline, who was described as a political hostess, housewife, and student of American history at Georgetown University. This might be a great peg for a magazine piece, Suero noted to himself that spring morning in 1954, and soon enough he was on his way to Washington to shoot a photo spread for *McCall's*.

The poetry of public life is often most evident in the before and after of fame: before society becomes obsessed with someone, and then again after the beast of celebrity has sated itself and slouched relentlessly onward. In the before and after, there is a cleaner shot at capturing the essence of a human being rather than the reflection of a myth. In the story of Jack and Jackie there was no after, and never will be, but there was a before, and we can see a poignant evocation of that in the photographs of Orlando Suero.

Of course, the title of a book displaying his rarely seen old photographs, *Camelot at Dawn*, should be warning enough that separating the Kennedys from myth is no easy task. The poses struck by the handsome young couple offer further notice: Here, page after page, are early variations of many of the motifs of the mythologizing that would follow (football, books, art, friends, family), with some obvious political forethought in the posing. Still, there is something natural about these pictures that no amount of worldly skepticism or factual realism can erase.

The Kennedys had been married only a few months and were living in their first home together, a rented town house at 3321 Dent Place in Georgetown. Suero arrived there on May 5, 1954, with an assignment that was changing before his eyes. His original concept—to record the daily life of the young political wife—was quickly overtaken by the fact that the husband did not want to be left out of the action. After inserting himself into the story ("He was very media wise," Suero recalled), Kennedy had only one further request: that he not be asked to

Jack and Jackie

do anything that would embarrass him or his office. In the end, Jackie proved to be the more cautious of the two, refusing to go along when some of her schoolmates bought Popsicles from the Good Humor man stationed outside the Georgetown University gate because she feared photos of the scene might be unbecoming.

In considering the pictures Suero took during his five days with the Kennedys—Jack and Jackie peering down from their balcony to chat with old pal Lem Billings, lazing around the living room looking at their wedding photos, Jackie floating down the stairs on the way to a dance, blossoming with a flower, glowing with a candle, the two of them striding together in the shadows of the U.S. Capitol, idling away a glorious weekend morning reading the paper and oil-painting and gardening out back, ambling down the middle of a quiet street with Bobby and Ethel to play touch football in the park—it is tempting to think that here were moments of innocence in an age of innocence. This is in part because they look so slender and tender and young (she was twenty-four; he thirty-six), in part because we know so well the rest of the story, the coming fame and tragedy, and in part because the past is constantly tempting us in that way. Innocence behind and innocence lost—it is at once true and false, the oldest deception in the human story.

Was it not wonderful that they spent so much time together? Yet Jackie was already chafing about how politics was taking her husband away so much. Who could look more elegant and radiant? Yet she thought she looked like a "monster" (except in Suero's rapturous frames). Did Jack not seem the picture of fitness and vigor in his classic quarterback pose? Yet his back was killing him and within months he would be on the operating table, near death. Who could appear more at ease and nonchalant? Yet the fire to become president burned inside. "He dragged me to Harry Truman's birthday party" that week, Suero remembered. "He wasn't inviting me as a buddy. He wanted to be photographed in that atmosphere."

There is Jack on a Saturday, the ramrod-straight signal caller in black high-tops, tossing the pigskin to Bobby, the gutsy little receiver circling toward a reception in his Bermuda shorts and polo shirt. A scene from the age of innocence? Compared to what? The newspapers on that gentle springtime morning long ago told of Joseph McCarthy in his full Red-hunting rage at the Army-McCarthy hearings up on

Capitol Hill, and of the French military, surrounded and defeated, surrendering at Dien Bien Phu in Vietnam—two of the seminal events of postwar history. Bobby was preoccupied with the hearings; he worked then as legal counsel for the Democratic minority on McCarthy's committee. That night, Jack went to a party at the home of columnist Joseph Alsop, who with his brother Stewart had just written a piece of morbid purple prose about the brave French colonialists holding on "against the murderous, terrible fire" in "the cruel mud"—what they called "one of the bright pages in the story of a glorious feat of arms." The headline in the column summed up the Alsop line: "They Fight for Us!" Senator Kennedy loved stories of derring-do, but he begged to differ on Vietnam. As he had declared in a Senate speech: "No amount of military assistance in Indochina can conquer an enemy which is everywhere and nowhere."

So much for innocence. At least the pace of life was slower then, right? Perhaps, but that was also the week that Roger Bannister broke the four-minute mile.

Pictures freeze moments, but moments are part of a continuum, one linked to the next. When Suero followed Jackie to her history course, he encountered Professor Jules David, whose lectures offered vivid accounts of statesmen and politicians making courageous if unpopular decisions. The theme intrigued not only Jackie but her husband, who only three years later would win a Pulitzer Prize for *Profiles in Courage*. It is safe to say that the seed of the book was planted in David's classroom. He also helped write it, and continued teaching at Georgetown through Kennedy's presidency and assassination and on through the sixties, eventually influencing another Georgetown student and Kennedy acolyte named Bill Clinton.

The Kennedys felt comfortable around Suero and were flattered by his pictures, and several times in the months after that May visit sent him letters encouraging him to come back for more. But he considered himself a news photographer, and there was always news elsewhere that his boss at the Three Lions picture agency wanted him to cover, so he never returned. There were times later when he considered the "if only"—if only he had followed up, he might have been the White House photographer. But that single assignment stayed with him for the rest of his career. He ended up in Hollywood shooting Lee Marvin, Brigitte Bardot, Jack Nicholson, and Jack Lemmon, but he thought he never shot a picture more radiant than the one of Jackie lighting the candles, and he never again found subjects quite the same, innocent or not, as the young couple living on Dent Place in the spring of 1954. "The camera loved the Kennedys," he said. "There wasn't a lens made for a camera that didn't love the Kennedys."

Part III

SPORTING PASSIONS

18

Ritual

Killeen, Texas

When the game ended and they had won, the boys who play football for the Killeen High School Kangaroos took off their helmets, jerseys, and shoulder pads and walked to midfield, carrying their equipment like cowboys bringing in their saddles after a hard ride on the range. The "Roos," as they are called in this agricultural and military city of fifty thousand near Fort Hood, were joined at the 30-yard line by cheerleaders, drill team Kangarettes, drummers, tuba players, and fans of all ages, several hundred Friday night victors gathered in a joyous semicircle under the blackland prairie moon. They hooked pinkie fingers and sang the school anthem, facing the west stands, where their words echoed back from several thousand more Killeen loyalists. Then the players formed an inner circle and slapped their thigh pads in syncopated rhythm to the chant *"Hee-roes. Hee-roes. Hee-roes."*

The head coach entered the circle carrying his young child in one hand, and when he fell to his knees, the players joined him, heads bowed. They began reciting the Lord's Prayer, tentatively at first, out of unison, then louder and more surely, their voices merging until the kingdom, the power, and the glory resounded through the stadium with spine-tingling force. In twos and threes, the young men sauntered off the field, followed by their girlfriends and little kids slipping imaginary tacklers in the dark shadows. The procession moved out the gates and up a hill a hundred yards or so to a one-story brick building, the home-team dressing room. The lights were dimming over the playing field below. The night air was sweet, ecstatic, and the boys wanted more of it. For the first time in their careers, they had defeated cross town rival Ellison. They were unbeaten and untied.

They lingered outside the dressing room, slowly removing shoes and socks as they sat at a long wooden bench paralleling the outer wall of their athletic sanctuary. Down the hill, a drumbeat sounded, and soon the marching band appeared in formation, six abreast, playing a fight song. Then the drummers started a jazz beat and the horns started jamming. The players, black and white, in white pants and T-shirts, danced on this hill in the heart of Baptist Texas, swaying in and out of the moonlight with a haunting effect of sensuality and violence.

A place defines itself by its rituals. In Texas, football is a ritual. It reveals more than the game, the scores and statistics. When Killeen faced Ellison on a recent Friday night, the city closed an hour before kickoff, and pregame traffic crawled for more than a mile toward Leo Buckley Athletic Complex. All of the ten thousand seats were sold, and hundreds of fans lined fences beyond the end zones. This was just an average game in Texas, nothing special. In Odessa—where if a linebacker goes on to play at a medium-sized college, he is taking a step down—a recent game was moved to Thursday night to accommodate television coverage. Up in Crowley, the focus was on Brownwood coach Gordon Wood, who gained his four-hundredth victory, a national record at any level. There were 964 Texas high school football teams in action that week, more than in any other state.

To say that cheating is part of the Texas football ritual might seem unfair, but this year has been imperfect, particularly for the state's universities. Five of the state's eight Southwest Conference schools have been accused of cheating or confessed to it. Players have been bought off with cold cash and sports cars. One of the great American myths is that football builds character. People in the Midwest and South seem particularly susceptible to that idea. Many Texans are not, for better or worse. In Texas, the traditions of teamwork and discipline compete with the frontier legacy of isolation and violence. The violence in Texas history has a direct connection to football, according to Bill O'Neal, a former football coach who became a scholar on gunfighters and Indian fighters in frontier Texas.

Frontier conditions prevailed in Texas for more than fifty years, until about 1870, longer than in any other western state or territory, O'Neal said, and the violent nature of that frontier cannot be underestimated. There were 846 recorded violent clashes between whites and Indians during those years, more than twice the number in Arizona, the second most violent territory. Of the 255 Western gunfighters and 589 shootouts that O'Neal has documented in the frontier West, Texas accounted for nearly half. Eleven of the top sixteen gunfighters did their bloody work in Texas: Killin' Jim Miller, Wes Hardin, Bill Longley, Harvey Logan, John Selman, Dallas Stoudenmire, King Fisher, Ben Thompson, Cullen Baker, Jim Courtright, John Hughes.

"The tradition can be traced quite clearly from gunfighting and Indian fighting into football in the twentieth century," O'Neal said. "Football deals with the same needs and outlets for manhood. And I suppose that one could make another correlation: If you didn't win on the frontier, you were dead. A lot of Texas coaches feel that way. It might account for some of the things that go on. . . . The finest high school football in the United States is played in Texas. As a consequence, college recruiters from across the nation raid the state of strapping young men who in an earlier time would have marched off eagerly to fight Indians or Mexicans or Yankees or each other. Thus, Texas has grudgingly adjusted to a more peaceful period, clinging unconsciously to the individualism of frontiersmen. The violent ways of a proud and harsh people have not yet vanished."

In Killeen, when the fighting is over, the boys take off their saddles and walk back up the hill.

This story was written in 1985, before Buzz Bissinger wrote his terrific book on Texas high school football, Friday Night Lights.

19

When Football Mattered

Vince Lombardi seemed haunted on his deathbed. A relentlessly proud man whose body was giving up, forty pounds lost in his struggle against colon cancer, he was embarrassed by his helpless condition. His face was so gaunt that he might have been unrecognizable if not for his top row of teeth, appearing larger than ever within his diminishing face, taking their gaps from left to right like Skoronski, Thurston, Ringo, Kramer, and Gregg at the line of scrimmage. His fingers—long, fleshy digits that were unforgettable to anyone who had ever been on the other side of one of his pointed lectures—now looked bent and withdrawn. The only part of him growing along with his cancer was his hair, untrimmed and free at last, as if to mock the myth of the Old Man, which is what his players and golfing buddies called him, even when he was dying young, at fifty-seven, in the last summer of 1970.

But it was not death that haunted Lombardi as much as life. Over the years, he had ordered the world around him so willfully that he had virtually forced life to make sense to him, but now it was spinning beyond his control. He expressed his sudden loss of equilibrium in odd ways. One night, as his wife, Marie, sat nearby in the stillness of his sixth-floor room at Georgetown University Hospital, the dying coach startled her by barking out a stern warning in his sleep. "Joe Namath!" he shouted. "You're not bigger than football! Remember that!" That was just like Lombardi. He was old in old ways. For the past three years he had been giving speeches lamenting what he considered to be the deceit of modern times. His argument was quintessentially Jesuit, instilled in him decades earlier at Fordham University in the Bronx.

In the rebellious sixties, freedom had become idealized against order, he said. The new against the old, genius against discipline. Everything was aimed at strengthening the rights of the individual and weakening the state, the church, and all authority. Now he feared that the battle had been too completely won and that society was reeling from the superficial excesses of freedom. This was not real freedom, according to Lombardi—that could be achieved only through order, discipline, and obedience. But who was listening to him? Not many of

Lombardi and Starr

Russel Kriwanek

the students whom he was trying to address and perhaps not even his beloved football players. They were changing too, speaking out, organizing, seeking their rightful money, power, and control of their professional lives, sporting long hair, flouting tradition, declaring themselves as individuals. Lombardi respected Namath's talent; before the opening kickoff of the 1969 Super Bowl in Miami, he had in fact seconded the white-shoed quarterback's bold prediction that the insurgent New York Jets would upset the Baltimore Colts. But Namath, a relatively tame character compared with what was to follow, nonetheless must have evoked something deeply troubling in the Old Man. It was as though, in his dying vision, he saw Michael Irvin and Brian Bosworth and Deion Sanders coming along behind Broadway Joe.

In an examination of Vince Lombardi and his place in American life, one speculative question resounds through the years: Could the greatest professional football coach ever, the one for whom the Super Bowl trophy is named, the only one to transcend his sport, could the flesh-and-blood Coach Lombardi prevail in today's world? Marie Lombardi, as it turns out, struggled with the question before anyone else and raised the first doubts. As he lay dying, she kept vigil in the room across the hall, drinking black coffee, chain-smoking Salems, and brooding over what might happen if he stayed alive. He loved the players above all else, yet circumstances would force him to turn away from them, as his sleep-talking warning to Joe Namath suggested. She predicted that he would plead with the owners to hold the line but that they would be incapable of doing so and the players would end up with too much freedom, tearing away at the order that held his world together and destroying his concept of team. "In the end," Marie told friends, "I think football will break his heart."

Though Marie would never have put it in such terms, there was a feeling that perhaps Vince Lombardi died at the appropriate time. He was in danger of being reduced to a convenient symbol then, his philosophy misused and misinterpreted by all sides in the political debates of that war-torn era. The establishment had turned him to stone even while he was alive, hoisting him up as a monument to righteousness, patriotism, and free enterprise. Counterculturists smashed him as a relic of old-line authoritarianism and a win-at-all-costs pathology. Both were wrong. Lombardi was more complicated, his philosophy more authentic, than either side could then appreciate. But if he had stayed alive, he would have faced more frustrations. The age of skepticism was coming with Watergate, combining later with the era of celebrity. Lombardi was meant for none of that, and so, the thinking goes, he left the scene just in time, remembered as a winner and more enduring as a mythic symbol of a lost past than if he had stayed alive as an increasingly frustrated coach fighting for relevance in the fickle and impermanent modern American culture.

Now, decades after his death, Lombardi's ghost is everywhere. Walk into the office of an insurance salesman in Des Moines or a hockey team president in New Jersey and there is the Lombardi credo, framed and hanging on the wall. Turn on the television during the football season and here he comes, all teeth and growl and camel-hair coat, once again prowling the sidelines in Nike ads. Look in the newspapers after the last Super Bowl, the one that returned the Packers to glory for the first time since he left Green Bay, and . . . what . . . over there in that photograph of the massive throng hailing the team at its victory parade, who is that figure standing alone on that mound of snow under the streetlight? The coat, the hat, the posture—Lombardi's ghost.

Green Bay's 1996 run to the championship certainly brought more attention to Lombardi, and would only increase the following year as the football world paid homage to the thirtieth anniversary of the Ice Bowl and his final championship. But he is always there anyway, lurking in the national psyche at a deeper level. Some go searching for the Old Man out of a sense of longing for something they believe has been irretrievably lost. Every time some sports act seems graceless and excessive, every time a player dances and points at himself after making a routine tackle, or a mediocre athlete and his agent hold out for millions, every year that these events seem more commonplace and accepted, the questions arise: What would Lombardi do about this? Why isn't there anyone like him out there anymore?

Another myth has to be dispatched before those questions can be considered rationally: the fallacy of the innocent past. Society has changed since Lombardi died, but the essence of human nature does not change. When Lombardi was a lineman at Fordham in the mid-1930s, grave concerns were raised about the commercialization of big-time college football, and players were being paid illegally almost as a matter of routine. At Ohio State, fifteen athletes were lured to play there with offers of easy jobs on the state payroll. Several of Lombardi's teammates were under par for a key game because they had been injured playing semipro ball illicitly across the river in New Jersey. When Lombardi was an assistant at West Point in 1951, nearly the entire football squad was expelled in a cribbing scandal. And at Green Bay in 1963, his favorite player, Paul Hornung, the Golden Boy, was suspended for a year for gambling on football games. There was nothing pristine about the football environment in which Lombardi operated, which is to say that some things never change, only the memories of them do.

What has changed most clearly from Lombardi's era is precisely what his wife foresaw: the dramatic shift in the balance of power between players and their bosses because of big money and free agency. Would that shift necessarily have led to the Old Man's failure and broken heart? Only if one believes that his leadership style was inflexible and wholly dependent on his not-so-benevolent despotism. But that is buying into the myth of Lombardi. The reality is that behind his seemingly quaint notions of spartan discipline, team love, and obedience to the leader, he was surprisingly adaptable. His entire football philosophy relied on adaptability above all else, reacting to conditions quickly enough to bend things his way. Had he lived longer, he would have persisted in that philosophy, adjusting to the changing times and in so doing making the times bend a little to him. It would have been a fascinating test of what he called will in action.

It was Henry Jordan, a defensive tackle for the old Packers, who uttered the memorable phrase "Lombardi treats us all alike, like dogs!" On the practice field perhaps, when he was barking at them during the dreaded nutcracker drills, but nowhere else. Lombardi was, in fact, an adept psychologist who treated each of his players differently. He rode some mercilessly but stayed away from others, depending on how they responded. Bart Starr, the sensitive quarterback, almost never got chewed out in front of the team. Marv Fleming, the impervious tight end, could hardly move without hearing it from the Old Man. Max McGee, the carefree wide receiver, was constantly being fined, but it was mostly for show. Since he was one of the coach's favorites, fining him was an effective way of getting a message across to the rest of the team. Lombardi's skills as a psychologist contradict the myth of his intractability, and they would serve him well today. He did not mind oddballs—his team was full of them—as long as they shared his will to win.

Would he have trouble with the showboating among today's players? When Travis Williams, the exhilarating kickoff return man on his 1967 team, danced a jig after scoring a touchdown that year, a modest ancestor of the elaborate celebrations so common now, Lombardi called him over and appealed to Williams's sense of pride. "Travis," he said, "try to act like you've been in the end zone before." That was all he had to say. It reinforced the message he gave his players at the beginning of training camp: You are professionals. You are Packers. You are above the rest. The glory-days Packers were in most respects no different from players of any era. They liked to drink and fool around. Lombardi established rules of behavior in Green Bay, but he also found ways to avoid confrontations. It was against his rules, for example, for a player to stand at a bar and have a drink. But when the Packers were on the road and Lombardi was heading back to the hotel after dinner, he would send one of his pals, former Packer Tony Canadeo, the TV color man, ahead to deliver a warning. Canadeo would stroll through the bar ahead of Lombardi and pass the word: "The Old Man's coming!"

The most significant and least appreciated aspect of Lombardi's leadership style was the way he trained his players to think for themselves and to respond intelligently to whatever they confronted. The myth of Lombardi is that he was a didactic autocrat with a simplistic approach to the game who told his players what to do, which is at once true and misleading, only part of a larger truth. Lombardi was a Jesuit in his football instruction, as in most other things. Like Saint Ignatius Loyola, the founder of the Society of Jesus, he believed in free will, that each man was at liberty to choose between action and inaction, good and evil, the right play and the wrong play. Lombardi made things simple for his players by taking nothing for granted. He repeated the same lessons to them over and over, every day, every week, every year. He kept the terminology understandable and used a small playbook. He would spend hours diagramming one play, the Packer sweep, so that his players knew how to adjust to whatever defense the opposition might employ. That was the point of his repetition and discipline—

freedom. His small playbook was not confining. It offered limitless variation. Starr, not Lombardi, called the plays. No coaches today give their quarterbacks that freedom. The offensive linemen called their own blocking assignments at the line. When the play began, every Packer knew how to respond, instinctively, to whatever the opposition did. The myth was that you knew what the Packers were going to run and yet they ran it so well that they beat you anyway. The reality was that the Packers beat you because they knew how to respond once the play began. They were, in that sense, free.

The players sometimes ridiculed Lombardi's fundamentalist coaching methods. At one training camp, when he began by saying, "Gentlemen, this is a football," Max McGee deadpanned, "Coach, could you slow down a little? You're going too fast for me." But they also believed in the deeper meaning of what he was doing and that all his yelling was balanced by a sense of love. "Leadership is not so much leading as having the people led accept it," Lombardi said a few months before he died. "You know how you do that? You've got to win the hearts of the people you lead." It was no accident, then, that so many of the old Packers went on to become independent thinkers and successful businessmen when their playing days ended.

Did Lombardi die at the appropriate time? Ask Dave Robinson, the great outside linebacker, who now runs a beverage distributorship in Akron, Ohio. Lombardi chewed him out nonstop for five seasons, most memorably after Robbie flushed out Don Meredith near the goal line and forced an interception that clinched the 1966 league championship against the Cowboys in Dallas. "You were out of position," Lombardi instructed him before embracing him during the postgame locker room celebration. Far worse if he ignored your imperfections; that meant you were a goner. When Lombardi died, Robinson flew to New York for the funeral and thought about how the Old Man reminded him so much of his own father, who also died young—and the tears started rolling down his cheeks. It was, he said—meaning it not as a sign of race consciousness but as honest feeling—the only time he ever cried at the funeral of a white man.

20

Ice

Ed Sabol could not sleep the night before a title game. He and his son Steve had been working pro football championships for NFL Films since 1962, and every year he was nervous, as if he had never done this before. Were his cameras in the right locations? Would there be a dramatic story line? Would the weather create problems again? By seven on the morning of December 31, 1967, he had already been awake for two hours, and now he was standing at the window of his hotel room, staring out into the northern darkness. Friday seemed unforgiving in Green Bay, with heavy snow and a fierce wind, but on Saturday there was a brilliant winter sun and the temperature had soared toward thirty. Local forecasters had predicted more of the same for today's one o'clock game.

The telephone rang. Steve, who had been asleep in the other bed, fumbled for the receiver.

"Good morning, Mr. Sabol."

The wake-up message came in a gentle singsong voice.

"It is sixteen degrees below zero and the wind is out of the north. Now have a nice day."

"Dad," Steve said. "You're not going to believe this!"

The same words of disbelief were uttered all over town. The phone at Paul's Standard Station on South Broadway had started ringing at five that morning, and the overnight man couldn't handle it, so Paul

Mazzoleni went in himself and took to the streets with his tow truck and jumper cables. One of his first stops was at the house of Willie Wood. The Packers free safety was standing next to his dead car, shivering, convinced that even when Mazzoleni brought his frozen battery back to life, he was not going anywhere. "It's just too cold to play," Wood said. "They're gonna call this game off. They're not going to play this." Chuck Mercein, the new man on the Packers, brought in at midseason to help fortify the depleted backfield, was alone in his apartment, semiconscious; his clock radio had just gone off. Had he really just heard someone say it was thirteen below? He must have misunderstood. Wasn't it near thirty when he went to bed? He called the airport weather station to see if he had been dreaming. "You heard it right. It's thirteen below and may get colder."

Lee Remmel of the *Green Bay Press-Gazette* had arranged a ride to the stadium with a cityside writer, one of eleven reporters the home paper had assigned to the game. His colleague called at seven with the question "Lee, do you know what the temperature is?" Remmel guessed twenty. No. Twenty-five? Go look at the thermometer. "I was aghast," he recalled. "The weatherman had been predicting twenty." Chuck Lane, the Packers young publicist, had grown up in Minnesota and was familiar with the telltale sounds of severe winter in the northland. As soon as he stepped out of his downtown apartment on Washington Street, he knew this was serious. "You can tell when it's cold by the sound of your foot in the snow. I could tell by the first stride that this was damn cold. The sound has got a different crunch to it." By his second stride he could feel something else—"the fuzz in your nose froze up."

Dick Schaap led a foursome of New Yorkers out to Green Bay for the big game, which he hoped would provide a narrative climax for the book he was writing with Jerry Kramer, the eloquent offensive guard. As Schaap and his editor, Bob Gutwillig, and their wives were driving downtown for breakfast, Schaap noticed the temperature reading on the side of a bank. It was minus thirteen. "Look, it's broken," he said. He had never seen a negative temperature and assumed that the bank got it wrong. Dave Robinson was in his kitchen, eating his traditional pregame meal: scrambled eggs, the filet of a twenty-ounce T-bone steak, toast, tea with honey. His little twin boys hovered in the next room, waiting for their dad to leave so they could eat the rest of the steak. His wife came in and gave him a kiss. "It's twenty below out there," she said. "Twenty above, you mean," Robinson said. "Can't be twenty below."

Not much was said about the temperature in the Lombardi house. There was barely any talking, period, that morning. "Everybody was uptight," Susan, the coach's daughter, recalled. Lombardi's two-year-old grandson had been up all night with a fever, distracting everyone, including the coach, who patted his grandson on the head before leaving for church. The cars were in the heated garage; Vince's Pontiac started right up. Silence on the way to Mass. The priest prayed for the Packers. All quiet on the way back. Then Vince and his son, Vincent, left, driving clockwise south to the bridge crossing the Fox River in downtown De Pere, then west to Highway 41, north to the Highland Avenue exit, and east to Lambeau Field.

The Sabols were already there, positioning eleven cameramen around the stadium. The parking lots were starting to fill up by eleven, two hours before game time, with many Packers fans insisting on going through their pregame rituals as though it were just another winter day in paradise. Not as many tailgaters as usual, but they were still out there. Folding chairs, card tables, brats, and beer. One concession to the weather: More of them than usual were huddled around fires. Jim Irwin, a local TV sports director, arrived at the press box two hours early and looked out and saw hundreds of people already stationed in their seats. "They didn't have to be in the stands," he noted. "They had reserved tickets. They chose to be out there when it was thirteen below."

Chuck Lane was heading out from the locker room to check the field when he met a group of assistants coming the other way. "Tell Lombardi that his field is frozen," one said. Tell Lombardi that his field is frozen? That, Lane thought, would be "like telling him that his wife was unfaithful or that his dog couldn't hunt." But that was his job, so he turned around and found Lombardi, who was leaving the locker room to check the field himself when Lane intercepted him. Lombardi seemed crestfallen, then angry and disbelieving. "What the hell are you talking about?" he thundered.

The field could not be frozen. The previous spring, in his role as general manager, Lombardi had paid $80,000 for a gigantic electric blanket. He loved inventions, and this electric blanket seemed to mean more to him than any play he had ever devised. It was working on Saturday when the crew pulled the tarp off to let the Cowboys practice. The ground was soft but not soggy. Lombardi had been so satisfied then that he had yelled over to the project engineer and given him the OK sign with his thumb and forefinger. Even Tom Landry, the skeptical Dallas coach, who hated to play in Green Bay, had deemed the field "excellent," though a little damp. But dampness was not the problem now. Parts of the field were indeed frozen—"As hard as a rock," reported Jim Tunney, the alternate referee.

In the locker room, Willie Wood took off his street clothes slowly, reluctantly, still convinced that the game would be canceled. "Man, it's too damn cold," he said to his teammates. "They ain't going to play in this shit." The room was full of smoke, cigarettes burning from the built-in ashtrays on almost every locker. Equipment man Dad Braisher passed out long underwear to everybody, even Lombardi. Coach said it was okay to wear it today, but he didn't want them stuffing too much underneath the uniforms; he had a thing about players feeling loose and easy. Linebacker Lee Roy Caffey and strong safety Tom Brown wanted to wear gloves, but Lombardi said no. Linemen could wear them, but no gloves for anyone who handled the ball. Dave Robinson walked over to the equipment manager when Lombardi left the room. "Give me a pair of those brown gloves and he'll never know the difference. I'm the only linebacker with brown hands anyway." Braisher agreed to the conspiracy, and Robinson wore gloves the rest of the day.

When the players took the field for warm-ups, most of them kept their hands tucked in their pants. Every deep breath was an arrow shooting into their lungs. Donny Anderson, a Texan, had never played in weather like this before, but he had no choice because Elijah Pitts, one of the other halfbacks, was out for the year. Pitts had been enjoying his best season until the game in Baltimore, when he suffered a severe ankle injury. Fullback Jim Grabowski had also been hurt during that game. He was slowly making his way back, and thought he might play against the Cowboys; the knee had felt good all week in practice. Then, during warm-ups, he went out on a pass pattern, planted his right foot, and felt something pop, and his comeback was over. Chuck Mercein, who had been cut from the Giants during the preseason and was plucked from forced retirement by a desperate Lombardi near season's end, would get most of the action at fullback.

It was not until the Packers returned to the locker room after warm-ups that the reality finally hit Willie Wood. "Well, it looks like we are going to play this game," he said to cornerback Bob Jeter. Then came another thought. If we're gonna play, we gotta make sure we're gonna win. We don't want to come out in these kinds of conditions and lose a damn ball game. Lombardi was of a similar mind, of course. He never wanted to lose any game, but especially not to Landry and the Cowboys. The two coaches had developed a friendly rivalry during their years together in New York in the 1950s, when Landry had directed

Ice

Vernon J. Biever

the defense and Lombardi the offense under the benign head coach Jim Lee Howell. Since then Lombardi had stayed one step ahead of his old Giants colleague. He became a head coach in 1959, Landry in 1960. He turned a losing team around in one year; it took Landry five years before he could get his expansion Cowboys to a winning record. But now the Cowboys were being cited as the team of the future, with the flex and the Doomsday Defense and multiple offense, their flashy uniforms and speedy receivers.

In his heart of hearts, Max McGee thought Dallas had the better team. "Not that they could beat us," McGee said. "We had their number. Lombardi had the hex on Landry."

Gary Knafelc, the old tight end, was in the press box that day. His playing career done, he could not stay away, and signed on as Lambeau Field's public address announcer. Looking out from his perspective atop the stadium, he was overwhelmed by the panorama. The players were the story, perhaps, and as the game went along, they would rivet his and everyone else's attention, but at first it was hard to take one's eyes off the crowd in the stands. "There was this incredible haze of breath, tens of thousands of puffs coming out. Like seeing big buffaloes in an enormous herd on the winter plains. It was prehistoric."

To many fans, attending this game was a test of their resourcefulness. Carol Schmidt and her husband, who worked in the oil business, sat in section 24 near the 20-yard line, where they snuggled inside a makeshift double sleeping bag made from the heavy felt used at the local paper mills. To warm their feet they turned a three-pound coffee can upside down, punched holes in the top, and placed a large candle inside on a pie plate. Bob Kaminsky arrived with his wife's twin brothers and took his seat in the end zone, oblivious of the weather. "This is what I wore," he reported. "Long johns. Work shoes. Over the work shoes I put those heavy gray woolen socks that came over the knees. Pair of galoshes over that. Flannel pajamas over the long johns. Work overalls. A T-shirt. Flannel shirt. Insulated sweatsuit. Heavy parka. Face mask with holes for mouth and eyes. Wool tassel cap. And then I climbed into a sleeping bag. I had foam on the ground and seat for my feet and butt. I was not cold."

Lombardi's golfing pal Jack Koeppler and his son wore deer hunting outfits (red and black in that era, not yet the glaring orange). Two

layers warmed their hands, first deer hunting gloves, then huge mit-
tens. At their seats near the 40-yard line they zipped two sleeping bags
together and slipped inside for the extra warmth generated by two
bodies. Jerry Van, owner of the Downtowner Motel, where Hornung
and McGee once lived, wore "two of everything." He cut up several
thick cardboard boxes into twelve-inch squares and put three layers on
the concrete floor to keep his feet warm. Lois Bourguignon, the wife
of Packers executive board member Dick Bourguignon, wore a plastic
garment bag under her winter coat to keep the heat in. Red Cochran,
the former assistant coach who had quit the year before, watched the
title game in the stands with his six-year-old son, both wearing bulky
snowmobile suits. Teenager Gary Van Ness, who had come to the stadium planning to sneak in, was given a ticket near midfield by a doctor
who had decided to leave, and found himself amid a group of rich folk;
he had never before seen so many fur coats.

Fur coats? They were plentiful at Lambeau Field, even in arctic
weather. The games were *the* social events of the year in Green Bay.
Many women bought their fall and winter wardrobes with Sunday
football games in mind and wore different outfits to every game. Mary
Turek, Lombardi's dentist's wife, sat in prestigious section 20, just
above the players' wives, in her heavy fur coat with fur-lined stadium
boots that extended over her calves. Around her she saw women in
less practical attire, many of them exposing their legs to the weather
in nylons and high heels. They tended not to last long. Tom Olejnic-
zak, the team president's son, took a date to the game who left for the
women's room midway through the first quarter and didn't come back
until the game was over. Lorraine Keck, Lombardi's assistant secretary,
got stuck in a restroom for more than a quarter, the door blocked by
paramedics treating a girl who had passed out. Throughout the game
bathrooms and passageways underneath the stands were jammed with
people trying to get warm. When Red Cochran took his young son to
the men's room, they got stuck in the human flow. It "was so mobbed,"
he said, "you had to go with the crowd, wherever it took you."

The temperature as kickoff approached was thirteen below, with an
estimated windchill of minus forty-six. The leather ball felt heavy and
airless. During their warm-ups, players said the field felt as if someone
had taken a stucco wall and laid it on the ground. Clumps of mud had
coagulated and stuck to the rock-hard turf. Blowers on the sidelines

shot warm air in the direction of the benches, but you had to be right next to one to feel it. Some players huddled in makeshift dugouts constructed from wood and canvas, like duck blinds. Lombardi paced the sidelines in his long winter coat and black fuzzy hat with muffs. No matter how cold the Packers felt, one look across the field made them feel superior. The Cowboys, said Chuck Mercein, "looked like Earthmen on Mars. The outfits they wore. Most of them had hooded sweatshirts on underneath their helmets, which looked silly as hell. And a kind of scarf thing around their faces with their eyes cut out. They looked like monsters in a grade-B movie."

For the first quarter and most of the second, the Cowboys played like anything but monsters. Their main receiving threat, Bob Hayes, known as the world's fastest human, also seemed to be the world's coldest, and unwittingly gave away every offensive play. If it was a run, he tucked his frigid hands into his pants as he lined up; if Cowboys quarterback Don Meredith called a pass play, Hayes pulled out his hands. "You can't catch a pass with your hands in your pants," said Tom Brown, the Packers strong safety. "We played eleven guys against ten whenever he did that. He was just stone cold."

The first time the Packers had the ball, Bart Starr led them on an eighty-two-yard drive that culminated in a touchdown pass to Boyd Dowler from eight yards out. In the second quarter he hit Dowler for another touchdown, this one of forty-three yards, and the score was 14–0. If a blowout seemed in progress, lingering in the back of everyone's mind was the memory of the previous year in Dallas, when the Packers had also bolted to a quick two-touchdown lead, then barely hung on to win the championship game on Tom Brown's last-second interception in the end zone. Could Dallas come back again? The weather argued no; conventional wisdom dictated that these Cowboys didn't know how to play in subzero weather.

Four minutes left in the half. Green Bay holds the ball on its own 26, first down. Starr drops back to pass. There is no protection, the entire Doomsday front line is roaring after him, he drops farther, turns away from tackle Bob Lilly, retreating nineteen yards, back to the 7, where Willie Townes hits him. Starr's hands are nearly numb, and he fumbles and Cowboys lineman George Andrie picks it up and plows into the end zone as he is being tackled by Forrest Gregg and Jerry

Kramer—and suddenly a seemingly secure lead is cut in half. A few minutes later, Willie Wood drops back to receive a Dallas punt. Wood has the surest hands in the league. In eight seasons as a return man, he has fumbled only once, during a rainstorm in San Francisco, and that time he recovered his own fumble. Now he is standing near the Packers 20, looking up, and Danny Villanueva's punt is fading on him. Wood is thinking too much: about how cold his hands are, about field position. Should he try to run it back or call a fair catch? He puts his hands up, fair catch, and the ball fades away, and when it hits his hands he can't really feel it. Fumble—Frank Clarke recovers for Dallas. Four plays later the Cowboys get a field goal, and they race for the warmth of the locker room at halftime, back in the game, trailing 14–10.

Ten points attributable to the weather. All ten for Dallas.

Lombardi had little to say at halftime. His assistant coaches did most of the talking. The offensive line coach was distraught over the way Dallas's front line was breaking in on Starr. Another assistant pointed out to Starr that Dallas's linebackers were dropping straight back on pass plays, so deep that he should be able to complete short passes to the backs—something to keep in mind. But mostly it was quiet, the focus on getting warm, having a smoke, a Coke, a section of orange.

The third quarter was nothing but frustration. Neither team scored. Bill Schliebaum, the line judge, had his whistle freeze to his lips and lost a layer of skin yanking it loose. Jim Huxford, working the chains, had to pull off his ski mask after part of it froze to his mouth. Linebacker Ray Nitschke refused to go near the blowers—he had a tradition of kneeling on one knee near the coach when the defense was off the field—and now he was starting to get frostbite in his toes. Chuck Mercein's left triceps felt numb after a tough hit in the second quarter. Steve Sabol, stationed on the ledge above the end zone stands, and shivering in his cowboy boots, discovered that his camera had broken, the focus wheel on his telephoto lens frozen at a thirty-yard distance. CBS television announcer Pat Summerall, whose assignment for the second half was to work the Green Bay sideline, was getting blistered every time he came near Lombardi. The fact that he had once played for the coach in New York made no difference. "Get the hell away from my bench!" Lombardi barked. "This is my office!"

The press box had its own share of discontent. Reporters stationed in the front row found that their portable typewriters were freezing on the ledge. The game was down there somewhere, but the writers and broadcasters were having an increasingly hard time seeing it through the big picture windows, which were either too steamed or too frosted. Writers took to scraping small patches of visibility in the windows with their credit cards. Chuck Lane had zipped across the street at halftime to buy some de-icer at the service station, and one press-box attendant was squirting de-icer on the windows like lighter fluid while another used a squeegee to clear away the condensation. Every time someone opened the side door, letting in a blast of cold air, *Milwaukee Sentinel* sportswriter Bud Lea yelled out, "Holy God, shut the door!" Ray Scott, calling the game for CBS with Jack Buck and Frank Gifford, insisted on having a window open in the booth. "You don't have the feel for the game otherwise," he said. Gifford was losing his feel for anything. "I think I'll take another bite of my coffee," he muttered famously on the air.

As the third quarter ended, Dallas had possession at midfield. The Cowboys were now dominating the game. Twice in the third quarter they had threatened to score, but one drive was thwarted when Lee Roy Caffey made Meredith fumble on the Green Bay 13, and another ended with a missed field-goal attempt. The Packers seemed inept, gaining only ten yards all quarter. On the first play of the fourth quarter, Cowboy running back Dan Reeves took the handoff from Meredith and ran wide to the left. Green Bay's defensive backfield played it as a run, and by the time they realized it was an option and Reeves was passing, receiver Lance Rentzel had slipped behind everyone, and Tom Brown could only chase him into the end zone. Dallas held the lead, 17–14.

Over the next ten minutes, the Packers had the ball twice but failed to score. Their one chance to tie the game fizzled when Don Chandler missed a field goal from the 40, wide left. Dallas picked up two first downs on its next possession, and held the ball for nearly five minutes before punting. Willie Wood thought of nothing but catching the ball this time. He cradled it safely at his 23, then burst nine yards upfield. The Packers were on their own 32, first down, sixty-eight yards to go for the winning touchdown, four minutes and fifty seconds remaining in the game.

CBS's Ray Scott had left the broadcast booth to work his way to the winners' dressing room. The quickest way to get there was to walk down through the stands to the field. He reached the Green Bay side-line just after Wood was tackled. The return team was running off the field and the offense was heading out to the huddle. Ray Nitschke, the emotional leader of the defense, had lost his voice. His toes were numb. Scott watched him as he rumbled off the field this one last time, his fist clenched, and yelled hoarsely but fiercely to the offense, "Don't let me down! Don't let me down!"

Dick Schaap had also left the press box with five minutes left, following a crowd of reporters to the field. He figured the game was over. Kramer had told him about one of Lombardi's favorite sayings: The Packers never lose, but sometimes the clock runs out. That's what would happen now, Schaap thought. At long last, the clock would run out on the Packers. Run out for this championship game, but also for the whole incredible run the team had been on since Lombardi came to Green Bay nine years earlier. The game was changing, these Packers were old, time was moving on. That was it, Schaap thought. He had the title for the book: *The Year the Clock Ran Out*. Great title, he said to himself as he walked down the aisle, through the primordial scene in the stands, the huge buffalo herd, fifty thousand puffs of breath, fifty thousand fans warmed by four quarters of brandy, bourbon, and beer. Still buzzing. Didn't they realize this was over?

Steve Sabol, his camera frozen and completely useless now, came down from his end zone perch to take a position near Green Bay's bench, as close to Lombardi as he could get. Sabol worshipped pro football and considered Lombardi the game's patron saint, the main character in the romantic story that he and his father were telling. The young filmmaker was among those who believed. He thought he was in a great spot to witness football history.

Before trotting onto the field, Starr had talked to Lombardi about what they would try to do. They had decided not to go for the quick score, but rather "just try to keep moving the ball." In the huddle, Starr seemed inordinately calm. "This is it," he said, looking directly at his teammates. "We're going in." Bob Skoronski, the tackle, had struggled all day to keep George Andrie out of the backfield. Earlier in the game, Lombardi had lit into him on the bench, accusing him of falling asleep. But now Starr's demeanor had a transformational effect.

Skoronski was fully awake and confident. He looked at Starr and saw Lombardi, the reminder of everything they had learned in nine seasons with the coach. All of Lombardi's schooling was for precisely this moment, all the hundreds of times that he had run them through the sweep, convincing them that no matter what the defense tried, they had the answer. There is nothing they can do to stop us, Skoronski thought.

Chuck Mercein, the fullback, after only seven games with the Packers, felt the same way. "The feeling I had was that we are going to score. I felt calm. I felt that everyone in the huddle was calm. I didn't sense any anxiety or desperation. Determination, yes, but not desperation. Bart just said a few words, 'We're going in,' but he had this tremendous presence. He was the on-field personification of Lombardi." Donny Anderson, the halfback, was more composed than any of his teammates had seen him before. He had tried to present himself as a latter-day Paul Hornung, the saturnalian golden-boy halfback of Lombardi's early championship years, but before this game the similarity had been most noticeable off the field. Now it seemed as though Anderson had grown up in one long, cold afternoon. "If you dump me the ball I can get eight or ten yards every play," he told Starr. The play had been there all afternoon, but as important as the sagacity of his observation was its fearless message: With the game on the line, he wanted the ball, just as the Golden Boy once had.

On first down it worked: Starr dumped a little pass to Anderson, good for six yards. Then Mercein ran around right end for seven more, and Starr hit Dowler for thirteen, and with those three successful plays the Packers had taken the ball into Dallas territory, forty-two yards from the end zone. Anderson lost nine on the next play, caught in the backfield by Willie Townes on a busted sweep, but he came back with two consecutive little gems, taking dump passes from Starr and picking his way cautiously down the ice-slicked field, eluding the linebackers for twelve yards and then nine more. Mercein had noticed something during those plays, and felt confident enough to bring it up with Starr. "I'm open on the left side if you need me." The ball was on the Dallas 30, only one minute and thirty-five seconds left. Starr went back to pass, Mercein swung to the left, Starr looked for Dowler and Anderson, then saw Mercein in the clear and went to him, the ball floating in the wind, behind Mercein and high, but he snared it on the run and slipped by the linebacker and was moving past the cornerback, nineteen yards and out of bounds at the Dallas 11. Gil Brandt, the Dallas personnel man, called that catch a killer, one of the best he had ever seen, given the conditions.

Then came what Starr considered the best call of the game. All week, Lombardi had told him to look for the perfect spot, and use it only when he really needed it. Now was the time. It was known as GIVE 54, an influence play. It looked like a variation of the Packer sweep, run from what was called the Brown formation, with the fullback lined up directly behind the quarterback, instead of Lombardi's preferred Red formation, in which the halfback and fullback were spread. On the sweep from this formation, the left guard pulled and the fullback was assigned to block the guard's man, which in this case would be Dallas's Hall of Fame tackle, Bob Lilly. Lilly was so quick and smart that he could shoot through the hole and bring down the runner from behind before the sweep unfolded.

The GIVE 54 was designed to take advantage of Lilly's aggressiveness. Starr would fake the sweep and hand the ball to Mercein, who would run through the hole vacated by Lilly. It could be a dangerous play. If Lilly held his ground, there was no one to block him. But when the guard pulled, Lilly followed, and Mercein came busting through. Skoronski made a clean block on the left end, sealing an alley, and a linebacker went the wrong way, and as Mercein came through he saw "a helluva great hole there." He thought that if he could only get behind Forrest Gregg for one more block he might take it in, but the field was almost all ice down in the shadows of the scoreboard, no footing at all, "like a marble tabletop," according to Starr. Mercein picked up eight crucial yards. "I can still hear the sound of his feet clicking on that ice," lineman Jim Huxford said three decades later. "You could hear it on the ice. He was slipping, but he kept going." All the way to the 3, where he stumbled into Gregg and fell to the ground.

On the next play, Anderson barely picks up the yardage needed for a first down. The Packers are one yard from the goal line. Anderson again, no gain. Second down. Twenty seconds left. Time-out. Anderson again. He slips on the ice as Starr hands him the ball, almost fumbling. Again, no gain. Third down. Green Bay calls its last time-out with sixteen seconds remaining, and Starr jogs to the sideline to talk to Lombardi.

A field goal would tie the game and send it into sudden-death over-time, but bringing in the field-goal team is not even discussed. Nothing needs to be said about a field goal. After playing for Lombardi for nine seasons, Starr knows what his coach is thinking. He is conservative, goes by the book, but he's a winner. Run to win. Lombardi had been preaching that motto to his team all through the final difficult weeks of this season, paraphrasing St. Paul's exhortation to the Corinthians: "All the runners at the stadium are trying to win, but only one of them gets the prize. You must run in the same way. Run to win." Also, Lombardi is freezing his tail off, like everybody else in the place.

Some on the Packers sideline think they should try a rollout pass; that way, even if it falls incomplete, the clock stops with time for one more play. They wonder whether Lombardi knows there are no time-outs left, but he doesn't seem to be listening. Starr says he wants to go with the wedge play, where the runner pounds between center and guard, but he wants to be certain that Jerry Kramer, who has to make a key block, can get good footing. It looks like an ice rink down there at the 1. Watching films of the Cowboys earlier that week, they had noticed that Kramer's man, Dallas tackle Jethro Pugh, stood the highest in goal-line situations, making him the easiest defender to cut down. Mercein is out on the field, he can't hear the discussion, but he's thinking the same thing, "one hundred percent certain" that they're going to give him the ball on the wedge, the simplest play in football.

"Run it!" Lombardi says. "And let's get the hell out of here." Starr trots back to the huddle.

Personnel director Pat Peppler rarely stands anywhere near Lombardi during a game, but now he can't help himself. He moves closer to the coach and asks, "What's he gonna call?"

"Damned if I know," Lombardi says.

Starr asks Kramer if he can get good footing.

"Hell, yes," Kramer says.

"Huddle up," Starr says. He calls the play. Brown right, 31 wedge. That's the 3 back (fullback) through the 1 hole (between center and guard). Mercein hears it and thinks, This is it. I'm going to score. But as Starr is calling the play, a thought flashes through the quarterback's mind: No matter how good the block is, if Mercein should slip, he won't be able to reach the hole in time. Starr remembers a game in

Milwaukee in 1966: On an icy field, at the end of a long drive, he called the wedge, then kept the ball himself and scored on a sneak. The Packers didn't even have a quarterback sneak in their playbook. Never practiced it. But the improvisation had worked once, why not now? I can just hug the block in there, just get one step and go right in, Starr thinks. He doesn't tell anyone. His teammates think Mercein is getting the ball.

The Packers break from the huddle. The Doomsday linemen—Lilly, Pugh, Townes, and Andrie—are kicking the ice at the goal line, desperate to find a patch of unfrozen turf so they can get a quick start off the ball. Jerry Kramer takes his position next to center Ken Bowman—and there it is, a soft spot on the ground, just for him. He digs in with his right foot, certain that he can cut Pugh at the snap. On the Packers bench, Willie Davis, the defensive end, is "thinking of all the possibilities, a bad snap or whatever." Aw, hell, he says to himself, and turns his head away. He can't watch. Willie Wood puts his head down. Looks hard at the ground. "Sometimes you don't want to see bad things," he will explain later. Lombardi wonders whether they'll have enough time to bring in the field-goal team if they don't make it.

Dick Schaap is still on the far end of the field, nearly a hundred yards away. He has no clue that his coauthor is expected to make the crucial block on the season's most important play. Vernon Biever, the Packers' official photographer, has been standing behind the end zone with his son John, his fifteen-year-old assistant. It makes no sense for them both to be shooting from the same spot, so he says to John, "You stay here. I'll change film and go to the bench area, so if they score I'll get the emotion over there." John Biever stays in the end zone and lifts his Nikon motorized camera, anticipating the final play coming his way.

One year earlier, in the championship game against the Packers in Dallas, the Cowboys were down near the goal line, threatening to score in the final seconds, and one of their linemen was penalized for moving before the snap. Now the Packers are in the same situation, and Kramer is coming off the ball hard and fast, and Jethro Pugh thinks that it is too fast, that Kramer is offside, but no call is made, and Kramer cuts Pugh off his feet, and then Kenny Bowman knocks Pugh back into a linebacker and Pugh falls on top of Kramer, and the wedge opening is there. Mercein gets a good start, no slips. "I'm psyched, I

want this thing to go right," Mercein recalls later. "I'm taking off and
. . . lo and behold, Bart's not giving me the ball. He's kept it and he's
in the end zone."

Mercein is coming right behind him, leaping over the line, and he
doesn't want the officials to think he's pushing Starr forward, which
would be a penalty, so he throws his hands above his head, trying to
say, See, I'm not assisting him, and it looks as though Mercein is signaling the touchdown in midair. John Biever clicks his Nikon and captures the moment for history: Kramer's block, Starr's sneak, Mercein's
dive. Vernon Biever is near the bench and gets a shot of Lombardi
lifting his hands jubilantly: Touchdown. Victory. Dick Schaap knows
that he has to change the title of his book. The clock did not run out.

The coach, it could be said, had nothing to do with the final drive,
in a game that would be remembered thereafter as the Ice Bowl. Starr
called the plays and scored the touchdown, Anderson and Mercein offered helpful advice and made the key runs and catches, Kramer and
Bowman threw the crucial blocks. Yet to every Packer on the field, and
to many of those watching from the sidelines and in the press box, that
final drive, more than anything else, was the perfect expression of Vince
Lombardi. The conditions were miserable, the pressure enormous, and
there were no fumbles, no dropped passes, no mistakes, just a group of
determined men moving confidently downfield toward a certain goal.
In his speeches, Lombardi talked about character in action, and here
it was, in real life. "Of all the games I've done," said Ray Scott, "that
final drive was the greatest triumph of will over adversity I've ever seen.
It was a thing of beauty."

The locker room was a jangle of cameras and lights when Lombardi got
there after the game. He evicted the press and talked to his men alone,
telling them how proud he was: for running to win, for persevering
and meeting their greatest challenge, winning three straight championships. He fell to his knees and led the team in the Lord's Prayer.
When he returned to his dressing room and began taking questions
from the press, he could not stop fidgeting in his chair. He rose, sat
down, got up again. He claimed with a touch of whimsy that the decision to gamble for the touchdown was dictated largely by the weather.
"I didn't figure those fans in the stands wanted to sit through a sudden

death," he said. "You can't say I'm without compassion, although I've been accused of it." But the story was "out there, not here," he told the media, nodding in the direction of the outer locker room.

Glacial tears burned the cheeks of Ray Nitschke. The offense had not let him down, and now he said he felt a deep sense of satisfaction. He was also cold and numb and had frostbite on both feet. He and several teammates were soaking their feet in a bucket of lukewarm water. The hot water in the showers disappeared quickly, and Tom Brown and Willie Wood came yelping out of the shower room when it turned cold. They decided to take their showers at home. Jim Grabowski, who had watched the game from the bench, wishing he could have contributed, now took in the postgame scene with feelings of loneliness and separation, as injured players always do, even in the midst of their teammates' joy. Grabo nonetheless sought out his replacement for congratulations. "Chuck, you just did a great job," he said to Mercein. "As good a job as I possibly could have done. Better, maybe."

Jerry Kramer could not stop talking. As Dick Schaap observed from the edge of the crowd, Kramer told one huddle of reporters after another about the last drive and the block, which CBS replayed in slow motion over and over. It was only then that Schaap was struck by the serendipity of the day's events. The last play of the biggest game, and his colleague had made the block, and now an enormous television audience was listening to him talk about it, and also about this special team and its uncommon coach. Kramer was the narrator of his diary, but he shared the role of main character with Lombardi, a looming presence in almost every scene. Kramer hated Lombardi and loved Lombardi, but he thought that he and his teammates knew him in a way that no outsider could. Weeks earlier, *Esquire* had published an article by Leonard Shecter that had portrayed Lombardi as a bully and a tyrant. "Many things have been said about Coach," Kramer now told his TV interviewers. "And he is not always understood by those who quote him. The players understand. This is one beautiful man."

A few weeks later Jerry Kramer was in New York as a guest at Schaap's journalism class at Columbia. He was describing his block on the final play of the Ice Bowl and how the television kept showing the play over and over. "Thank God for instant replay," Kramer said.

Aha, Schaap thought. There's our title.

Instant Replay would become one of the best-selling sports books of all time.

A few months later the crowd that would gather in Lombardi's basement after home games reassembled there, now to watch the highlight film of Green Bay's championship season produced by Ed and Steve Sabol. They draped a bedsheet against the wall to serve as a makeshift screen, then turned off the lights. The film, titled *The Greatest Challenge*, was narrated by John Facenda, who was being phased out as a newscaster at Channel 10 in Philadelphia when Ed Sabol asked him to be the voice of NFL Films. With his deep and melodramatic tone, Facenda became known as "the voice of God." He read his scripts without ever looking at the pictures that accompanied them.

At the climax of the film about the 1967 Packers, Jerry Kramer said that he played pro football because of all the men who had been his teammates during the Lombardi era. "I'll tell you in a nutshell, if you can understand this: I play pro football because of Emlen Tunnell, Bill Quinlan, Dan Currie, Paul Hornung, Fuzzy Thurston, Max McGee, Henry Jordan, Herb Adderly, Ray Nitschke, Dave Robinson, Bart Starr." Then came Facenda's voice: deep, reverberating, sentimental. "They will be remembered as the faces of victory," he said. "They will be remembered for their coach, whose iron discipline was the foundation on which they built a fortress. And most of all, they will be remembered as a group of men who faced the greatest challenge their sport has ever produced—and conquered."

When it was over, the room stayed dark and the projector ran on and on, film flapping noisily over the reel. Someone belatedly turned on the light switch, and there stood Lombardi. He had been watching football film for decades, and he had run this projector himself, the old pro. But this time he was not grading the blocking technique of his players with ones or twos or zeroes. He had a handkerchief out, and he was crying.

21

The Passion of Clemente

Most athletes fade into oblivion after their playing days, but Roberto Clemente's story has grown in the decades since his death. There is even a movement now to have his No. 21 retired from the game and honored at major-league ballparks alongside Jackie Robinson's No. 42, its proponents arguing that Clemente carries the same legendary status in the Latino world as Robinson does for African Americans and for people of any color shamed by the racism that kept blacks out of America's pastime until 1947. However that debate plays out, the larger comparison of Robinson and Clemente is fascinating, especially in light of the recent dominance of Spanish-speaking players and the corresponding decline of black Americans in organized baseball. Clemente was both Latino and black, an intensely proud and passionate man who struggled furiously to succeed amid the crosscurrents of race, language, and culture.

Born near the sugar fields of Carolina, Puerto Rico, on August 18, 1934, Roberto Clemente Walker played right field for the Pittsburgh Pirates for eighteen seasons before dying in a plane crash on New Year's Eve, 1972, while trying to deliver medical aid and food to Nicaragua after a devastating earthquake. Like Robinson, he was a stirring athlete whose charismatic style lifted his team and transcended the statistics that define the game.

His totals were exceptional enough (exactly three thousand hits, the magic number to assure enshrinement in the Hall of Fame, along with a .317 career batting average and twelve Gold Gloves as the league's finest right fielder), but again like Robinson, he was great and inimitable while not the all-time best. And unlike Robinson, Clemente was not the first of his kind. Several Latinos, white-skinned Cubans, had already played in the majors. The first Puerto Rican to make it was Hiram Bithorn, a burly pitcher from Santurce who won eighteen games for the Chicago Cubs in 1943. There were also a few black Latino stars preceding Clemente, including the dashing Minnie Miñoso from Cuba and fellow Puerto Rican Vic Power, a balletic first baseman.

Yet Clemente alone has emerged as the seminal figure in the baseball history of Latinos. There is a stadium named for Hiram Bithorn in San Juan, but few know the rest of his story, how he suffered a mental collapse after that one fine year in Chicago and was eventually shot to death, penniless and alone, by a corrupt cop in rural Mexico. Clemente's memory still burns bright in all of Latin America. When the Baltimore Orioles went to Havana in 1999, they learned that Clemente was as honored there as any Cuban. Ozzie Guillen, the Venezuelan who managed the Chicago White Sox to the World Series championship in 2005, revealed afterward that he kept a shrine at his home for Clemente, whom he admired above all others. In Nicaragua, where he died, and Puerto Rico, the homeland island to which he always returned, he is regarded with the reverence of a saint, a perspective reflected by the thirty-foot cenotaph in Carolina where the center panel portrays him holding a lamb. Partly this is because of how he died—on a humanitarian mission to help strangers, the plane plunging into the sea, his body never found. And partly it is because of how he lived and played—with the same relentless force, and pride in who he was and where he came from, that fueled Jackie Robinson.

In the Puerto Rico of Roberto Clemente's childhood, there were no legal or overt social barriers separating the races. Years before they integrated the majors, American blacks, led by Josh Gibson, the fearsome slugger of the Negro Leagues, played in the Puerto Rican Winter League. Clemente rooted for the San Juan Senadores, and his idol as a teenager was Monte Irvin, a graceful outfielder who was just getting a shot with the New York Giants after starring for ten seasons with the Newark Eagles. Irvin recalled decades later that young Clemente, shy and without a ticket, would get into the games by carrying Irvin's suit bag to the locker room—a small gesture that captures the long-stand-

Linda Maraniss

Clemente cenotaph

ing symbiotic relationship of blacks and Latinos in baseball. Puerto Rico also served as the training ground for the first black manager in the major leagues, Frank Robinson, who got his start with the Santurce Cangrejeros, eventually broke the managerial color barrier with the Cleveland Indians in 1975, and three decades later was in the dugout for the Washington Nationals.

When Clemente began his baseball migration to the mainland, he followed in Jackie Robinson's footsteps. He was signed by the same Brooklyn Dodgers and like Robinson was sent to play for its triple-A club the Montreal Royals. The following winter, when the Dodgers failed to protect him on the forty-man roster, he was stolen by Pittsburgh in a supplemental draft, and it was for the Pirates in 1955 that he began his major-league career. Eight years had passed since Robinson desegregated the game, and the *Pittsburgh Courier,* a black newspaper, took note of the gains that had been made by what the paper called "Tan Stars." By 1955 there were twenty-eight black regulars on major-league teams, including future Hall of Famers Robinson, Larry Doby, Roy Campanella, Hank Aaron, Ernie Banks, and Willie Mays, along with thirteen black rookies. Five years later the *Courier* reported there were forty-nine blacks on National League rosters and fifteen in the American League. The numbers would increase year by year into the mid-1970s.

From the start of his career, Clemente faced a double barrel of discrimination as a Spanish-speaking black man, and constantly raged against the inequities he faced. During Florida spring training for his first seven years with the Pirates, he was forced to live with a black family in the Dunbar Heights section of Fort Myers while his white teammates enjoyed hotel rooms downtown. When the team held its annual golf outing at the local country club, Clemente and his few black teammates were not invited. He found it humiliating to have to stay on the bus while his white teammates stopped at roadside restaurants on Grapefruit League road trips, and finally forced the Pirates management to let the black players travel in their own station wagon. Enduring spring training, he once said, was like being in prison.

He was also infuriated by stereotypes. In a *Life* magazine preview of the 1960 World Series, in which he got a hit in every game of Pittsburgh's stunning upset of the New York Yankees, he was criticized for what was called his "Latin American variety of showboating," although the example used was of him rounding third base and barreling over his coach on the way toward an inside-the-park home run, a play that might have been seen as an example of grit and determination if he had been a white player. And he hated being quoted in broken English by sportswriters who did not know a word of Spanish. When he drove in the winning run and was named most valuable player of the 1961 all-star game in San Francisco, the headline in the *Pittsburgh Press* the next day read "I Get Heet" and the wire service account quoted Clemente as saying, "When I come to plate in lass eening . . . I 'ope Weelhelm [Hoyt Wilhelm] peetch me inside."

Late in his career, Clemente got his sweet revenge, and he did so in a way that solidified his reputation as the most revered of Latino ballplayers. The moment came in the locker room after the seventh game of the 1971 World Series. The Pirates had defeated the favored Baltimore Orioles, with Clemente playing brilliantly at the plate, on the base paths, and in the field—an all-around performance that the pitch-perfect baseball writer Roger Angell described as "something close to the level of absolute perfection."

For all his career to that point, Clemente had felt misunderstood and underappreciated. Now he had proved himself, and the network microphones and cameras, and the nation's attention, were focused on him alone. And what did Clemente do? He said that before he answered any questions, he wanted to say a few words of thanks in Spanish to his aging parents back in Carolina. The symbolic meaning of that moment reverberated through the Spanish-speaking world and down through the years.

That same year, 1971, the Pirates broke another barrier by fielding the first all-black-and-Latino lineup in major-league history. Rennie Stennett at second, Gene Clines in center, Clemente in right, Willie Stargell in left, Manny Sanguillen catching, Dave Cash at third, Al Oliver at first, Jackie Hernandez at short, and Dock Ellis on the mound. Nearly a quarter century after Jackie Robinson broke the color line, the racial transformation of baseball was so advanced that the moment went virtually unnoticed. It turned out to be not a sign of things to come, but an unlikely turning point.

Over the next three decades, the number of African Americans in baseball declined steadily, down from 23 percent to below 9 percent today. The Houston Astros in 2005 went to the World Series without a single black American on their roster. Basketball, which could be played more easily in urban settings, and football, which offered more speed and action, became more appealing to young black athletes.

The number of Latinos, by contrast, rose dramatically over the same period. In 2005 there were 204 Latinos in the majors, about one-fourth of all players. Rodriguez, Martinez, Ramirez, Ortiz, Guerrero, Rivera—these are the names of twenty-first-century baseball. And some will end up in Cooperstown, joining the six Latinos already there: Tony Perez of Cuba, Rod Carew of Panama, Luis Aparicio of Venezuela, Juan Marichal of the Dominican Republic, Orlando Cepeda of Puerto Rico, and the legend among them, paving the way into the Hall of Fame for others to follow, the only player besides Lou Gehrig to be enshrined before the normal five-year waiting period—Roberto Clemente.

Baseball will certainly undergo more transformations this century. The sport is already declining in Clemente's Puerto Rico, overtaken by basketball and faster-paced sports, for the same reasons that led black Americans away from baseball. The Dominican Republic and Venezuela surpass Puerto Rico now in the number of major leaguers. A new wave is coming from Japan and Korea, and perhaps China after that.

But through it all, Clemente's role cannot diminish. The mythic aspects of baseball usually draw on the clichés of the innocent past, the nostalgia for how things were. But Clemente's myth, like Jackie Robinson's, arcs the other way, to the future, not the past, to what people hope they can become.

22

Out of the Sea

Three days before Christmas 1972, holiday revelers strolled along the narrow streets of Managua's old city late into the night. Colored lights festooned the shops along Avenida Central and glowed from the pyramid-shaped Hotel Continental up on the hill. For days it had been hot and oddly still, but just after midnight a sudden wind blew in, cold and strong. The animals sensed something. So did Pedro Chamorro, editor of the opposition newspaper *La Prensa*. The leaves rustled as if in warning, Chamorro thought. Then came the first tremor, and the earth shuddered. Soon there was a second rumble, as if some gargantuan creature were bursting to the surface from deep underground. Later came a third quake, more violent than the second, and in a thunderous spasm the city collapsed. Three hundred and fifty square blocks were flattened, with pipes erupting, fires flashing, soot and debris choking the air, people running, screaming, ripping off their burning clothes. The clock atop the Cathedral of the Immaculate Conception stopped at 12:27 a.m.

Nicaragua's strongman, Anastasio Somoza Debayle, was at his sprawling ranch house on a hill above town with his wife and three of his five children. The second and third tremors bounced them around so much, Somoza said later, that "we thought we were pieces of ice in a cocktail shaker." When the rumbling ended, Somoza climbed into a car and began working the radio, contacting police and the headquarters of the National Guard, Nicaragua's army. He learned that the Guard building downtown had been destroyed, with massive casualties, and the national communications center inside the presidential palace had been knocked out. He set up emergency headquarters at his house, which had suffered only minor damage. Somoza was not Nicaragua's president, but he ran the country from his position as commander of the armed forces, and now, with the earthquake crisis, he dropped all pretense and seized full control.

Roberto and Vera Clemente, at their house in Puerto Rico, awoke on the morning of December 23 to news of the deadly temblors. To them this was not some distant tragedy. Roberto had spent three weeks in Nicaragua in late November and early December as the manager of the Puerto Rican national team in the amateur baseball world series. He had stayed at the Hotel Continental, and every morning, he went down to the front desk, got change for a twenty-dollar bill, and walked around with a bagful of coins searching out poor people, listening to their stories, and giving them some money. Now he wondered what was happening to all those characters he had met in Managua. He found a ham radio operator who was picking up detailed reports of the earthquake from a Managuan identifying himself as "Enrique." What did people need? Clemente asked. Everything, was the answer: food, clothing, medical supplies. That night, he and Vera went to a San Juan hotel for a banquet at which the ballplayer was to receive an award. Ruth Fernandez, a singer and political activist who had just been elected to Puerto Rico's Senate, was there, along with Luis Vigoraux, a local television personality. Vigoraux suggested that as well-known figures in the community the three of them should take prominent roles in the relief effort. What came to be called the Comité Roberto Clemente Pro-Nicaragua was born.

The next morning, Christmas Eve, Richard Nixon called Somoza from his vacation compound at Key Biscayne. The president was worried that chaos in Nicaragua might lead to civil disturbances and possibly a Communist uprising. Along with medical teams and army engineers, Nixon dispatched a battalion of paratroopers, ostensibly to help keep order in Managua. In San Juan that day, Clemente and Fernandez made a plea for assistance on television and announced that the parking lot at Hiram Bithorn Stadium, the ballpark of the San Juan and Santurce winter-league baseball teams, would be used to collect aid throughout Christmas Day. By then Clemente had a direct ham radio contact to a hospital in Masaya, thirteen miles from Managua, and learned of its need for medicine and X-ray equipment. Refugees from the capital had nearly doubled the population of Masaya to more than six hundred thousand. Conditions there were dire. Clemente decided to lease a plane to get supplies to Nicaragua faster.

By Christmas morning troops were stationed at street corners in downtown Managua, notably outside banks and government buildings. The stench of death was overwhelming. On some blocks hundreds of decaying bodies littered the streets, and many more remained trapped under debris. Health officials were concerned about the spread of typhoid and other diseases. Most of the old city had been declared a contaminated area. Service agencies were instructed by the Somoza government to stop feeding the poor and hungry in the center of town. A six o'clock curfew was imposed, but late into the night the old city echoed with gunfire. Some looting had begun, and Somoza directed guardsmen to shoot looters on sight.

Dawn on the morning of December 26 "broke with the arrival of parachutists," recalled Chamorro, the opposition newspaper editor. They were American troops from Panama, sent to supplement Somoza's Guard. But the tension only increased. Chamorro described "the thousands and thousands of hands extended toward emptiness, asking for food, which was kept . . . under custody of the government tanks. They didn't give the food out." A massive tent city was rising on the edge of town. U.S. Army engineers began clearing the old city in hundred-degree heat. Demolition crews used bulldozers and dynamite to level anything that stood after the quake. Lime was spread over the rubble as vultures circled overhead.

Clemente spent the day at the parking lot of Hiram Bithorn Stadium. His committee had leased a Lockheed Constellation called the *Super Snoopy* for three round-trips to Managua, each at a cost of $3,700. Volunteers in San Juan worked overnight loading donated goods and medical equipment. The plane's first trip was scheduled for early the next morning. Raul Pelligrina, a major in Puerto Rico's National Guard, had agreed to accompany the crew to Nicaragua. The Clementes went to the airport to see them off in the dark, misty chill. Vera looked over at her husband and wondered whether she saw a tear in his eye.

Nicaragua is the largest country in Central America, about the size of Iowa, but one of the least populated. In 1972 it had about two million citizens, a quarter of them in metropolitan Managua. More than half of the populace was illiterate. The Somoza family had controlled Nicaragua since General Anastasio Somoza García seized power in 1936. He was assassinated in 1956, but power was passed along to his sons. Anastasio Somoza Debayle, the last in the family line, had taken control in 1967. He spoke fluent English, having gone to prep school in the United States and graduated from West Point. What he excelled at was using power for financial gain. By 1972 he and his family controlled an estimated 25 percent of Nicaragua's gross national product. They held cattle ranches, coffee and sugar plantations, sugar mills, distilleries, auto dealerships, textile mills, hotels, an airline, and vast stretches of real estate. A commission on Central America chaired by Henry Kissinger declared in 1984 that the general's "achievements gave new meaning to the term kleptocracy, that is, government as theft."

By two days after Christmas, Red Cross volunteers in Managua were wondering where all the arriving aid was going. Money seemed to disappear. Major Pelligrina returned to San Juan that night after delivering the first cargo of aid from Puerto Rico and could barely contain his disappointment. It was awful, he told Clemente. The moment they landed, Somoza's soldiers surrounded the plane and tried to take everything. Pelligrina had told the soldiers that if they didn't let him through, he would reload his aircraft and fly back to San Juan to tell the great Roberto Clemente what was happening. Somoza's son, Tachito, a Guard officer, came to see who was giving his troops trouble. Upon hearing Clemente's name invoked, Tachito let the Puerto Rican crew go on to Masaya, but it seemed to Pelligrina that most other supplies were being diverted.

Clemente, his voice reaching a high pitch, said they had to do something to get the aid to the people who needed it. If he had to travel to Managua himself to make certain that Somoza and his Guard were not stealing it, then that is what he would do.

To several friends in those final days of 1972 Clemente made the same request: "Come with me. I'm going to Nicaragua." Orlando Cepeda, nearing the end of his career, recently released by the Oakland A's, told Clemente he wanted to stay in Puerto Rico to get in shape for the next major-league season and to enjoy the holidays. Clemente's Pirates teammate had ball games to play with the San Juan Senadores. Then there was Osvaldo Gil, Clemente's compatriot on the baseball trip to Nicaragua. "Valdy, will you go with me?" Clemente asked. Sure, Gil said. But that night when he told his wife, she fled the bedroom and cried. They had been married for just a few months when he left for Nicaragua the first time, and now he wanted to go again? "I talked to my wife," Gil told Clemente the next day, "and I'm not going."

"You're right," Clemente said. "You shouldn't go. I'll go by myself."

In the wide world of aviation there are dark little corners of desperation. One of them during the early 1970s was a back lot of Miami International Airport known as Cockroach Corner. It was said that you could buy anything for a song at Cockroach Corner, occasionally even planes that had a decent chance of taking flight. The place looked like a mechanical graveyard, creaking with rickety old surplus DC-3s, DC-6s, Lockheed Constellations, and DC-7s, but in fact it was more of a winged bazaar. What were known in the industry as tramp operators did business there, buying, selling, and leasing planes to anyone looking for a cut-rate deal. It was at Cockroach Corner that a twenty-six-year-old operator named Arthur S. Rivera bought another old plane on July 12, 1972. This DC-7, powered by Curtiss Wright 988 engines with Hamilton Standard propellers, would double Rivera's cargo fleet, supplementing his twin-engine DC-3 in hauling goods between San Juan, Puerto Rico, his home base, and other Caribbean islands.

Rivera had obtained a commercial pilot's rating four years earlier but knew nothing about DC-7s, so he could not fly his new plane back to San Juan. It remained at Cockroach Corner until sometime in September, when he finally found a pilot. When they ferried it from Florida to the island, Rivera rode along in the right seat as copilot. They parked the aircraft at a cargo ramp at San Juan International Airport on Isla Verde, and there it remained throughout the fall. Word soon spread about Rivera's folly, the only DC-7 on the airfield. The plane seemed anything but airworthy. Among other deficiencies, its No. 3 propeller was said to be feathered, indicating engine malfunction. "It was never seen to fly," Michael Pangia, a Justice Department aviation lawyer, observed later, "and everybody wondered what Mr. Rivera was going to do with the plane."

What Rivera did was spruce up the exterior. He painted the fuselage silvery white and added the bravado touch of lightning bolts, orange with black trim, on both sides and below the cockpit. The same color scheme was applied to the tips of the propellers, creating the effect of tiger stripes. With that superficial remodeling, Rivera placed ads in local newspapers announcing that his outfit, American Air Express Leasing Company, had a DC-7 available for use. The phone in his home office on Loiza Street in Santurce did not ring off the hook.

From the moment he had come down from Atlanta and begun transporting cargo out of San Juan in November 1969, Rivera had been an irritant to inspectors at the Federal Aviation Administration's district office. Despite repeated warnings, he had refused to obtain the proper certification for a commercial operator, acting instead as though he were merely flying planes for his own personal recreation. This allowed him to avoid more frequent inspections and the strict flight standards of commercial aviation. The FAA compiled a list of sixty-six illegal trips that Rivera had made and issued an emergency order in 1971 revoking his pilot's license. Rivera appealed the revocation order, arguing that the government should not deprive him of his livelihood, and a judge eventually reduced his penalty to a 180-day suspension.

That fall, the FAA had issued a regulatory action that came to be known as the Southern Order, covering the agency's southern region, including Puerto Rico. The order read as though it had Arthur Rivera in mind, calling for continuous surveillance of all aircraft "that cannot be readily identified as bona fide air carriers." Air-traffic controllers were directed to contact field inspectors whenever a suspicious plane arrived or departed. The inspectors were then to see that the pilot was in compliance with commercial regulations, that the plane was airworthy, and that the load was balanced. Different districts responded to the order in different ways. The San Juan FAA chief instructed his eight-man inspection staff to conduct surveillance only on incoming flights, not departures, claiming that he did not have sufficient staff to do both.

On the morning of Saturday, December 2, Rivera and a relative, who knew even less about DC-7s than he did, took the plane out for what was called a runup, meaning they would taxi around the airstrip, warming up the engines, but not try to fly it. Rivera forgot to close a hydraulic device and lost control of the steering, rolling the plane into a drainage ditch. If aviation officials needed a reminder to keep close watch on the comings and goings of Arthur Rivera, this was it, but with his aviation history, one might assume that no further warnings would have been needed. After the DC-7 was towed out of the ditch, the FAA inspectors determined that it had sustained considerable damage: two blown tires, bent blades on the No. 2 and No. 3 propellers, sudden stoppage of the No. 2 and No. 3 engines, broken hydraulic lines on the right landing gear, and damage to the No. 3 engine oil scoop. Rivera enlisted two mechanics to make minimal repairs. He ignored an inspector's suggestion that he replace all the engines, which had been in use longer than the manufacturer recommended.

In the days leading up to New Year's Eve, the Clementes worked on the earthquake relief from early morning to long past midnight. On the Puerto Rican end, at least, the effort was a heartwarming success. More than $100,000 had been raised. Food, clothing, and medical supplies were coming in as quickly as they were going out. The *Super Snoopy* had made its second run to Nicaragua, and Roberto was even more enraged when he heard that the supplies had been held up again by soldiers at the Managua airport. At nine thirty on the morning of December 30, Roberto and Vera were at the south ramp of the airport's cargo area as the plane was being readied for its third flight. Mountains of boxes were stacked on the tarmac, far more than could be loaded for this trip, and more supplies were on the way. Arthur Rivera saw an opportunity. "He came over and introduced himself to us," Vera Clemente recalled. "He told Roberto that he had a plane, a DC-7, for cargo. He said, 'I'm available anytime.'"

Rivera then invited the Clementes to see his plane. The DC-7 was freshly painted. A mechanic dressed in a white uniform stood near the steps. Vera stayed below while Roberto climbed inside. It looked okay to him, although he knew little about airplanes. Rivera said that for $4,000 he would provide the crew, and they would wait in Nicaragua for as long as it took Clemente to do his business. Clemente and Rivera shook hands on the deal. They would leave the next day. While the Clementes returned to their house in the suburb of Rio Piedras, Rivera began scrounging, because he had no crew. A few hours later, an old prop plane arrived from the Virgin Islands and taxied to a stop near Rivera. The pilot, Jerry Hill, noticed the DC-7 as he walked by and said, "I used to fly one of these."

Again, Rivera seized the opportunity. "Hey," he said to Hill. "Want a job?"

Vera Clemente stood in the kitchen fixing lunch. It was late Sunday morning, the last day of the year, and the house on the hill was silent. The three boys were staying with her mother in Carolina. Roberto was in the bedroom, shades drawn tight, trying to rest before his trip to Nicaragua. Angel Lozano, a member of the relief effort who would accompany Clemente on the mission, had called several times that morning with the same news. He was near the DC-7 at the cargo area and nothing was ready; it would be hours before the plane left. Out the big windows of her kitchen, Vera could look north across the treetops toward the airport on Isla Verde and the Atlantic Ocean beyond. The winter sky hung low and gray; the sea looked green. In the stillness, as she prepared the meal, a song looped in her mind. It was the "Tragedia del Viernes Santo," a popular ballad about a DC-4 that crashed into the ocean on Good Friday 1952 after taking off from San Juan on the way to New York.

> *Que triste fue el Viernes Santo*
> *Que horas de anguista y dolor*
> *Sufrieron nuestros hermanos*
> *Que volaban a New York*

"How sad was Good Friday / What hours of anguish and pain / Our brothers suffer / Who were flying to New York." In the silence, the haunting lyrics and melody ran through Vera's mind, but it was just a song, something that slipped into the subconscious without her thinking about what it meant.

When lunch was ready, Vera went to fetch Roberto, who had barely slept, as usual. As they ate, they reviewed their plans for the next few days. Friends were coming from Pennsylvania, but Roberto would not be there. He would miss New Year's Eve, a major holiday in Puerto Rico, a time to be with friends and family. There had been so many special days that Roberto had missed lately. He had missed their eighth wedding anniversary in November and then Thanksgiving because of the amateur baseball world series in Nicaragua. He kept saying that he hated to be separated from his family and yet he kept leaving. Vera didn't ask him directly not to leave again, but the message was there as she cited his absences.

"Don't worry," Roberto said. "When you are healthy and you are happy, every day of life is the same."

"That's true," Vera said. She understood what he meant. That every day of life was special, none better than the others. And so many times she had heard him repeat his mantra: If you have a chance to make life better for others, and fail to do so, you are wasting your time on this earth. In going to Managua, she thought, he was doing something good for humanity. She didn't feel great about him leaving, but she was not going to make a big deal of it. He'd be back in a day, soon enough.

Rivera's new pilot, Jerry Hill, had returned to San Juan after a quick hop to Miami and back. He had not slept and would need some rest before leaving for Managua, so he dozed in the cabin of the DC-7 as it was being loaded with supplies. Rivera would serve as Hill's copilot, even though the sum of his experience with this plane had been the first flight from Cockroach Corner and then the disastrous taxiing episode. Rivera had not bothered to check Hill's background. According to FAA records, he was in jeopardy of losing his commercial license, facing a hearing on thirteen violations of his own. In need of a flight engineer, Rivera recruited a mechanic who had no qualifications for the assignment.

The plane was already full—198 packages of rice, 312 cartons of evaporated milk, 320 cartons of beans, 70 cartons of vegetable oil, 90 cartons of luncheon meat, and 60 cartons of cornmeal—when a small pickup truck arrived with a final load of sugar, milk, toothpaste, and medical supplies. A ramp inspector for the airport police helped load the cargo with his supervisor. With no space remaining in storage, they stacked this load haphazardly in front of a steel-mesh net near the bulkhead, then placed a large spare tire on top of the pile. No attention was paid to the plane's center of gravity. The plane's total weight was not supposed to exceed forty thousand pounds. It was, officials would later determine, now more than four thousand pounds over the allowable load.

Cristobal Colón, the regional sales manager for Goya Food Prod-
ucts, who had been helping with the relief effort, drove the Clementes
to the airport. They arrived around four that afternoon. Colón took
a good look at the DC-7 and did not like what he saw. The plane was
so heavy that the landing wheels were squashed almost flat, and it was
so unbalanced that the nose tire was almost off the ground. "I complained to Roberto and advised him that the aircraft was unsafe and
improperly loaded," Colón said later. As Vera would recall, "Roberto
said, 'Don't worry. They know what they're doing.' " Vera said goodbye to her husband and went to meet a flight bringing friends from the
United States in for the holidays.

At nine, according to FAA records, Rivera's plane, registration
No. N500AE, was cleared for runway 7. As the aircraft reached the end
of the runway, Antonio Rios, working for Eastern Airlines at gate 12,
heard several loud backfires about five seconds apart on the left wing.
A mechanic near Rios in the cargo area said he heard "three backfires
. . . changing engine noise, and a very big explosion. Then silence."

The plane struggled into the air. It barely cleared the palm trees on
the eastern edge of the airport before witnesses lost sight of it. In the
air-traffic tower, ground controller Gary Cleaveland noticed that the
DC-7 was not gaining altitude as it flew about a mile past Punta Maldonado and then banked to the north and out over the ocean. By his
estimate the plane was no more than two hundred feet above water. It
appeared to be descending.

The radio scratched. "Tower, this is five hundred Alfa Echo coming
back around," Hill reported from the DC-7.

Cleaveland could not hear the transmission clearly. He said, "Five
hundred . . . uh . . . Alfa Echo say again."

Nothing but silence. Traffic controller Dennis McHale, tracking
the flight on radar, watched as N500AE curved north and then disappeared from the Brite-1 display screen.

When the Eastern Airlines flight from New York had arrived in San
Juan earlier that evening, Vera Clemente was at the gate waiting for
her friends Carolyn and Nevin Rauch and their daughters Carol and
Sharon. They all went out to dinner, and afterward they drove to the
house of Vera's mother in Carolina. The boys were asleep now, though

Robertito had fussed before going to bed. *"Abuela,"* he had said to his grandmother. "Why is Daddy leaving? That plane will crash."

Robertito had been anxious for days. One of the last things he had done at his parents' house the day before was to sneak into their bedroom and look in a little dresser drawer where his dad usually kept his plane tickets. Robertito once tried to hide the tickets in a futile effort to keep his father at home. This time there had been no tickets. The boy had warned his father not to leave. His grandmother told him not to worry, everything would be fine. But later she was overcome by an odd sensation herself. She went into the kitchen and cried. Something bad is happening, she thought. Melchor Clemente, Roberto's father, who lived nearby, was also haunted by dark feelings. He had had a bad dream about his son.

The radio was on at Vera's mother's house, but no one was listening. The room was full of people talking: Vera, her mother, her brother, and his wife. The Rauches. Neighbors. A few times Vera thought she heard the radio announcer say the name Roberto Clemente, but he was in the news every day for his relief work. The telephone rang constantly. A close friend of Vera's called three times. She seemed tentative, evasive, asking how Vera was, then hanging up. Then Vera's niece Fafa called. She was crying. "Are you listening to the news?" she asked Vera. Something about a crash of an airplane going to Nicaragua. Vera's sister-in-law called the airport and got the first confirmation. It was a cargo plane with five people bound for Managua. Robertito, in the far bedroom, heard his mother's cry.

In Puerto Rico, New Year's Eve is celebrated with fireworks, vibrant music, and street dancing. But Orlando Cepeda felt something eerie in the air long before he heard about the crash. "It was quiet and sad," he recalled. "The night felt different. There weren't many people celebrating. No stars were out." Cepeda, who had revered Clemente since Cepeda was a bowlegged batboy for the Santurce Cangrejeros team in 1954, was with his wife at a brother's house when he got the news. Roberto Clemente cannot die, he thought. And he remembered how Clemente had wanted him to go along on the flight to Nicaragua.

Osvaldo Gil, who would have accompanied Clemente on the mercy flight had his wife not talked him out of it, was celebrating with his family when word of the crash reached him. He remembered what

Clemente had said only a few days earlier: Nobody dies the day before. You die the day you're supposed to. Pirates infielder José Pagan was asleep at his family's home in Barceloneta, Puerto Rico, when his father came into his room and told him the news. Pagan remembered when Clemente had fallen asleep on the team plane once but had been jolted awake by a dream in which a plane had crashed and he had been the only one killed.

Seconds after N500AE disappeared from the radar screen, San Juan's air-traffic control tower activated the emergency accident notification system, a sequence of twenty telephone calls. The second call went to the U.S. Coast Guard Rescue Center in Old San Juan, nine miles from the airport. One Coast Guard vessel and two planes went out on the first call, but search officers had not yet plotted the Probability of Detection area, so the rescuers were operating on guesswork, in the dark, and found nothing.

Not long after sunrise on New Year's Day, it became obvious that this was not just a routine search. From Isla Verde to Punta Maldonado, the shore was lined with people who had come to bear witness. The two-lane roads leading to the water became more congested as the day progressed until by afternoon there was a bumper-to-bumper traffic jam of pilgrims flocking toward the place where their hero had fallen. "That night on which Roberto Clemente left us physically, his immortality began," the Puerto Rican writer Elliott Castro later observed, and here was the first manifestation of the transformation from man to myth. Although Governor Louis A. Ferré had declared a three-day mourning period, many Puerto Ricans refused to believe that Clemente was dead. The vast crowds at the beach waited, as though expecting him to come walking out of the sea. It took nearly a week for the search team, reinforced with more divers and sophisticated sonar and salvage equipment, to locate most everything that was to be found.

First they dragged up the body of the pilot. Then portions of the cockpit, and some fuselage sections, and melted medical equipment. Then the tail section, intact, from the tip to the large cargo loading doors. And nearby a twenty-five-foot section of one wing, with the landing gear attached and in the down position. Following an underwater line perpendicular to the tail section, they spotted three engines, all separated from the wings. On the No. 2 engine two propellers were bent and one sheared off. These remains offered more telling clues to investigators for determining the cause of the crash. Rivera's DC-7 was a death trap even before it rolled down runway 7, but it appeared from the wreckage that there was a final human error. Hill had overboosted the engines, pushing them beyond their limits. His crewmates, there to monitor the instruments and throttles, were not trained for the task.

At the end of the long, bleak week—after Clemente's people by the thousands had lined the Atlantic shore and thousands more had made pilgrimages up the hillside to shuffle past his house as if it were a shrine, and the U.S. Coast Guard, with all its boats and planes and divers and equipment, had slowly dragged up the wreckage and debris—at the end, on a coral reef a mile east of Punta Maldonado, they found one sock, and Vera knew that it was Roberto's. One sock, that's all, the rest to sharks and gods.

23

One Guy

There is only one person alive who knows what it was like to be a black ballplayer integrating the white world of the major leagues during the historic summer of 1947. If you are young or only a casual follower of baseball, perhaps you have not heard of him. Larry Doby is seventy-two now, and his calm manner seems out of style in this unsporting age of self-obsession. He is neither a celebrity nor the stuff of myth, simply a quiet man with an incomparable story to tell. This season, as the national pastime commemorates the fiftieth anniversary of the breaking of the color line, the attention has focused inevitably on the first black player of the modern era, Jackie Robinson, who shines alone in baseball history as the symbol of pride against prejudice. But Doby was there too, blazing his own trail later that same year. He was brought up by the Cleveland Indians on July 5, 1947, three months after Robinson broke in with the Brooklyn Dodgers. Some of the strange and awful things that happened to No. 42 in the National League happened to No. 14 in the American League as well.

"I think I'm ahead of a lot of people because I don't hate and I'm not bitter," Doby says softly now. He has spent a lifetime "turning negatives into positives," but he is also sharp and direct in pointing out what he considers to be the myths surrounding the events of a half century ago. Jackie Robinson in death has gone the way of most American martyrs, transformed from an outsider struggling against the prevailing culture into a legend embraced by it. In the retelling of this legend it sometimes sounds as though most people always loved him. Doby knows better. He was there and he remembers.

After that first season, he and Robinson barnstormed the country with Negro Leagues all-stars. They rarely discussed their common experience in white baseball ("no need to, we both knew what the situation was"), but a few times late at night they stayed up naming the players in each league who were giving them problems because they were black. It was a long list. "Many people in this world live on lies. Know what amazes me today?" Doby asks, his deep voice rising with the first rush of emotion. "How many friends Jackie Robinson had fifty years ago! All of a sudden everyone is his best friend. Wait a minute. Give me a break, will you. I knew those people who were his friends. I knew those people who were not his friends. Some of them are still alive. I know. And Jack, he's in heaven, and I bet he turns over a lot of times when he hears certain things or sees certain things or reads certain things where these people say they were his friends."

Playing and traveling in the big leagues that year was a grindingly lonely job for the two young black men. Which leads to Doby's second shattered myth: the notion that Robinson, by coming first, could somehow smooth the way for him. "Did Jackie Robinson make it easier for me?" Doby laughs at his own question, which he says is the one he hears most often. "I'm not saying people are stupid, but it's one of the stupidest questions that's ever been asked. Think about it. We're talking about eleven weeks. Nineteen forty-seven. Now it's fifty years later and you still have hidden racism, educated racist people. How could you change that in eleven weeks? Jackie probably would have loved to have changed it in eleven weeks. I know he would have loved to have been able to say, 'The hotels are open, the restaurants are open, your teammates are going to welcome you.' But no. No. No way. No way."

There was no transition for Larry Doby, no year of grooming in the minors up in Montreal like Robinson. One day he was playing second base for the black Newark Eagles, and two days later he was in Chicago, pinch-hitting for the Cleveland Indians in the seventh inning of a game against the White Sox. "We're in this together, kid," Bill Veeck, the Indians' owner, had told him at the signing, and that was enough for Doby. He trusted Veeck, then and always. Doby was only twenty-two years old, and his life to that point had been relatively free of the uglier strains of American racism.

At East Side High in Paterson, New Jersey, he had been a four-sport star on integrated teams. He remembers being subjected to a racist insult only once, during a football game, and he responded by whirling past the foulmouthed defensive back to haul in a touchdown pass. That shut the guy up. In the navy on the South Pacific atoll of Ulithi during World War II, he had taken batting practice with Mickey Vernon of the Washington Senators and found him to be extremely friendly and encouraging. Vernon later sent him a dozen Louisville Slugger bats and put in a good word for him with the Washington club. Wishful thinking. It would be another decade before the Senators broke their lily-white policy, but Veeck, who had both an innate empathy for underdogs and a showman's readiness to try anything new, was eager to integrate the Indians as soon as possible.

Doby was not the best black player (that honor still belonged to old Josh Gibson), but he was young and talented. Through the Fourth of July with the Newark club in 1947, he was batting .414 with a league-leading fourteen home runs. His Newark teammates gave him a farewell present, a kit with comb, brush, and shaving cream, but there was no celebration when he took off to join the Indians. "We looked at it as an important step as far as history was concerned, but it was not the type of thing you would celebrate in terms of justice for all, because you were going to a segregated situation," Doby says. "Maybe someone smarter than me would be happy about that, but I wasn't. You know you're going into a situation where it's not going to be comfortable. That's what you're leaving. What you're leaving is comfortable because you are with your teammates all the time. You sleep in the same hotel, you eat in the same restaurants, you ride in the same car."

When Doby was introduced to the Cleveland players that afternoon of July 5 a half century ago, most of them stood mute and expressionless, essentially ignoring his existence. There were a few exceptions. Second baseman Joe Gordon told him to grab a glove and warmed up with him before the game, a ritual they continued throughout the year. Catcher Jim Hegan showed he cared by asking him how he was doing. And one of the coaches, Bill McKechnie, looked after him. "He was like Veeck, but there every day on the road—nice man," Doby recalls. But there was no roommate for him on the road, no one in whom he could confide. In every city except New York and Boston, he stayed in a black hotel apart from the rest of the team. Equally troubling for him, he rarely got the chance to play. After starting one game at first base, he looked at the lineup card the next day and was not there. Same thing the rest of the year. The manager, Lou Boudreau, never said a word to him about why he was on the bench. He was used as a pinch hitter, and could not adjust to the role. He finished the year with only five hits and no home runs in thirty-two at bats over twenty-nine games.

After the last game of the season, he was sitting at his locker, wondering if that was the end of the experiment, when McKechnie came over to him and asked whether he had ever played the outfield. No, Doby said, always infield, in high school, college at Long Island University for a year, Negro Leagues, the streets, wherever. "Well," Doby recalls McKechnie telling him, "Joe Gordon is the second baseman and he's going to be here awhile. When you go home this winter get a book and learn how to play the outfield." He bought a book by the Yankees outfielder, Tommy Henrich, and studied the finer points of playing outfield: what to do on liners hit straight at you (take your first step back, never forward), throwing to the right base, hitting the cutoff man. He started the next season in right, and within a few weeks was moved to center, where he developed as an offensive and defensive star, a key figure in the fearsome Indians teams from the late 1940s to mid-1950s. With Doby driving in more than a hundred runs four times and tracking down everything in center, the Indians won the World Series against the Boston Braves in 1948 and lost to the Giants in 1954 after winning a league-record 111 games during the regular season.

It was during the 1948 season that Doby set several firsts. After batting over .300 during the regular season, he became the first African American to play on a championship club and the first to hit a home run in the World Series. His blast won the fourth game that fall against the Boston Braves. In the locker room celebration afterward, a wire service photographer took a picture that was sent out across the nation showing something that had never been seen before: a white baseball player, pitcher Steve Gromek, hugging the black player, Doby, who had won the game for him. Doby says he will never forget the embrace. "That made me feel good because it was not a thing of, should I or should I not, not a thing of black or white. It was a thing where human beings were showing emotion. When you have that kind of thing it makes you feel better, makes you feel like, with all those obstacles and negatives you went through, there is someone who had feelings inside for you as a person and not based on color." It was a rare situation that went easier for the black person than his white friend. Gromek received hate mail and questions from his neighbors when he went home. What are you doing hugging a black man like that? *Hey, Doby won the game for me!* was his response.

But the world did not embrace Doby as warmly as Gromek had. In St. Louis one day, McKechnie restrained him from climbing into the stands to go after a heckler who had been shouting racist epithets at him the whole game. His anger erupted one other time, in 1948, when he slid into second base and an opposing infielder spit in his face. "I didn't expect to be spit on if I'm sliding into second base, but it happened. I just thank God there was an umpire there named Bill Summers, a nice man, who kind of walked in between us when I was ready to move on this fella. Maybe I wouldn't be sitting here talking if that hadn't happened. They wanted to find any way they could to get you out of the league."

Al Smith, a left fielder who joined the Indians in 1953 and became Doby's roommate and close friend, said there was one other way opposing teams would go after black players. Whenever Al Rosen or some other Indian hit a home run, the pitcher would wait until Doby came up, then throw at him. "They wouldn't knock down the player who hit the home run, they'd knock Doby down." Common practice in those days, says Doby. He and Minnie Minoso, a Cuban-born outfielder who was an all-star seven years despite not becoming a regular in the majors until he was twenty-eight, and Roy Campanella, a three-time National League most valuable player after playing for the Baltimore Elite Giants of the Negro Leagues, were hit by pitches ten times more often than Ted Williams, Stan Musial, and Joe DiMaggio. "You don't think people would do it simply because of race," Doby says. "But what was it? Did they knock us down because we were good hitters? How you gonna explain DiMaggio, Williams, and Musial? Were they good hitters? So you see, you can't be naïve about this kind of situation." But there was one situation where Doby and the other blacks on the Indians later felt protected—when teammate Early Wynn was on the mound. "Whenever Early pitched we didn't have any problems getting knocked down. Early, he would start at the top of the opposing lineup and go right down to the bottom. They threw at me, he'd throw at them."

The segregation of that era offered one comforting side effect. Black fans in the 1940s were directed to the cheap seats, the bleachers in left, center, and right. They were a long way from the action, but closer to Doby. "When people say, 'You played in Washington,' well, I had a motivation factor there. I had cheerleaders there at Griffith Stadium. I didn't have to worry about name-calling. You got cheers from those people when you walked onto the field. They'd let you know they appreciated you were there. Give you a little clap when you go out there, and if you hit a home run, they'd acknowledge the fact, tip their hat."

At the 1997 all-star game at Jacobs Field in Cleveland, all of baseball will finally tip its hat to Lawrence Eugene Doby. Finally, he will emerge from the enormous shadow of the man he followed and revered, Jackie Robinson. The American League, for which he works as an executive in New York, has named him honorary captain of its team, and he has been selected to throw out the first pitch. The prospect of standing on the field in front of a sellout crowd to be honored has led Doby to think about what has changed since he broke in with the Indians. "A lot of people are complaining that baseball hasn't come along fast enough. And there is much work to be done. But if you look at baseball, we came in 1947, before Brown versus the Board of Education, before anyone wrote a civil rights bill saying give them the same opportunities everyone else has. So whatever you want to criticize baseball about—it certainly needs more opportunities for black managers, black general managers, black umpires—remember that if this country was as far advanced as baseball it would be in much better shape."

Doby rises from his chair and walks around his den, taking another look at history. Here is a picture of him at the first of seven consecutive all-star games. He is posed on the dugout steps with three other black players. "There's Camp and Newk and Jackie," he says. "I'm the only American Leaguer, fighting those Dodgers." Nearby is the photo of "Doby's Great Catch," taken in Cleveland in a game against Washington on July 20, 1954. "What a catch," he says softly, sounding modest even in praise, as though someone else climbed that fence to make the play. And in the corner is a picture of the football team at Paterson's East Side High back in the early 1940s. One black player in the crowd—the split end. "I was always the one guy," he says, looking at the image of his younger self. Sometimes he was overshadowed, or all but forgotten, and the history books say he came second, but Larry Doby is right. He was always the one guy.

Larry Doby died in June 2003, six years after this story appeared in the Post. *I was living in New York City that summer of 1997 conducting research for the book on Vince Lombardi and decided to go across the river to Montclair, New Jersey, to talk to Doby before he was honored at the all-star game. Doby had a deep meaning to me. He was one of the great players on the first team I knew as a five-year-old boy, the Cleveland Indians, during the one year my family lived in Cleveland.*

24

Diamond in the Rough

El Paso, Texas

Is this America or what? You want baseball, hot dogs, and the Stars and Stripes? How about Wall-ball, Jalapeño Burrito Dogs, and the Green Wienie Flag? Forget about Disney World, this is a real fantasyland—an ancient, bright yellow, adobe ballpark where the public address announcer sounds like Bob Barker, the fans act as if they're on *Let's Make a Deal,* the pitchers complain about bum arms and sore heads, and the hitters—wow, the hitters! Wait . . . the owner's on his feet in the press box. Could it be? Yes! He shoots his hands up in the touchdown signal as the home club scores its seventh run of the inning. And the bases, as they say again and again, are still FOD. Full of Diablos.

Come on down to the Dudley Dome, also known as the House of Thrills, home of Your El Paso Diablos, the Class AA farm club of the Milwaukee Brewers and defending champions of the most colorful league in the bushes, the century-old Texas League. When people here say they are going to the circus, this is where they end up, for an evening of sights, sounds, smells, surprises.

Whack! George "Panama" Canale, an All-American first baseman from Virginia Tech just called up from Class A ball, cracks a grand-slam home run. He rounds third, toes the plate, and heads directly toward the box seats, where he holds out his helmet as little kids fill it up with dollar bills, an El Paso tradition.

What's that odor? It must be Mona the Elephant across the way in the zoo. Sometimes, when the Diablos really need a comeback, the fans start their "Wake up, Mona!" chant. Sometimes Mona wakes them up. Whiff. Or maybe it's the nearby sewage treatment plant. Depends on which way the wind blows.

Who's that codger up near the press box waving the Green Wienie Flag? That means a rally is in progress, good for at least two more runs. The whole place is vibrating with the shrieks of an old-fashioned Diablos whistle rally. Annie "the Fanny" Tudor, the Yugoslavian baseball nut, can make an inordinate amount of noise from her seat along the third-base line.

Left fielder La Vel Freeman, who sports a modest .401 batting average, slaps a double off the wall. Up steps Eeeeeeasy Ernie Riles, the Brewers shortstop sent to El Paso to recover from an injury. He pokes one to the top of the Green Monster, the thirty-six-foot wall atop a center-field slope that keeps a canal from flooding the field. Ever seen an outfield fence like this one? Forty-two wall ads, double-decked from left to right, all hand-painted in bright colors against a garish yellow background.

Time to gaze into the visitors' dugout, the one with "ENEMY" painted on top in big, bright letters. There goes the San Antonio Dodgers manager out to the mound. His pitcher has given up five doubles, a triple, a grand slam, two walks, and eight runs in two-thirds of an inning. Not a bad outing, here. His earned run average might even go down. The public address announcer urges fans to listen in as the Dodgers congregate on the hill. Then he plays the Abbott and Costello routine "Who's on First?" over the sound system. As pitcher and manager depart, two thousand fans pull out white hankies and wave them to the accompaniment of "Bye-Bye Baby."

After three innings, the home club leads 19–3, but there is no comfortable margin in the Dudley Dome. The week before, against the Midland Angels, one of the promising young arms in the Brewers chain took a 14–3 cushion into the late innings and failed to gain a decision. Isn't that the same guy pitching again tonight? Yogi Berra must have been to El Paso before he said, "It ain't over till it's over." And that is usually a long time from now. In the Midland series, a Texas League record was set for longest nine-inning game: four hours and fifteen minutes.

The air is dry and light here, and the outfield fences are no more than 330 feet away in the power alleys of left-center and right-center. That explains part of the zaniness of the hardball devils. Devils is English for Diablos, and about 65 percent of the fans are Hispanic. All of the fans are bilingually loony, none more so than Jim Paul, the owner. He bought the club in 1974 for $1,000 plus $52,000 owed to seventy-two creditors. The most important employee then, Paul said, was the groundskeeper, who had to wake up a few hundred dozing fans each night when the game ended. The essence of Paul's personality is that he hates to be bored. It took him two years to revive the dying franchise. He held promotions every night, giving away everything from pizzas to caps to television sets to cars. He brought in cheerleaders to dance on the dugout. He recruited the Chicken from San Diego. He hired the loudest, craziest announcer he could find to lead the fans in cheers. He made it fun to go to the ballpark for everyone—except the visiting team. When Joe Frazier, who later managed the Mets, was here as the manager for a visiting team, he became so enraged at the announcer's antics that he climbed the fence and started bullying his way toward the press box before being restrained by an officer of the law.

There remain a few purists who believe that Paul and other gimmick-masters have hurt the game, but they are in a minority. Last year, the Diablos won the President's Trophy as best-run franchise in the minor leagues, and Paul's ideas have been at the forefront of a bush-league revival. In the last ten years, about two-thirds of the 144 minor-league teams have been transformed into moneymakers. Paul does not worry about how it plays in New York or Boston. It plays in El Paso.

The Brewers have to believe that the pluses here—weather, crowds, management, enthusiasm—outweigh the one big minus: the psychological damage inflicted on young pitchers. A few years ago, Harry Dalton, general manager of the Brewers, visited El Paso specifically to assess the pitching staff. The Diablos were playing the Beaumont Golden Gators; in honor of the visiting dignitary, they put on a real Texas League show. The final score was El Paso 35, Beaumont 21, a league record for runs scored in one game. In the ninth inning, when Beaumont scored its final run, some people in the press box expressed puzzlement as Dalton clapped and cheered.

"Why are you cheering?" Dalton was asked.

"Because thirty-five to twenty-one is a better football score," he answered.

In fact, the score was transmitted on the sports wire that night, followed by the parenthetical note "(NOT A FOOTBALL SCORE)." They have to use that quite often in El Paso. This is fun for the fans, but decidedly not for the pitchers. "Pitching for this team is tough," says Rick Parr, the general manager. "If you can pitch here, you can pitch anywhere." If you can get out of here, that is. One of this year's pitchers is Alan Sadler, who starred in football and baseball at the University of Maryland. What's it like to pitch in El Paso, Alan?

"Terrible. It just screws you up totally. You jam a guy inside, a good pitch, and the wind blows it out. Every day, I look in the papers and see that somewhere there are scores of two to one and three to two. Not here. I can't think of another place worse to play, for a pitcher. The hitters love it here. You get a home run and they give you dollar bills. You pitch a shutout and they say the pitcher can pass his hat, but who's gonna be around to give him money after the game? And I've never seen a shutout anyway."

Sadler was on the disabled list with a sore elbow. He has a 1–5 record with an earned run average of 8.37. His worst outing? "I got them one-two-three in the first but never made it out of the second. You can't walk anybody down here. The wall is so close. I gave up three and left with the bases loaded, and a guy hits a double off the wall and clears them. I still haven't gotten over it. I don't know if I ever will."

Everything is topsy-turvy in the Dudley Dome. It was named in 1978 when, night after night, rain fell on every section of the city except within the friendly confines of the ballpark. Whenever a rainstorm approaches, the announcer says it's time to put on the dome, and he makes weird screeching noises as an imaginary roof closes overhead. It works. Twice during the San Antonio series, rain pelted everywhere but inside the dome. Play had to be stopped twice because of sandstorms blowing from left field, but the rain never fell, and the hitters never stopped hitting.

One night, the Diablos had three touchdowns, kicked two extra points, made a two-point conversion, and booted a field goal for twenty-five points. The Dodgers scored a touchdown, an extra point, and two field goals for thirteen—25 to 13 (NOT A FOOTBALL SCORE). How would you like to score thirteen runs and lose by twelve? But you know what they say at the Dudley Dome: You can never get enough.

25

When Worlds Collided

More than half of the 305 athletes who would represent the United States in the Rome Olympics were in New York City on August 15, 1960, for a send-off rally at City Hall. Besides Mayor Robert Wagner, a military color guard, and a stairwell full of politicians, there was retired five-star general Omar Bradley, stirring echoes of a time when Americans had swept through Europe as liberators. World War II was a mere fifteen years gone, and its aftereffects were still evident in Italy. Yet the conflict seemed as remote as the Roman Empire to many of the U.S. athletes, whose lives had been shaped by a relentlessly forward-looking postwar culture.

Rafer Johnson was chosen to speak for his teammates. "It is the goal of each of us to win a gold medal," he told the crowd. "Naturally, that's not possible for all. But we hope to do the best job possible of representing our country." Simple words, even prosaic, but with Johnson the whole was often greater than the sum of its parts. He sounded self-assured yet humble. No one looked sharper in the U.S. Olympic team's travel dress uniform: McGregor-Doniger olive-green sport coat, Haggar slacks, Van Heusen beige knit shirt. Johnson flawlessly called out the names of the dozens of teammates who stood at his side. He had a firm grasp of the occasion, and team officials took notice. His performance in New York, along with his stature as the gold-medal favorite in the decathlon, convinced the officials that Johnson should be the U.S. captain in Rome and the first black athlete to carry the U.S. flag at an Olympic Opening Ceremony. There could be no more valuable figure in the propaganda war with the Soviet Union, which wasted no opportunity to denounce the racial inequities of the United States.

Beneath his composed exterior, however, the twenty-five-year-old Johnson was a jumble of emotions: joy, pride, anticipation, gratitude, determination, and anger. He refused to be manipulated, yet he could not escape the burden of other people's expectations. He was aware, he later said, of the irony of representing a nation that treated people of his color as second-class citizens, but he also felt he could advance their cause most effectively by doing what he did best, which was to excel at his sport and comport himself with dignity.

That night, after an informal reception at the Waldorf-Astoria, three busloads of athletes set out for Idlewild International Airport and the flight across the Atlantic. One plane, a prop DC-7C, carried the cyclists and weightlifters, some of whom spent the night drinking and gambling. Another flight took the heavyweight crew and the women's track team, which included eight members of the Tigerbelles, the runners of little Tennessee State University. The white rowers and black track stars spent the night playing whist and pinochle together. The fleetest of the Tigerbelles was Wilma Rudolph, known to her friends as Skeeter, a nickname her high school basketball coach had given her for the way she buzzed around the court. The twenty-year-old sprinter, whose track career had been interrupted by pregnancy and childbirth, had left behind her two-year-old daughter, Yolanda, with her parents in Clarksville, Tennessee.

A third plane carried the Olympic boxing team, including an obstreperous eighteen-year-old light heavyweight from Louisville named Cassius Marcellus Clay. In Manhattan that week he had told *Newsweek* sports editor Dick Schaap that he would win a gold medal and be "the greatest of all time," but his fear of flying was so strong that it took all his teammates to persuade him to board the plane. *"If God wanted us to fly,"* he repeated over and over again, *"he would give us wings."* According to light middleweight Wilbert McClure, Clay spent the night "talking about who would win gold medals and dada-dada-dada." Not for the last time, the man who would become Muhammad Ali was running his mouth and boasting to overcome his own fears.

In the annals of the modern Olympics, other years have drawn more notice, but none offers a richer palette of character, drama, and meaning than 1960. The Rome Games, during eighteen days in late August and early September, shimmered with performances that remain among the most golden in athletic history, from the marathon triumph of Ethiopia's barefoot Abebe Bikila to the domination of the U.S. basketball team led by future NBA stars Jerry West, Oscar Robertson, and Jerry Lucas. But beyond that, the forces of change were at work everywhere. In sports, culture, and politics, interwoven as never before, an old order was dying and a new one being born. The world as we know it today, with all its promise and trouble, was coming into view.

These Summer Olympics were staged during one of the hottest periods of the Cold War. Just before the Games began, Francis Gary Powers, the U.S. U-2 pilot whose plane had been shot down over Soviet territory on May 1, was convicted by a Moscow court on espionage charges. A few days before the Closing Ceremony, Soviet premier Nikita Khrushchev set sail for New York, where he would pound his fist and rail against the West at UN headquarters. In between, as athletes from East and West Germany competed as a combined team in Rome—a united façade that had been ordered by Avery Brundage, the International Olympic Committee president—officials in East Berlin closed their border temporarily, laying the first metaphorical bricks for what, months later, would become the all too real Berlin wall. The debate over the Two Chinas raged, with Red China boycotting the Games because of the presence of Taiwan, whose athletes, including the great C. K. Yang, were forced to compete for their island alone.

Television, money, and drugs were altering everything they touched. Old-boy notions of amateurism, created by and for upper-class sportsmen, crumbled in the Eternal City and would never be taken so seriously again. Rome brought the first commercially broadcast Summer Games, foreshadowing today's multibillion-dollar Olympic television contracts; the first Olympic doping scandal, with the death from heatstroke of a Danish cyclist, Knud Enemark Jensen, after his trainer apparently gave him an illicit doping drug to boost blood circulation; the first reports of anabolic steroid use, by Soviet bloc weight lifters; and the first runner paid to wear a brand of track shoes in Olympic competition, hundred-meter gold medalist Armin Hary of Germany.

New nations were being heard from, notably in East Africa, whose distance runners emerged at the 1960 Games. And in Rome as throughout the world, there was mounting pressure to provide equal rights for blacks and women after generations of discrimination, which was reflected in the swell of cheers for the U.S. delegation as it marched into the Stadio Olimpico during the Opening Ceremony with Rafer Johnson bearing the flag. Johnson's movements were rhythmic, precise. Keep in step, he told himself. Don't drop the flag. He cradled it, one observer thought, like a baby.

Among the dignitaries at the Opening Ceremony was air force general Lauris Norstad, supreme commander of NATO forces in Europe, a quintessential cold warrior who had developed the air defenses for Western Europe against possible Soviet attack. Norstad wrote to an associate about the sight of the U.S. delegation striding onto the track:

> *What an impressive experience! By far the greatest and warmest applause was for the American contingent. Our group flag bearer and leader was Rafer Johnson, and he looked magnificent. I discreetly inquired from people of several nationalities about their reaction to this colored boy being in the lead, thinking that there might be some feeling that this was arranged for political purposes, but I found that the case was quite the contrary. It was generally believed that he had been elected by his teammates, but that even if he had been appointed by officials, it was in recognition of the fact that he was a very fine man and perhaps the world's outstanding athlete.*

Johnson was not concerned about why he was chosen. He knew that he had won the respect of his athletic peers, and thought he could make no stronger statement in support of civil rights than to be captain of the U.S. delegation at a time when it was still acceptable for a white official to refer to him as a "colored boy."

Before the Games, Ed Temple, the coach of the Tennessee State Tigerbelles and the U.S. women's track team, held the modest hope that one of his runners would get on the medal stand. A single bronze would do. But then, on September 2, Wilma Rudolph won gold in the hundred-meter dash, enthralling not only fans inside the Stadio Olimpico but also millions of Americans back home, who viewed the event hours later on CBS. With that one race, Rudolph shot from relative obscurity to international stardom. It was not just the way she ran—so lithe and flowing—but the combination of her speed, her biography, and her winning personality. Long before it was commonplace for the media to build Olympic coverage around personalities, attention was suddenly lavished on the Wilma Rudolph story: how she had overcome childhood polio, teenage pregnancy, and unwed motherhood to triumph on the Olympic stage.

After her gold-medal win, wherever Rudolph went on the streets of Rome adoring fans pushed forward to be photographed with *la Gazzella Nera*—the Black Gazelle. For a self-described lazybones, the hoopla should have been too much. Rudolph had lost ten pounds in the searing Roman heat, and one of her ankles was tender from a training mishap in which she stepped into a sprinkler hole. Then there was the distraction of having watched her boyfriend, Ray Norton, who had entered the Olympics billed as the next Jesse Owens, finish dead last in the men's sprints, sending reporters to the thesaurus in search of synonyms for Armageddon. But worrying was not Rudolph's style. She had been so relaxed before the hundred-meter final that she'd taken a nap in the holding room.

Rudolph became a symbol to her teammates and to all women in sports. Anne Warner, one of the so-called Sweethearts from the Santa Clara Swim Club who combined to win six gold medals in Rome, said the swimmers "had read the stories about her fight against polio. She was really a hero for a lot of us." Warner remembered facing her own polio scare before she entered kindergarten, when there was a widespread belief that the disease spread in swimming pools. "I think when I was five I went swimming at a local pool and got a high fever, which was a sinus infection, and my mother rushed me to the doctor. My pediatrician's wife had been taken to the hospital that day to an iron lung from which she never came out. The fact that Wilma Rudolph had become such a magnificent runner was remarkable."

Just as Rudolph had overcome the odds, so had her coach and teammates from Tennessee State, the historically black school in north Nashville. Women's track and field was a forlorn outpost on the frontier of U.S. sports in 1960. Only a few colleges, mostly black schools in the South, had track-and-field programs for women. There were no scholarships. When Temple was named head coach at Tennessee State in 1950, it was because nobody else wanted the job. His first budget was under $1,000. Ten years later, even after he had placed eight runners on the U.S. Olympic team, the Tennessee State athletic department still would not give him an office or even a desk. He shared a cubbyhole with his wife, the campus postmistress, and borrowed her desk.

For years, while competing in the South, Temple's team had traveled not by bus but in two station wagons, one driven by him, the other by the photographer Earl Clanton, who had coined the nickname Tigerbelles, a felicitous melding of "tiger" and "Southern belle." Their road trips ventured deep into Jim Crow territory, and it was best if they filled the gas tanks beforehand; getting service at filling stations along the way couldn't be guaranteed. At some point there would be a shout from the back of a wagon: Time to "hit the fields," meaning pull over so the girls, not allowed to use restrooms reserved for whites, could scramble into the darkness for relief. Near the end of the trip, an order would come from the front: Get your stuff together. This meant rollers off, lipstick on, hair brushed, and clothing straightened. "I want foxes, not oxes," Coach Temple told his runners. They perfected the art of emerging from the least comfortable rides looking as fresh as a gospel choir, for which they were often mistaken.

In Rome the Tigerbelles earned the recognition they were denied back home, led by the wondrous Wilma. As Rudolph and five other competitors stepped onto the track on the afternoon of September 5 for the two-hundred-meter final, Temple, who had been so nervous before the hundred-meter final that he couldn't watch, had a good feeling. Rudolph, he would say later, "was a better two-hundred runner. She could just run the curve so well, plus when she hit the straightaway she could open up with her long legs and her fluid stride." Before a qualifying heat she had been so confident that she asked Temple if it would be okay for her "to just loaf" if she had a good lead. Give it your all for 150 meters, the coach said, then look around, and if you have a good lead, go ahead and coast. That is exactly what Rudolph did, but she coasted to an Olympic record time of 23.2 seconds.

In the final she not only faced a wet, slow track and a swirling wind but was also handicapped by being slotted in the far inside lane, where the curve is tighter and more difficult for a long-limbed runner to negotiate. At the gun Rudolph was slow out of the blocks, but at the curve she surged past the field, and down the straightaway she lengthened her lead with every stride. In the stands even the German fans, who had been chanting in unison for their blond countrywoman Jutte

Heine in lane 3, joined in the roar for the American at the sprint's end.

It was an unspectacular time, 24 seconds, but the victory was historic. From a crowded little red house in Clarksville, from an extended family of twenty-one kids, from a childhood of illness and leg braces, from a small black college that offered no athletic scholarships, from a country where she could be hailed as a heroine and yet denied lunch at a department-store counter, Wilma Rudolph had swept the sprints in Rome, the second of three gold medals she would win on her way to Olympic immortality.

The joke was that an hour after that victory she ran harder than she had down the track. As she and her teammates Lucinda Williams, Barbara Jones, and Martha Hudson approached the Olympic Village, a mob of fans spotted Rudolph and started toward her. But she had done enough for one day, and an electrical storm was about to hit Rome, so she and her fellow Tigerbelles just took off, sprinting away toward their dorm. They easily outdistanced their pursuers, one local columnist noted, "including the rain, which they beat by fifteen yards."

When darkness fell that night, the action moved across Rome to the Palazzo dello Sport for the boxing finals. The new arena was packed with a standing-room-only crowd of more than eighteen thousand raucous boxing fans. The dominant claque was Italian—vociferous, on edge, ready at any time to burst into song ("as if every man in the audience was a Caruso," the British writer Neil Allen noted in his diary) or to unleash harsh whistles. They had come to cheer the home squad, which had six men going for gold out of ten weight classes. The United States had three.

In the middleweight match, after two Italians had lost and one had won, Wilbert McClure of the United States out-pointed Italy's Carmelo Bossi in a decision that the home crowd found hard to dispute but nonetheless intensely disliked. That was the situation when Eddie Crook, a U.S. Army sergeant based at Fort Campbell, Kentucky, entered the ring to face Poland's Tadeusz Walasek. Yanks in the stands sensed anti-American sentiment bubbling up in the crowd. To Pete Newell, the U.S. basketball coach, it seemed rooted in ideology. He believed there were many Italian Communists in the arena. Whether it was politics or merely boxing's combustible mix of mob psychology and controlled violence, there was no doubt as to the hostility in the arena.

Crook boxed deliberately, using his left to keep Walasek away while dodging the Pole's occasional errant swings. Most boxing writers thought Crook outboxed Walasek and were not surprised when he was declared the winner. But the Italian crowd, having rooted loudly for Walasek, jeered the decision. When Crook took the podium to accept his medal, he looked around in astonishment as the audience kept whistling and hissing.

The protest persisted even as the U.S. flag rose to the rafters. American fans stood to sing the national anthem with uncommon vigor. *Washington Post* writer Shirley Povich focused on the loudest singer of them all: "A visitor in Rome named Bing Crosby . . . unloaded with a fierce Ethel Merman bust-down-the-roof vigor that could get him thrown out of the crooners union."

Cassius Clay heard the commotion from his dressing room. He was next up for the United States, coming out to face another Pole, Zbigniew Pietrzykowski, for the light-heavyweight title. The booing strengthened Clay's resolve as he made his way to the ring. Although only eighteen, he did not lack experience. By the time he reached Rome, he had fought in 128 amateur bouts. Early in his career he exhibited an urgency to be in the spotlight that made him at once charming and irritating. Nikos Spanakos, his teammate on the Olympic squad, remembered an incident when he and his brother Pete, another boxer, were getting off a plane with Clay after a Golden Gloves meet in Chicago. "Photographers came out to take our pictures, and Cassius actually pushed us aside and got in the middle so he could be the center of attention," Spanakos said. "That was Cassius."

Traditionalists thought his style in the ring could also be a bit much. In late April 1959, at the Pan American Games Trials in Madison, Wisconsin, Clay approached John Walsh, the University of Wisconsin's veteran coach, to brag about a first-match victory during which he had danced and taunted his opponent before knocking him out in the second round. Had Walsh seen it? Clay asked. "I couldn't stand it," Walsh replied, according to boxing writer Jim Doherty. "I got up and left."

In Rome, Clay found everything new and exciting, even the bidet in his suite at the Olympic Village, which, according to Spanakos, he mistook for a drinking fountain and tried to take a swig. Within a few days Clay had established himself as the young clown prince of world athletes. He seemed to be everywhere, shaking hands, telling tall tales, boasting about his prowess, joshing with Olympians from Europe, Asia, and Africa. Francis Nyangweso, a boxer from Uganda, recalled coming back from training one afternoon and being approached by athletes wearing USA uniforms. "One of them, very tall and big, spoke to us in an American accent," Nyangweso said. "When I got used to his English, our conversation ranged over topics including wild animals, forests, and snakes. Before we parted, this gentleman advised us that the boxer on our team who happened to be drawn against him should duck on medical grounds and should not try to fight him, for he, Cassius Clay, would not like to demolish a young brother from Africa."

Reporters dubbed Clay "Uncle Sam's unofficial goodwill ambassador" and were especially taken by his "solid Americanism"—a trait he reinforced in an exchange with a foreign journalist. "With the racial intolerance in your country, you must have a lot of problems," the reporter said. "Oh, yeah, we've got some problems," Clay was quoted in response. "But get this straight—it's still the best country in the world."

Over eleven days there had been 280 Olympic boxing matches among competitors from fifty-four countries, and Nat Fleischer, editor of *Ring* magazine, claimed to have watched them all. Several U.S. boxers, Fleischer thought, had fallen victim to Cold War politics, with Soviet bloc judges ruling unfairly against them. Clay against Pietrzykowski was the final America vs. Iron Curtain bout. Pietrzykowski had been the European champ three times and a bronze medalist at the 1956 Olympics in Melbourne. In the dressing room Fleischer gave Clay a piece of advice. "I told [him] that if the fight went beyond two rounds," the editor would recall, "he had to go all out to win."

"I'll do that," Clay said.

The first two rounds were close but uneventful. Pietrzykowski, a tall lefty, stayed back, trying to find openings for his long reach. Clay was so quick that he could dodge the Pole's left even with his gloves down. He danced left, skipped right, hands down, and then darted in for a punch. Most of his lefts landed just short. The boxing writers talked about what a showman Clay was but questioned whether he could really take a punch. Neil Allen thought Pietrzykowski won the first round, in which "there was some neat defensive work by both." Shirley Povich agreed, recording that Clay "was taking a beating from

Ziggy." Most observers felt otherwise, as did the judges, who gave the round (barely) to Clay. In the second round a furious exchange in the last thirty seconds also favored Clay, but going into the final round, the fight was still close. Fleischer's warning registered in Clay's corner. "You have to go out there and get him now," he was told.

"The whole picture changed in the third and last round," Allen recorded in his diary. Clay came to life "and began to put his punches together in combination clusters instead of merely whipping out a left jab. He pummeled Pietrzykowski about the ring, blood came from the nose and mouth of the Pole, and only great courage kept this triple European champion on his feet." Povich wrote that suddenly "Ziggy's whole face was a bloody mask. Clay was throwing punches from angles that were new and he had the Pole ripe for a knockout but in his eagerness and greenness he could not put his opponent away." Still, in the opinion of *Ring*'s Fleischer, "Clay's last-round assault on Pietrzykowski was the outstanding hitting of the tournament."

By the time it was over, even the Italians in the arena were on Clay's side. One of them was Rino Tommasi, a young boxing promoter and writer. "It was a great night," he said. Clay was both an attractive boxer and a great actor, characteristics equally admired by the Italians. Years later Tommasi would interview Pietrzykowski, who told him that he knew before entering the ring that Clay would beat him and that he was glad he lasted three rounds.

There were no whistles when Clay was announced the unanimous winner. "That was my last amateur fight," he said afterward. "I'm turning pro." He had intended to keep his USA trunks as a souvenir, he added, but "now look at them!" They were streaked with the Pole's blood.

The next morning, September 6, everyone seemed to be up and about early in the Olympic Village. Clay paraded around before breakfast, gold medal dangling from his neck. "I got to show this thing off!" he exulted. His coach said Clay had slept with the medal, or at least gone to bed with it; the young boxer had been too excited to sleep. Visions of his future flashed in his mind.

"Fool, go someplace and sit down," Lucinda Williams chided him lovingly, like a big sister, when he approached the Tigerbelles and started blabbing that he was the greatest. Clay was always hanging around the Tigerbelles; he had an unrequited crush on Wilma Rudolph.

Dallas Long, the bronze medalist in the shot put, said nothing when he came across Clay that morning. He thought, This guy is such a jerk. He's never going to amount to anything. But many other athletes reacted to the young boxer with amused tolerance, not least among them the U.S. captain, who was about to compete for a gold medal of his own.

Rafer Johnson was an exemplar of sound mind in sound body. Intelligent and movie-star handsome, he was the student body president at UCLA. He stood six-foot-three and weighed two hundred pounds, with long legs on a muscular, classically sculpted frame. While he was

Rafer and C.K.

International Olympic Committee

ferociously competitive, he was not as self-centered as most athletes; he had a broad perspective that came in part from having grown up black in a historically Swedish town in central California.

Kingsburg, out in the San Joaquin Valley, was about as flat, hot, and white as America got. The Johnsons were the only black family in town. They had a small one-story house near the railroad tracks in the shadows of a cannery. A legend arose later that they had lived in a boxcar—not quite, though the narrow house looked like one. In the summers, Rafer and his siblings worked the fields near the cannery, picking grapes, plums, and peaches. With one exception, Rafer felt embraced by the community, where, he said, "everyone knew everyone." That lone exception was the police chief, who reflexively suspected the Johnsons when anything went wrong. "Every time something was taken . . . a bicycle missing . . . they came to our house looking for it," Johnson recalled. "We weren't taking anything."

But the prevailing sensibility in Kingsburg, a community that showered attention on its children, was a boon to Rafer. "The parents would build the fields and drive young people back and forth to different competitions," he remembered. "They were the coaches. It was a wonderful community for young people." His best sport was football, but he also starred in basketball and track and field.

Much of Rafer's athletic skill came from his mother, Alma, who could outrun him until he was a teenager. She was also the person he most admired. His father, though a hard worker, drank too much. "There were very few Monday mornings when my father was not at work, but there were a lot of weekends when the family suffered because of his drinking problem," Rafer said. "At athletic events, sometimes, honestly, he could be a little disruptive. My mother was able to keep him calm for the most part, but there were times when she couldn't control him and no one else could."

When Rafer was a junior in high school, Kingsburg Vikings track coach Murl Dotson drove him down to watch a decathlon meet in Tulare, California, the hometown of Bob Mathias, the 1948 and 1952 Olympic decathlon champion. Mathias was the hero of the valley. Although there were no decathlons in high school, Rafer returned from Tulare determined to compete in as many of the discipline's individual events as possible and build up his skills so that someday he might succeed Mathias to the title of best all-around athlete in the world.

His first attempt came at the 1956 Olympics in Melbourne, and it resulted in the most painful loss of his career. The twenty-year-old Johnson had gone to Australia as a gold-medal favorite but pulled a muscle while warming up, and although he gutted his way through the punishing two-day decathlon, he was slowed just enough to finish second. Failing to win the gold shattered him. The normally stoic Johnson broke down in the arms of UCLA coach Elvin "Ducky" Drake, crying inconsolably. Drake talked to him long into the night, and from that discussion Johnson emerged with a deeper understanding of what it took to become an Olympic champion.

"When you finish second you have to take a real close look at how you performed, how you thought, and how these thoughts caused you to feel," Johnson said later. "We broke those things down." He had heard the words before, but now he absorbed them: "You have to do it on that day. You have to do it at the time when they fire the gun. You have to be fully aware and prepared for anything that might happen."

Now here he was, four years later, nearing the end of the decathlon competition in Rome, fighting for survival against Taiwan's C. K. Yang, his UCLA teammate and close friend. Few Olympic athletes knew one another as thoroughly as Johnson and Yang. It was not just that both had trained at the same college for the same event. A deeper shared sensibility seemed to be at work, a blend of admiration and competitiveness that pushed them to greater accomplishments than they might have achieved apart.

Track experts had virtually awarded the gold medal to Johnson before the Games, and Johnson himself had been quoted as saying that Yang would finish second, but privately, he would say later, he was "nowhere near as cocky as that statement suggests." They knew each other's strengths and weaknesses intimately, as did the coach they shared. Drake, who had not been appointed to the U.S. track staff, came to Rome officially as Yang's coach, but he tried to show no partiality for either of his two great decathletes, devoting equal time and attention to each. It had come down to a two-man competition, he told them—one would win gold, the other silver.

Eight events down, only the javelin and the 1,500 meters to go.

Darkness had fallen by the time the decathletes got to their final javelin throws. A full moon glowed over the Stadio Olimpico. Yang, chilled by the night air, wrapped his shoulders in a blanket. Johnson knelt patiently, chewing a wad of gum. The competition had been intense all of this second long day of the decathlon. Yang had snatched the overall lead after the 110-meter hurdles, then Johnson had taken it back with the discus, then he had watched his margin shrink with the high jump. The javelin, the penultimate event, usually provided Johnson's safety cushion; with it he amassed enough points to withstand any charge in the closing 1500-meter run. He tried to turn his mind off and just perform, but his approach on his final throw was too slow, and he felt sluggish. He would have to settle for just under 230 feet, six feet better than Yang but not enough to make Johnson feel comfortable. Here came the 1500, and Johnson was leading by only 67 points.

He and Yang were in the same heat. Fluent in the decathlon's arcane scoring system, both men calculated that if Yang won the race by ten seconds or more, the gold medal was his. This was far from improbable; Yang's best time was 4:36.9, while Johnson's was 4:49.7—a spread of nearly thirteen seconds.

In the front row of the Stadio Olimpico stands, near the 330-meter mark, sat Ducky Drake. Go about your work with a quiet confidence that cannot be shaken, he had often told Johnson during anxious moments. Johnson's confidence was not shaken now, but he felt he needed more advice, so he approached his coach at the edge of the stands. How should he run this most important race of his life? The key thing, Drake said, is that when Yang tries to pull away—and he will try—you have to stay with him. At some point Yang will look back to see where you are, and you have to be right there.

Easier for Drake to say than for Johnson to do, but still, it was perhaps the only plan that could save him. Johnson nodded in agreement and walked back toward the track. About halfway there, he turned around and saw none other than Yang approaching the same spot at the edge of the stands. Drake, after all, was his coach too.

"Ducky said to me, 'C. K., you run as fast as you can. Rafer cannot keep up with you!' " Yang later recalled. Drake was like a master chess player competing against himself. He saw the whole board and was making the best move for each side.

But Yang was not convinced. He knew how competitive Johnson was. Even if Yang was so much better at this distance, he felt uneasy. What if he tried to pull away and got a cramp, as he had at the Olympic Trials a few months earlier in Oregon?

They approached the starting line at 9:20 p.m. "The pressure was on. I don't know if I've ever felt more pressure than I felt starting that race," Johnson recalled. "It's like I couldn't breathe."

There were four other runners in the race, but they were inconsequential, like ghosts. All eyes were trained on Johnson and Yang. After a late workout, Newell and some of the U.S. basketball players took seats near Drake to watch the climax. Most of the Tigerbelles were there too, rooting hard for Johnson. Lucinda Williams said she and her teammates all had crushes on their captain, "but he was too focused to look at anybody. He was the greatest."

The darkening night, the sense of autumn coming, of something ending, added to the tension. As the race got under way, *Sports Illustrated*'s Tex Maule jotted down his impressions of Johnson: "His strong, cold face impassive, the big man pounded steadily through the dank chill of the Roman night. Two steps in front of him, Formosa's Chuan Kwang Yang moved easily. In the gap between them lay the Olympic decathlon championship."

Johnson ran the first two laps with determination. "I stuck to him like a shadow, dogging his footsteps stride for stride," he said of Yang. Midway through the race, Yang picked up the pace, but Johnson stayed with him, shifting his position from Yang's left (inside) shoulder to his right shoulder. He wanted to be fully visible when Yang turned around. Just as Drake had predicted, Yang did turn around. He was stunned to see Johnson at his right shoulder. Not only that, Yang would recall, but "he looked like he was smiling."

Johnson did indeed smile, but it was pure acting. "I just wanted to let him know that this was going to be different," he would say later. "I could have had my head down and dragging, because I was feeling that kind of fatigue and pressure, but I smiled as big a smile as I could."

By the final lap, memories of the Oregon Trials seeped into Yang's head. He worried that he might cramp up again. But how else could he shake the big guy? He had no choice but to try one more acceleration, one final push to break clear. It seemed to work for a short time, but then Yang felt his body weakening. Coming around the turn, he looked back again, and there was Johnson, clinging to him, only three yards behind.

Johnson tried not to think about the ache in his legs. He was "struggling so hard," noted Neil Allen, "that we in the stands could almost feel his pain." But he knew he had one crucial edge over Yang. "My huge advantage was that this was the last time I was going to do this," he recalled. "And C. K., he had several more times; this was not his last race. I kept saying to myself, This is it. Just this one more time. I can do this one as good as I've done it. I would never run the fifteen hundred again. Never. Never. More important, I would never run it at the end of doing nine other events."

Maule called that fifteen hundred "the tensest five minutes of the entire Games. And it grew and grew until it seemed like a thin high sound in the stadium." Down the homestretch, Yang was bobbing and struggling, while Johnson was moving mechanically, sheer will driving him forward. They crossed the line only 1.2 seconds apart, Yang at 4:48.5, Johnson at 4:49.7. Johnson had tied his best time ever.

Yang knew he had lost the decathlon. A few steps after finishing, his close friend and tenacious foe caught up to him. Johnson felt at once jubilant and sad. "I never in my whole life but that once competed against someone where I had a little bit of ambivalence about beating him," he would explain later. "I was exhilarated that I won and totally depressed that C. K. lost."

As they came to a stop, Johnson put his head on Yang's shoulder. Yang bent down to catch his breath, and Johnson bent with him, hands on knees, as officials and photographers rushed toward them in the artificial light of the stadium. Johnson straightened and walked around, arms akimbo, smiling and shaking hands with well-wishers, utterly out of breath. Yang slipped over to a bench and put his head in his hands in despair. He got up, jacket around his shoulders, head bowed, and found a Taiwanese official who hugged him and patted him on the back.

A few seconds later Yang was bending down again when Johnson appeared, lifted him up, and stood with him arm in arm. "It was a moment of such beauty," Neil Allen wrote in his diary, "that I was not surprised to see one friend in the press box with tears in his eyes and I for one, for the first time in my life, found that my hands were trembling too much to type."

At eleven that night, after back-to-back fourteen-hour days of competition—ten events, draining humidity, evening chill, rain delays, unbearable tension, and the accumulation of an Olympic record—Rafer Johnson left the Stadio Olimpico for the last time, retracing the steps he had taken nearly two weeks earlier as the captain and flag-bearer for the U.S. Olympic team. As he trudged, exhausted, along the moonlit Tiber and over the bridge, C. K. Yang, now just a friend, no longer a competitor, walked once again at his side.

26

Still the Greatest

Berrien Springs, Michigan
No words at first. The greeting comes from his eyes, and then a hand-shake, light as a butterfly, followed by a gesture that says follow me. He has just popped out the back door of his farmhouse, wearing green pants and a light brown wool pullover with sunglasses tucked coolly into the mock turtleneck collar. He is carrying an old black briefcase. His hair is longer than usual and a bit uncombed. He starts walking toward his office, a converted barn on the lower end of the circular driveway.

He moves slowly, lurching slightly forward as he goes, never a stumble but sometimes seeming on the verge of one, as though his world slopes downhill. He opens the door and stands aside, following, not leading, on the way upstairs to his second-floor office. Halfway up, it becomes clear why. He sticks out his hand and catches his visitor's foot from behind. The old trip-up-the-stairs trick. Muhammad Ali loves tricks.

At the top of the stairs is the headquarters of GOAT. Another trick. It is the playfully ironic acronym for Greatest of All Time, Incorporated. Ali wants the world to know that he is just another goat, one living thing in this vast and miraculous universe. But also the greatest that ever was. He is fifty-five, his mouth and body slowed by Parkinson's disease, yet still arguably the best-known and most beloved figure in the world. Who else? The pope? Nelson Mandela? Michael Jordan? Ali might win in a split decision.

Even the most dramatic lives move in cycles of loss and recovery. Last summer in Atlanta, when Ali stood alone in the spotlight, the world watching, his hands trembling, and lit the Olympic flame, he began another cycle, perhaps his ultimate comeback, as emotional as any he had staged in the ring against Joe Frazier or George Foreman. For sixteen years he had been retired from boxing. During that time he had gone through periods of boredom and uncertainty. He kept going as best he could, his health deteriorating, spreading goodwill with his smiling eyes, trying to keep his name alive.

Then his moment arrived again, first at the Olympics, next at the Academy Awards, where he bore silent witness to *When We Were Kings*, the Oscar-winning documentary about his dramatic heavyweight championship fight in October 1974 against Foreman in what was then Zaire. The shimmering house of movie stars seemed diminished, their egos preposterous, when Ali rose and stood before them. Yet some saw in that appearance a hint of the maudlin: poor Ali, enfeebled and paunchy, dragged out as another melodramatic Hollywood gimmick. Was he real or was he memory? What was left of him if he could no longer float or sting?

Quite a bit, as it turns out. No sorrow and pity from the champ. He says he cherished his performances at the Olympics and the Academy Awards more than anyone could know. Publicity is his lifeblood, more important to him than any medicine he is supposed to take. "Press keeps me alive, man," he says, with an honesty that softens the edge of his ego. "Press keeps me alive. Press and TV. The Olympics. Academy Awards. *When We Were Kings*. Keeps me alive."

When the producers sent him a videotape of *When We Were Kings*, he stuck it in his VCR at home and watched it day after day. At a recent autograph extravaganza in Las Vegas, he conducted his own poll by comparing his line to those for Jim Brown, Paul Hornung, Bobby Hull, and Ernie Banks. Twice as long as any of them. Staying alive. And the biggest lifesaver of all: that night in Atlanta last July, thirty-six years after he had first danced onto the world scene in Rome as the brash young Olympic light-heavyweight champion, Cassius Marcellus Clay.

Long after the torch scene was over, Ali would not let go. He went back to his suite with his wife, Lonnie, and a few close friends. They were tired, emotionally drained from the surprise, anxiety, and thrill of the occasion, but Ali would not go to sleep. He was still holding the long white and gold torch, which he had kept as a prized memento. He cradled it in his arms, turning it over and over, just looking at it, not saying much, sitting in a big chair, smiling, hour after hour.

"I think the man was just awed. Just completely awed by the whole experience," Lonnie Ali recalled. "He was so excited. It took forever for him to go to bed, he was on such a high. He found it very hard to come back down to earth. There was just such a fabulous response. No one expected that. None of us did."

By the time Ali and Lonnie returned to their farmhouse in southern Michigan, the mail was already backing up, flooding in at tenfold the previous pace. Letters from everywhere. The return of a trembling Ali had unloosed powerful feelings in people. They said they cried at his beauty and perseverance. They said he reminded them of what it means to stand up for something you believe in. Disabled people. Old sixties activists. Republicans. Black. White. Christian. Jewish. Muslim. A little boy from Germany, a boxing fan from England, a radiologist from Sudan, a secretary from Saudi Arabia—the multitudes thanked him for giving them hope.

When Ali reaches his office, he takes his customary chair against the side wall. There is work to be done, the room is overcrowded with things to be signed for charity, and his assistant, Kim Forburger, is waiting for him with a big blue felt pen. But Ali has something else in mind right now.

"Mmmmmmm. Watch this, man," he says. His voice sounds like the soft, slurred grumble-whisper of someone trying to clear his throat on the way out of a deep sleep. Conversing with him for the first time, one unavoidably has to say, "I'm sorry, what?" now and then, or simply pretend to understand him, but soon enough one adjusts, and it becomes obvious that Parkinson's has not slowed his brain, only his motor skills.

Ali walks toward the doorway and looks back with a smile.

"Oh, have you seen Muhammad levitate yet?" Forburger asks. She suddenly becomes the female assistant in a Vegas act. With a sweep of her hand, she says, "Come over here. Stand right behind him. Now watch his feet. Watch his feet."

Ali goes still and silent, meditating. His hands stop shaking. He seems to radiate something. A mystical aura? Ever so slowly, his feet rise from the floor, one inch, two inches, six inches. His hands are not touching anything. "Ehhhh. Pretty heavy, mmmm," he says. His visitor, familiar with the lore of Ali's levitations, yet easily duped, watches slack-jawed as the champ floats in the air for several seconds.

Come over here, Ali motions. To the side. "Look," he says. He is not really levitating, of course. He has managed to balance himself perfectly, Parkinson's notwithstanding, all 250 pounds of him, on the tiptoes of his right foot, creating an optical illusion from behind that both his feet have lifted off the ground.

The tricks have only just begun. He hauls out a huge gray plastic toolbox, opens it, and peers inside. His hands now move with the delicacy of a surgeon selecting the correct instrument from his bag. For the next quarter hour, he performs the simple, delightful tricks of an apprentice magician. Balls and coins appear and disappear, ropes change lengths, sticks turn colors. "Maaann! Maaann! Heavy!" he says.

Then he turns to slapstick. Close your eyes and open your hand. The champ places something soft and fuzzy in it. "Mmmmm. Okay. Open."

A fuzzy toy mouse.

Ali beams at the startled reaction.

His voice becomes louder, higher, more animated. "Ehhh!" he shrieks. "Kids go 'Ahhhh! Ahhhh!' "

Try it again. This time it's a fake cockroach.

And again. This time fake dog shit.

Ali closes his gray toolbox and puts it away, satisfied.

What is going on here? In part it is just Ali amusing himself with magic tricks that he has been doing over and over for many years for anyone who comes to see him. But he is also, as always, making a more profound point. He has transferred his old boxing skills and his poetry and his homespun philosophy to another realm, from words to magic. The world sees him now, lurching a bit, slurring some, getting old, trembling, and recalls the unspeakably great and gorgeous and garrulous young man that he once was. He understands that contrast. But, he is saying, nothing is as it appears. Life is always a matter of perception and deception.

Poets and philosophers contemplate this, and boxers know it intuitively. (Ali, ghost boxing before the Foreman fight: "Come get me, sucker, I'm dancin'! No, I'm not here, I'm there! You're out, sucker!") Back when he was Cassius Clay, he pretended that he was demented before fighting Sonny Liston because he had heard that the only cons who scared big, bad Sonny in prison were the madmen. By acting crazy, he not only injected a dose of fear into Liston, he took some out of himself. Life is a trick.

The Islamic religion, to which Ali has adhered for more than thirty years, disapproves of magic tricks, but he has found his way around that problem, as usual.

"When . . . I . . . do . . . a . . . trick," he says now. He seems more easily understandable. Is he speaking more clearly or has the ear adjusted to him? "I . . . always . . . show . . . people . . . how . . . to . . . do . . . it."

He smiles. "Show . . . people . . . how . . . easy . . . it . . . is . . . to . . . be . . . tricked."

Perception and deception. He has returned to his chair in the office, with his black briefcase on his lap. Slowly and carefully he opens it . . . click . . . click . . . and looks inside as though examining its contents for the first time. His passport is tucked in the upper compartment. Parkinson's has not slowed his travels. He's at home no more than ninety days a year. Washington, D.C., Los Angeles, Louisville, Las Vegas in a week, doing good deeds. He visits schools, campaigns against child abuse, for more Parkinson's funding, for peace and tolerance. Everyone wants to see the champ. Germany is clamoring for him. Its national television network just ran an hour-long documentary on him. Next to the passport is a laminated trading card. He lifts it out and studies it. There's Ali next to Sugar Ray Robinson and Joe Louis.

"Two of the greatest fighters in the world," he says. Pause. "Mmmmmm. Both dead."

Ali thinks a lot about death. Aging and death and life after death. His philosophy is at once selfish and selfless. Publicity keeps him alive. He wants to stay alive so that he can make people happy and do good deeds. And "good deeds are the rent we pay for our house in heaven."

He is teaching and preaching now. A new poetry, slower, no rhymes, stream of consciousness, deeper meaning.

Twice a month they call us to sign autographs
Make two hundred thousand a day
Signing. Hundred dollars a picture
Long lines. Bring in millions of dollars
I'm not fightin' no more
I'll sign for nothin'. Give it to charity
Get the money, give it to the homeless
Give it to soup lines
If I see someone who needs some
Here's a hundred. Here's fifty
Soup vendor. Wino. Old woman with varicose veins
Good deeds. Judgment
I'm well pleased with you my son. Come into heaven
That's eternal life. Maann! Maann!
Look at all the buildings in downtown New York
People built them. They're dead
Buildings still standing
You just don't own nothin'. Just a trustee
Think about it. You die
This life's a test. I'm tryin'
Warm bodies. Shake hands. Gone
All dead now. President Kennedy
Whatever color you are
No matter how much money you have
Politics. Sports. You're gonna die
Sleep is the brother of death.

Ali closes his eyes. He starts snoring. Reopens his eyes. "Turn over now. It's morning."

Back to the black briefcase. Stacked in rows along the bottom are a collection of little leather books, five of them, in red, pink, and green. It turns out they are Bibles. Why he needs five is not clear. What he does with them is part of the mystery of Muhammad Ali.

During the past several months, he and Lonnie and Thomas Hauser, author of his authorized biography, have made appearances around the country promoting the cause of universal understanding and tolerance. Ali and Hauser, Muslim and Jew, put together a little book titled *Healing* that they distribute at every stop. It contains quotations on tolerance from Cicero, Voltaire, Thoreau, Ali. The book was inspired by Ali's habit of combing through the Koran and other books and writing down phrases that he found moving. Hauser chose the title when he studied a series of words and noticed A-L-I in the middle of H-E-A-L-I-N-G.

This crusade seems natural for Ali now. In the sixties, when he shed the name Cassius Clay, which he dismissed as his slave name, and refused to be inducted into the military to fight in Vietnam, temporarily giving up his freedom and wealth and title in the process, he became what Hauser called "a symbol of divided America." Now his popularity transcends politics, race, country, and religion. He is universally accepted as a man who stood up for what he believed in, paid the price, and prevailed. He has endured enough intolerance to give the message deeper meaning. His shining eyes are the prize of peace.

Ali takes the leather Bibles out of his briefcase and places them on a table beside him. He peers inside again and comes out with a stack of paper. Each page has a typed message. He hands over the first page. Could these be the quotations of tolerance and understanding he writes down each day?

Read it, Ali indicates wordlessly, nodding his head.

If God is all perfect his revelation must be perfect and accurate. Free from contradiction. . . . Since Holy Scripture is from God, it should be impossible to find mistakes and conflicting verses. If it doesn't you can't trust it 100 percent. There are many conflicting verses in the Bible.

Ali smiles, gestures to take that piece of paper back, and hands over one page after another of contradictions he has found in the Bible. Some contradictions in numbers, some about what Jesus was purported to have said. "All in the Bible," Ali says as he puts the stack of papers back in his briefcase. "Heavy." He points to a filing cabinet behind the desk, which is overflowing with similar papers. It turns out that this is one of his favorite intellectual pastimes, searching his little leather Bibles for thousands of contradictions of fact or interpretation that have been cited by Islamic scholars. There seems to be no malice in his hobby, though it is hardly what one might expect from a missionary of universal healing.

What is going on here? The question is later put to Lonnie Ali. She is his fourth wife, wholly devoted to his well-being, a smart, funny, and gracious woman, a graduate of Vanderbilt University, who started cooking for him when he was getting sick, married him twelve years ago, and is serving more and more as his public voice. She knows that he is not perfect, but she also appreciates his larger meaning to the world. Muhammad, she says, is greater than his individual parts. He means so many things to so many people, and she is determined to preserve that, sometimes in spite of him. She has known him since she was six years old, growing up in Louisville in the house across the street from his mother, Odessa Clay. Why is Ali doing this?

She shrugs. It is, she says, "part of the dichotomy that is Muhammad. Even when Muhammad was in the Nation of Islam where they considered whites devils he was putting little white kids on his lap and kissing them and loving them. Muhammad could really care less if a person is of another religion. But Muhammad found out that there are contradictions in the Bible and he's hooked on that. If he can get you to say, 'Oh, look, I never knew that,' then it's like he has accomplished victory. Muhammad is a warrior. And he finds these little things to battle over."

There certainly seem to be more important battles now for Muhammad Ali. Perception and deception. How sick is he?

Ali began showing signs of trouble as far back as 1980, when he lost the heavyweight title in his sixtieth and next-to-last fight, against Larry Holmes. He visited several medical experts over the next few years and finally parkinsonism, a syndrome related to Parkinson's disease, was diagnosed. Parkinson's is a slowly progressive disease, suffered by an estimated 1.5 million Americans, that causes cells in the middle part of the brain to degenerate, reducing the production of the chemical dopamine and leading to tremors, slowness of movement, memory loss, and other neurological symptoms. Its cause is unknown. People who suffer from parkinsonism have many of the same symptoms but in a milder and usually undegenerative form. Until recently, most of his doctors believed Ali had the syndrome, not the disease. Over the past eighteen months that diagnosis has been changing and the belief now is that he might have the disease.

Some doctors who have examined Ali remain convinced that his ailment was brought on by the pounding he took in the ring, especially the brutal fights late in his career against Frazier, Foreman, and Holmes. Mahlon DeLong, his Parkinson's physician at Emory University in Atlanta, and other experts argue, however, that Ali must have had a predisposition to the disease. They note that most "punch drunk" fighters do not show signs of Parkinson's, but more often suffer from something known as Martland's syndrome, with intellectual deficits that Ali does not show. His disorder, in any case, is not as debilitating as one might suspect from catching a brief glimpse of him. He is agile enough to dress himself each morning. He knots his ties perfectly. He lifts his legs to put on his socks. Laces his shoes. Slips on his Swiss Army watch. Feeds himself. Opens doors. Performs magic tricks. Reads his Bibles and Korans. Writes legibly. Talks on the telephone. Understands everything said to him and around him. Flips the remote on the television to watch CNN and Biography and the Discovery Channel. Misses some spots on his chin when shaving, but only because he is nearsighted.

Ali is on the move now, heading down the steps and out onto the grounds of his eighty-eight-acre farm. It is an unexpected paradise at the end of the road in the middle of Middle America, between South Bend, Indiana, and Benton Harbor, Michigan. It once belonged to Al Capone, a mobster's hideaway. "Found . . . machine . . . guns," Ali says.

There is a gentle pond, a gazebo where he prays to Allah, a playground for the youngest of his nine children, six-year-old Assad, whom he and Lonnie adopted at birth; acres of sweet-blooming perennials, woods at the edge of the field, the St. Joe River rolling by, white picket fences, and white and green barns. On his way down the looping driveway, Ali cannot resist some playful sparring. His hands stop shaking as he bobs and weaves and dances backward. His condition seems irrelevant, or at least that is the point he wants to make. He could knock you out in ten seconds. His middle looks soft until it is felt: like steel.

At the turn in the driveway he reaches the far garage and his beige-on-brown Rolls-Royce Corniche sedan. He slowly eases himself into the driver's seat, then struggles out and onto his feet again, and starts fishing in his pockets for the keys. He pulls out a set, examines them, picks a key, settles back into the car, tries to insert it into the ignition. He starts over again, pulling more sets of keys out of his deep pocket. Two sets. Three sets. Four sets. Which is it? None fit. He gets out again and walks to the rear of the car and points to the license: Virginia plates with a '93 sticker. "Haven't driven it in four years," he says. He leaves the garage and walks toward the fence, where a black Ford pickup is parked. The seat is too close to the steering wheel for him, and he has a difficult time squeezing in. It takes him a few minutes, but now he is there, behind the wheel, and he has a key that fits and the engine starts and he motions to climb in. As the truck reaches the front entrance, Ali stops, waiting for an electronic gate to open. His eyes close. He starts snoring. He can fall asleep any time of day, his doctors say, but he often only pretends to, and people around him can never be sure if he is dozing or duping.

Only a trick this time. The gate opens. The black pickup flies up the road, free and swaying. He always loved to speed. In the old days he might take the wheel of the press bus at training camp and scare the daylights out of the boxing scribes. He is doing it again. What is going on here? No reason to fear. Muhammad Ali is heading out to see the world. He is hungry, and knows what he wants: some love and affirmation and a Quarter Pounder with mustard and onions at the local McDonald's.

The love is there the moment he pulls into the parking lot. Everyone wants an autograph, and he joyfully obliges. People call him champ and hero, pat his back, shake his hand, kiss him, smile at him, show him pictures, stare at him. They talk about how much he means to them. They say they will miss him if he moves, as he and Lonnie plan to do before the year is out, down to Louisville, his hometown, where he is setting up a Muhammad Ali center. He smiles back with his eyes. No need to feel sorry for the champ, he wants you to know. "My life is a party," he says softly, chewing his Quarter Pounder. "Every day. Imagine. Every day. Things are quiet here. Imagine how it must be when I go to New York. Harlem. Detroit. Philly. Walk into a gym. The streets. Look at me. Imagine what it's like."

After lunch, Ali returns to the farm and resumes a tour of the grounds. He comes to a barn, slides open the door, and looks inside. Trophies, one bigger than the next, line the hayloft beam, gathering dust. And attached to the wall: an oversized black-and-white blowup of the young Ali, gloved hands aloft in triumph, after one of his title matches with Frazier. He stares at his own image, the greatest of all time.

People often wonder about the past; how beautiful it would be if they realized the present. Ali turns and steps out of the barn. He slides the wooden door to the right. Is it closed? He notices an opening on the left. He slides it to the left. Now there is an opening to the right. He decides to leave it that way, a ray of light filtering in, and walks down the path to his home.

Part IV

———————

The Arc Toward Home

27

Alamo Flags

San Antonio

Let's get the goldamn flag back! A Texan—who else?—issued that
vainglorious battle cry. It was in the winter of 1984, down at oilman
Claude D'Unger's place in Corpus Christi. He and an old navy pilot,
Clay Umbach, were shooting the breeze, two Sons of the Republic
reliving great moments in Texas history. Eventually they hit upon the
battle of the Alamo and a book titled *A Time to Stand*, in which the
author revealed that the flag captured by Santa Anna on the morning
of March 6, 1836, was still stored in a brown filing cabinet in the basement of Chapultepec Castle in Mexico City.

For D'Unger, the vision was painful: Imagine the battle flag of the
Alamo, symbol of Texas's victory-or-death tradition, filed away in a
dank museum chamber in that inscrutable southern land. It seemed
a hostage, not a spoil of war, and it needed to be recaptured and carried over the foreign mountains, deserts, and traditions to its rightful
place at the little mission in downtown San Antonio. What better gift,
said D'Unger, than to bring it home for the Texas Sesquicentennial,
the 150th anniversary of freedom from Mexico. That celebration is at
hand, the flag is not, and therein lies a lesson of sorts for modern Texas:
Even in this place of mythic optimism, you can't always get what you
want.

When D'Unger and Umbach sought to get the flag back, they did not organize an armed brigade and head across the Rio Grande on a liberation march.

They petitioned Congress.

"We wanted the flag so bad we knew we had to play it straight and not offend anyone," said D'Unger, an aggressive fellow by nature. "From the get-go, we damn near walked a path of appeasement with the Mexicans." Anything to get it back. Two House members from south Texas, Democrats Solomon Ortiz and Henry Gonzalez, gave their blessing to the venture, and D'Unger went on to recruit the rest of the Texas delegation and nearly a hundred members from nineteen other states. He appealed directly to patriotism and local pride. Most of the heroes of the Alamo, after all, were from elsewhere: David Crockett from Tennessee, William Travis and James Bonham from South Carolina, James Bowie from what is now Kentucky.

Texan Jim Wright, the House majority leader, suggested that it would be more appropriate to ask Mexico to return the flag on loan, rather than give it back permanently. Republican senator Phil Gramm took the hard line, saying the flag represented, in the words of press secretary Larry Neal, "what Texas is, what it was, and what it always shall remain." Gramm and other Texas politicians broached the subject with Mexico's ambassador to the United States, Jorge Espinosa de los Reyes, and diplomatic approaches were made to President de la Madrid.

Mexico, as it turned out, had heard this before. It seems that every generation of American patriots had rediscovered the Alamo flag and sought its return. Twenty-five years ago, the Texas legislature directed the state to enter into negotiations with Mexico on the flag. Governor John Connally vetoed the measure, citing a fact of which Texans often need to be reminded: Texas is a state, no longer a republic with its own diplomatic service.

In 1965, the capture-the-flag movement hit Congress. D'Unger's role was played by a wealthy real estate man from Amarillo who persuaded Senators John Tower of Texas and Sam Ervin of North Carolina to sponsor S.R. 112, in which the State Department was asked to obtain the flag's return so that it could "rest in honored glory." It was noted then that Mexico had a moral obligation because the United States under the Truman administration had returned the Mexican flag captured by its troops during the Mexican War. The Mexicans never said *sí* or no. They just kept the flag.

There are several historical points of dispute concerning the battle of the Alamo, and one is whether the banner Santa Anna sent back to Mexico City was in fact a battle flag that was flying above the mission on the morning of the slaughter. There was no Texas flag as such that day, for it had only been a few days since Texans declared independence at Washington-on-the-Brazos, an event unknown to the 188 men under siege in San Antonio. Most historians believe that there were at least two flags at the Alamo: the Mexican Flag of 1824 and the flag of the First Company of Texan Volunteers from New Orleans.

The Texas revolutionaries honored the Mexican Flag of 1824 because it symbolized the constitution that Santa Anna abandoned. But it was the New Orleans flag that Santa Anna sent to Mexico City, along with a note saying the flag proved that the Texas rebellion was being fueled by what he called "perfidious foreigners."

Charles Long, curator at the Alamo, is among those who believe that the New Orleans flag was not a battle flag but a ceremonial guidon and that Travis and his men must have flown the Flag of 1824 on that morning 150 years ago. But D'Unger disagrees, citing the diary of one of General Santa Anna's assistants, José Enrique de la Peña.

In de la Peña's account, the New Orleans flag, or something resembling it, is said to be flying over the Alamo. But if his rendition is trusted, then it follows that its account of David Crockett's exploits during the fight would have to be accepted as well. The beloved, mythologized Davy—bear tamer, congressman, Indian fighter extraordinaire—is said to have killed fifty to two hundred Mexican troops during the ninety-minute battle. No one knows for certain because the only surviving combatants were Mexicans, and to them all the coonskinned Tennesseans looked alike. Still, the legend persists. In Walt Disney's version, Fess Parker stands tall to the end, the last of the 188 heroes to fall. In several historical versions, authors state that someone "who could have been Crockett" was seen fighting off eighteen Mexicans at a time.

De la Peña tells it differently. He says that "a David Crockett, well-known naturalist from Tennessee," was among a small group of defenders who hid during the final stage of the battle and eventually surrendered, only to be executed by the enraged, despotic Santa Anna. But the Alamo must be more myth than reality. It evokes the image of valor, not the oversized souvenir shop that dominates the modern-day shrine. And so it is with the flag, regardless of history.

The last American to examine the flag was curator Long, who traveled to Mexico City in 1979. He noticed that it was no longer on display and asked its whereabouts and whether he could photograph it. "They took me down to the basement of that musty castle," Long recalled, "and we spread out some paper on the floor and then laid the flag over it. I shot down at the flag and got several pictures. It seemed tattered, but they were doing a beautiful job of restoration. It was odd-sized, with gold fringe, faded light blue-gray in color."

Long did not seek the flag's return to his museum. "My standard saying is, 'It is theirs, not ours,'" he said. "It was captured in war. Those are the rules of war."

Lest Texans get too riled over Mexico's possession of the Alamo flag, perhaps they should consider life from the other side of the river. The Mexicans want their cork leg back.

They lost it during a skirmish in the Mexican War. It was the cork leg of none other than the ubiquitous Santa Anna, who had lost his real leg during the Pastry War of 1838, an odd little military action against France that began when some Mexicans invaded a French pastry shop in Veracruz, locked up the proprietor, and ate his goods. Santa Anna lost a leg, then gave it a full burial, and got an artificial one made of cork.

Around noon on April 18, 1847, Santa Anna was with his troops near Cerro Gordo. He was sitting in his carriage; the horses were untied. The battle, or so the general presumed, was being carried out some distance away, so he settled down for a picnic lunch of roast chicken. He took off his cork leg, for it was uncomfortable to wear it in the carriage. Then, suddenly from the brush appeared a regiment of men from the Illinois Third. The volunteers rushed toward the carriage. One of Santa Anna's aides carried him off on horseback before he could be captured. The carriage was left behind. The Fighting Illini wolfed down the roast chicken, pocketed some gold doubloons they found on the carriage floor, and sped off with the cork leg. It remained in the possession of three soldiers from Pekin, Illinois, who took it home after the war and used it to make money.

They traveled from town to town in the Land of Lincoln, charging folks ten cents a peek at the artificial leg of the famed Mexican general. Eventually the cork leg was placed in the trust of the state, and for a century it rested unseen in a vault in one of the executive office buildings in Springfield. All efforts by Mexico to get the cork leg back were rebuffed. The Illinois General Assembly almost handed it back during a special session in 1942, but the Democratic-backed resolution was ridiculed by the Republicans, who said that if the measure passed, "the Democrats won't have a leg to stand on."

In 1970, Colonel Carl Johnson, director of public affairs for the Military and Naval Department of Illinois, was asked to set up a museum display of military artifacts at the Camp Lincoln Illinois Military History Museum in Springfield. He hauled Santa Anna's leg out of the vault and put it on display, where it has been ever since. Johnson recently got a call from officials in Texas, who said they wanted the cork leg for their sesquicentennial. "I'm not sure if it's going anywhere," he said. "It's ours, you know."

28

Roadside Distraction

New Orleans

Dead animals on the side of the road are an unfortunate part of American mobility, so much so that the other day, as I was driving northwest along Interstate 10 between New Orleans and Baton Rouge, it took me a while to realize the magnitude of the carnage passing before my eyes. For a mile or more, the carcasses must have been registering only in my subconscious, as though they were telephone poles or night reflectors—five, ten, fifteen, twenty. Then I reached a dead animal tolerance threshold, and the decaying lumps took on a new and tragic meaning. I saw the slaughter in its totality (death everywhere, by the score, evoking a battlefield) and in its individualism. As the dead animals became real and thus important to me, I was struck by something else—I had no idea what they were. They might have been muskrats, but they were too big; or small beavers, but for their rodentlike tails.

And so it was, out of nausea and concern, that I learned the improbable story of Louisiana's nutria.

Nutria is Spanish for fish otter, and if nature had been left alone—that is a big if; it rarely is—these creatures would not encounter many highways. Their native habitat is among the remote rivers, ponds, and marshlands of Argentina and Chile. They are brown-furred, twenty-pound, web-footed, herbivorous rodents. And while they do resemble beavers and muskrats, they have an exclusive place in the animal world as the only members of their family, the Myocastoridae. They are also known as coypu, Greek for mouse and beaver and the preferred designation of biologists.

Their fur, though hardly in the mink category, is of some value, and that is how and why they got to Louisiana.

In the 1930s, modest numbers of them were introduced to North America and Europe for breeding. Among the experimental breeders was E. A. McIlhenny, millionaire Tabasco sauce baron and naturalist, who secured twenty nutria from a friend in Buenos Aires and penned them at his place on Avery Island on the Louisiana coast south of New Iberia.

McIlhenny was just starting his nutria fur farm when a hurricane struck: Who could have imagined then that the most permanent environmental effect of that storm would be the release of a small number of nutria into the marshy wild? To say that they took to south Louisiana—with its vast wetlands and temperate climate—would be an understatement. From their hurricane-emancipated past, the nutria population exploded into the millions, reaching a peak of perhaps twenty million by the late 1960s. Greg Lipscombe, a research biologist at the Louisiana Department of Wildlife and Fisheries, said exponential growth of that sort is common among exotic animals when they are placed in an

Nutria

environment that suits their lifestyle and is at least temporarily void of natural enemies.

Nutria had escaped or been released from farms in several parts of the country, but in most places the climate and geography conspired to kill them off after a few years. They cannot stand cold weather—their tails have been known to freeze and fall off after a few days below twenty degrees. But for better or worse, they thrived down here, especially in what is known as Cajun country, the geocultural trapezium whose points are New Orleans, Houma, Cameron, and Lafayette. At times they have thrown the ecology out of balance, gnawing at sugar and rice crops, damaging marshes by overeating the aquatic vegetation, and pushing the muskrat out of its natural habitat.

But the population has been controlled to some extent by trapping. In Louisiana, which, despite its dominant oil rigs and petrochemical plants, has some justification in calling itself the Sportsman's Paradise, trapping is not only permitted but encouraged for both economic and ecological purposes.

"People think nature controls these things," said Lipscombe. "Well, that is true and not true. Nature will eventually control it, but the population can build to such levels that it denudes the environment before it crashes. By the time nature controls it, the damage has been done. That's why we believe very strongly in managing the population by trying to promote the fur."

While the reddish brown nutria fur has never been popular in the United States, it developed a strong following in parts of Europe, where women use it for fur coats and gloves. Furriers praise the nutria coat especially for its warmth and the ease with which it can be dyed. Because of its ability to meet Europe's nutria demand, Louisiana has emerged in recent years as the No. 1 fur-trapping state in the country. Of the two million wild pelts the state provides each year—including muskrat, raccoon, bobcat, red and gray fox, and beaver—about 1.3 million are nutria. The trapping of most of those other animals is controversial even here, but for some reason no one seems too concerned about trapping the nutria. Rare is the creature that provokes disinterest in the environmental world, but this rodent comes close. Most naturalists consider it a pest whose introduction into North America has done more harm than good.

Perhaps that is true—for everyone but the six thousand backwater

Cajuns who live off the land catching nutria and alligators. The trapping season begins in December, when the nutria fur thickens for winter, and lasts until mid-February. Entire families move into the marsh and work together as units in large trapping camps. The children are let out of school for those two months and bring homework with them.

The price of nutria has declined in recent years from a high of fifteen dollars to today's four dollars per pelt, prompting some trappers to concentrate on alligators and shrimp. That may answer part of the riddle "Why did the nutria cross the road?" It could be overpopulation in that area, or it could be that one side of the marsh was drying up for lack of rainfall. It could be that they were forced from burrows by chemicals dumped illegally on roadsides at night—the not unheard-of practice known as midnight dumping.

In any case, the nutria, slow-moving waddlers not known for their brainpower, are making a mess of things on the roadside. "I don't want to sound cold about it, but it's been going on for years," said state wildlife official Dave John. "The dang things just can't get to the other side."

29

Dad and Ron Santo

One of the joys of visiting my parents in Wisconsin during the final years of their lives was rummaging through the wide-ranging collection of magazines and newspapers that piled up on their couch and spilled over to the floor below. The *Nation* and the *Packer Report*. The *New Yorker* and the *Sporting News*. The *New York Review of Books* and *ESPN the Magazine*. The *Progressive* and the *Packer Plus*. The *American Prospect* and *Baseball America*. The *Capital Times* and *Sports Illustrated*. The *Washington Post National Weekly Edition* and *Baseball Weekly*. If you wanted to know about my dad, Elliott Maraniss, his reading tastes told much of the story.

A lifelong newspaperman, he was always interested in history and politics. The books he checked out from the local library and stacked near the magazine pile tended to be about European writers, Civil War generals, American presidents, British diplomats. But what satisfied him as much or more, I think, was reading about a rookie defensive tackle showing promise in training camp with the Green Bay Packers or another phenom left fielder out in El Paso (when the Diablos were in the Brewers farm system) who was knocking the stuffing out of the ball. Earl Warren, the former chief justice of the United States, was known, among his other greater accomplishments, for saying that when he got the newspaper in the morning, he turned to the sports section before the front page. I'm not sure that sports came first with my dad, but he certainly turned to it most often.

He was not a statistics guy. He had little interest in the Sabermetrics approach to baseball analysis in which everything is reduced to numbers. He loved baseball more as a story with characters and drama. It didn't have to be elegiac, or melodramatic, or even particularly elegant. Maybe that's because he spent his adolescence in Coney Island rooting for the Brooklyn Dodgers when they were the "Lovable Bums." (Family legend has it that he was holding me and listening on the radio when Bobby Thomson hit the home run, and dropped me in disgust—or maybe he just threw some crackers.) His baseball was the sort described by Mark Harris in *Bang the Drum Slowly* and *The Southpaw*. Just salt-of-the-earth kids, some dumb, some smart, making their way through the vagaries of baseball life. He was from the Ring Lardner school. I had a tendency to make things up when I was a kid and had an excuse for every wrong thing I did. My dad called me Alibi Ike long before I realized that he was at once chewing me out and letting me know that he loved me. In my family, where my mother and siblings were scholars, "The sun got in my eyes" held as much literary merit as any quotation from Shakespeare.

There were some apparent contradictions in my dad's view of sports. As a tough-minded journalist, he was fearless in pushing reporters to challenge the traditional wisdom of coaches. He was always skeptical, questioning whether universities were running honest programs and whether sports icons were all they proclaimed to be. He took pride in the fact that one of his reporters at the *Capital Times* in Madison broke a story that Bob Knight was leaving West Point to coach at the University of Wisconsin, and that Knight got so upset by the scoop—it was supposed to be kept secret for two days—that he backed away from the deal. Untold thousands of Badger fans who endured decades of losing seasons at the UW Field House in the ensuing decades might have felt that the story wasn't worth all that suffering, but in fact the wound-tight Knight never would have fit in Madison anyway. Elliott also hired the first woman sportswriter at the newspaper, and the first African American sportswriter, and he was constantly pushing at the traditions of the profession. Even though he was born in Boston, he taught me never to root for the Red Sox, because they were the last major-league team to integrate. His preference for the National League

in the 1950s and 1960s was due in large part to the league's more progressive recruitment of black and Latino players, from Jackie Robinson
to Hank Aaron to Roberto Clemente to Rico Carty to Felipe Alou,
those last two among his favorite hitters from the last days of the Milwaukee Braves.

Yet in his personal tastes, when he was on the side porch in his
boxer shorts and T-shirt listening to a ball game on the radio on a summer's night, his preferences ran completely to the babbling, incoherent,
lovable homers. The newfangled announcers were either too bland or
narrow-mindedly aggressive, from his perspective. He even had the
temerity to criticize Vin Scully, who was one notch too glib for him.
To be completely honest, his disdain for Scully might also have had
to do with the fact that Scully sashayed out of Brooklyn with Walter
O'Malley and made his name with the new Dodgers in Los Angeles,
and that marked him as a traitor, but I still think my dad would rather
hear Harry Caray or Jack Brickhouse obliterate the English language
than listen to Scully recite a perfectly literate paragraph without so
much as an "er" or an "uh." He felt that announcers like Caray and
Brickhouse and Lou Boudreau weren't making more out of the game
than what it was; they were closer to Ring Lardner and Mark Harris.

Which brings me to the balm of Ron Santo.

Many people, even some Cubs fans I know, might make the reasonable argument that Ron Santo, the old third baseman, ranks among
the least articulate announcers ever to call a game. He made Caray,
even in his drunken dotage, seem erudite. My dad would agree, but
could not care less. He loved Ron Santo, first as an underrated ballplayer, but even more as the voice of Cubs radio with his partner, Pat
Hughes. Anyone can call balls and strikes, or offer an astute observation on the erratic play of the second baseman during a road trip in
June, or coin some distinctive way of calling a home run, but who
besides Santo can produce so many central European guttural sounds
of agony as his team is on its way to blowing another game? *Ahhhhhh-
hhhrrrgggguuuuuuuuhhhhgggooooh.*

For most of his life, Elliott lived by the motto "It could be worse."
That was in the real world. In the world of baseball his sensibility was
that it was going to get worse, no matter how good things seem right
now, and Santo was his favorite poet of imminent demise. From homer
to Homer.

I'll never forget what Santo did for my dad one July day in 2001 when Elliott was starting to show his own first signs of mortality. He and my mother had taken a Badger bus from Milwaukee to visit my wife and me in Madison, where we were spending the summer researching a book on the Vietnam era. As my dad stepped down off the bus, he said, "Dave, I'm sick. I've got to get to bed right away." We drove across town to the house and put my dad on a cot with a radio. The Cubs were playing a day game. I can't remember anymore who they were playing, either the Phillies or Cards, I think. I do remember the Cubs were leading 10–1 in the third or fourth inning. And as soon as my dad heard the score, he muttered, "Uh-oh. The Cubs are gonna blow it." For the next two hours, Elliott and Santo were on the same wavelength. Santo moaning, my dad laughing, as the Cubs did what they were destined to do and relinquished a nine-run lead. I was as into the game as either of them, but didn't care about the score or the final result. What made me deliriously happy was how much joy Santo was unwittingly bringing to my ailing dad. What drug, what surgical operation, what wisdom from what physician, what felicitous phrase from the Santo antipode Vin Scully could have been better treatment for a sick old baseball guy? The answer is absolutely none. Two hours of joy and laughter, and he was up and ready for dinner.

30

Uncle Phil's Brain

My mother was newly married and living in New York when she learned of the mental breakdown of her brother, Philip Dever Cummins. Sixty years later, the moment remained fixed in her memory. She was sitting on a bed in the living room of their cramped apartment, reading a letter from her mother in Ann Arbor. The report from home was at once warm, understated, and devastating. Irrational behavior. Depression. Hospitalization. All of it took my mother by surprise. A great sadness washed over her, and she began weeping for her brother and how terrible it must have been for him.

There is a story of mental illness in almost every family. My uncle Phil is the central character of ours, the foremost troubled mind emerging from our particular mix of history and genetics. Many relatives were burdened by depression or other disorders before and after him, but Phil carried the heaviest load. He was, in a sense, the exaggeration of us all. The same impulses that others struggled with occasionally, but that could be controlled or concealed enough for them to function in everyday society, overwhelmed him much of his life, starting with that long-ago spring when he was hospitalized at age twenty-two for what experts today might classify as schizoid affective disorder.

By the time I got to know him, when I was about eleven, Phil was living with my grandparents at their modern farmhouse on the western edge of Ann Arbor. He had his own hideaway room in the basement, down the hall from the white lift-up freezer where my grandmother kept her black-walnut cookies. When we visited at Christmas or on summer vacation, the bedrooms filled quickly and I'd be sent down to Phil's room to sleep on a cot. I considered it an honor to be let into his special space. It signified that my uncle approved of me, which meant something, because he did not approve of much. Some of my strongest childhood memories are of nights spent in that dark subterranean lair: Phil on the edge of his bed, flicking the drooping end of his cigarette onto a ridged white saucer, soft yellow light filtering from his radio, his brow furrowed, a faint smile taking shape, and then a series of questions, beginning with, "Dave, who has the strongest arm from right to third: Kaline, Clemente, or Colavito?" I was amazed and secretly heartened by the way he took my answers seriously.

I had only a vague awareness then of the dimensions of Phil's mental history. My family had a strong humanist tradition that honored every person, and preferred poetic souls to self-satisfied ones, so this was not a matter of shame. There was nothing to hide in that respect, no embarrassment about having a crazy uncle. But along with the family's sensitivity came a powerful respect for privacy and a tendency to avoid acknowledgment of irreversible pain. My mother is the sort who would apologize and say it was her fault if you backed a car over her foot. It was from those impulses that Phil's story was left mostly untold.

There were some obvious ways that he differed from other adult males in the family. He never married. He lived with his parents. He did not work regularly and kept odd hours, often staying in his room during daylight and then shuffling through the house in the middle of the night in his robe and slippers. His brown hair was usually wet and slicked back. He sometimes seemed to be chuckling at a joke understood only by him. I heard him now and then criticizing, or even ridiculing, my little grandmother, which simply was not done. But almost all that I knew about his history of hospitalization came from a few color slides among the scores of family scenes that my grandfather would show us on his projector. They were of Phil standing in the countryside near an old bridge in a faraway place. I was told they were taken when my grandparents visited him during his long stay in North Carolina.

An old brochure describes such a beautiful place: Highland Hospital. Asheville, North Carolina. From the grounds Phil looked out on a vista of "nearby hills, with their soft green slopes, gradually blending with the more distant, rugged ranges till the skyline is broken by the pearly haze of far-off peaks." From the tap he drank water of "crystalline clearness, perfect purity, complete softness and cool mountain freshness." At the cafeteria his body was nourished with a "rational, scientific, wholesome, vitamin-rich, yet dainty, dietary." From the moment he arrived at the hospital in 1941, Phil was in the care of "a corps of over a hundred workers" overseen by Duke University professors of neuropsychiatry who believed they could determine the "present disorder and its causative factors" and then provide treatment for "the removal of both cause and effect." The regimen included frequent examinations and discussions, regular hardball games between two teams of patients and doctors—the Blues and the Golds—light gardening and farming, work in the storehouse, hikes in the hills, horseshoes, table tennis, volleyball, board games, and dances.

Such serene surroundings, such a healthy environment. But for every sign of improvement there came a corresponding spell of despair. When Phil's mood and behavior worsened, doctors would jolt him back with insulin shock therapy and electric shock treatments. The positive results in every case proved ephemeral. He remained hospitalized for seventeen years, the prime of his life, during which time the cause and effect of his troubles persisted and the only thing removed was part of his brain.

It was only recently, several years after Phil's death, that I began to appreciate the daily struggle of his long stay in Asheville. My awakening came when my aunt Jean, the family genealogist, sent me a box of documents from Phil's life. Inside were letters to Phil from his parents (my grandparents, Andrew and Grace Cummins) and a lesser number of letters from Phil to them, as well as voluminous correspondence between my grandparents and various doctors at Highland Hospital. In some ways these papers seem anachronistic, evoking a time long gone from the mental health scene. The transforming world of psychotropic drugs was yet to be discovered. Doctors resorted more often to long-term institutionalization and such things as seizure-inducing shock treatments, often performed without anesthesia. The diagnostic vocabulary psychiatrists used then also had an archaic ring, the words less technical, more poetic. (In their reports on Phil, they often noted that he was "too philosophical in his thinking.") But the story that emerges from that box is timeless nonetheless. There can be nothing outdated about a wounded mind and a family trying desperately to mend it.

Among the scores of letters, one provides the context for the others. It was from Phil to his parents, postmarked April 2, 1945. He was twenty-seven then and entering his fourth year at the hospital. The previous fall he had sent a fairly upbeat letter home describing his daily routine, but then followed five months of silence. Now the explanation, the most thorough written account of his despair:

> *Dear Mom and Dad,*
>
> *I am sorry to be so tardy in writing you, but it is difficult when one feels that anything one has to say is going to be a burden on the reader. I only hope that things aren't actually as bad or rather as hopeless as they seem to me at present. I know that one should be careful in saying a thing like this. I could go on writing about what is going on here, baseball, work, etc., but that would be just holding back on the things that are uppermost in my mind. For I have been feeling pretty terrible and despondent for a long time now and without any signs of improvement. Dr. Billig [Otto Billig, Highland Hospital's chief psychiatrist] says that he is convinced that I have improved greatly and am still getting better, but to tell you the truth, I feel worse than I did when I came down here and that after four years of so-called hospitalization, I just feel that I am doomed to gradual incapacitation of a more or less general nature, being regarded as something of a subhuman species halfway between a gorilla and a man. For I am pretty much all by myself in the world, have difficulty making friends and adjusting myself with no ideas practically, nothing to say and getting no enjoyment or satisfaction out of anything I do. I am also tired most of the time, worried, apprehensive, and very unhappy. It's just downright torture, that's all it is.*

One shudders to imagine being a parent reading that letter from your son. Not much room for encouragement, but my grandfather, a construction engineer, searched his rational mind for angles of hope. In his next letter to Phil, he argued that the brutally realistic nature of Phil's self-analysis in itself represented an improvement from the bizarre and delusional behavior that had led to his hospitalization in the first place. "To have reached that point has been a wonderful accomplishment," Grandfather wrote. With enough effort and time, he said, "a reasonable amount of happiness would come, although nobody probably is happy all of the time." He noted that tests showed that Phil had an exceptionally high IQ of 150, meaning that he "could accomplish a lot worthwhile for society" as soon as he felt secure and confident. To counter Phil's sense of being alone in the world, he recited a list of his son's old friends and then argued, "After all one only has a very few real friends." And he closed the letter by inviting Phil back to Ann Arbor for a visit. The peas, radishes, and onions were up.

Phil eventually got away from Asheville for three weeks. According to a letter Grandfather later wrote to Dr. Billig, the visit to Ann Arbor was normal and routine, at least on the surface. He saw his brothers and sisters, talked about his condition, went to shows, bowled, played table tennis and bridge, went to basketball and hockey games at the University of Michigan, and "voluntarily helped around the house." He also spent "quite a bit of time" reading Thomas Mann's *The Magic Mountain* in German. Perhaps Asheville was his Davos.

As engaged as he was in Ann Arbor, Phil could not forget his worries. "On the whole his sense of well-being was not good," his father reported. "He complained of headaches and tiredness and evidently thinks a lot about his difficulties." He was indeed a chronic hypochondriac, a trait that would later become all too familiar to many of his younger relatives, including my brother, Jim, and me and several of our children. During Phil's visit home, he read his father's magazines and took particular note of insurance company ads from which he would get "ideas about physical ailments" and "magnify the symptoms." He also read an article about mental illness in *Newsweek* that reinforced his feelings about the hopelessness of his situation and left him further depressed.

My grandfather suffered from minor depression himself and had reached some conclusions over the years about the best way to counteract it. For the most part he had been successful, at least to the extent that he rarely showed his inner struggle to his family or society. In letters to his son, one can see him hoping upon hope that what worked for him could help someone he loved who was in a far more debilitating mental state. One night in February 1946, after paying a working visit to a Morton Salt plant in Manistee, Michigan, he took out the desk stationery from the Hotel Chippewa and wrote his son a letter filled with his homegrown psychology. It read in part:

> *I would suggest that you concentrate the mind on something other than yourself. You will feel better and time will go faster. I found that out at the hospital when I was hurting. Effort I believe will make it possible to minimize the pain due to trouble or any other reason. You know Phil if in your letters you did not say you were having trouble one would never know it. I am not saying that as a suggestion that you don't mention it, in fact I want you to feel entirely free to say just what you do feel. I mentioned it only to emphasize how rational, reasonable, sympathetic and intelligent your letters are. You know what FDR said during the Depression viz. "The only thing we have to fear is fear itself" and I believe that applies in your case. The biggest obstacle confronting you is the fear you have of the future. Yet your I.Q., your general conduct and ability it seems to me does not warrant that belief. In any case don't give up. Also try to see as many funny things in life as you can . . . I'm making a collection of jokes. Tell me any new ones you have heard. Here is one for you . . .*

He then recounted a corny old story involving the producer Darryl Zanuck and a would-be actor who stuttered. If only a joke collection could have been enough.

The next several months were better for Phil, but he took another turn for the worse in the summer of 1946, a regression documented month by month in reports from the Highland doctors to my grandfather. First, a report that Phil exhibited "a sense of unreality." Next he was showing "great concern about other people's influence upon him." By September he was displaying "bizarre behavior" that compelled the staff to confine him to the building and resume treatments of sub-shock doses of insulin. All of this was received with ever deeper sadness and concern by my grandparents, who refused to give up hope that some treatment could return Phil to a relatively normal life. In the spring of 1947, my grandfather's search for cures led him to ask, for the first time, about the possibility of a brain operation. In a letter to Dr. Billig, he asked: "Do you think that this holds any promise in his case and does such a procedure call for a special diagnosis as well as special surgery available only at certain hospitals?"

Literature teems with tales from asylums and mental hospitals that are cold or brutal warehouses where patients are mistreated or regarded as the very "subhuman species" that Phil feared he had become. Highland Hospital seems not to fall into that category. As I examined the letters sent to my grandparents, it struck me from both the frequency and the substance of their reports that these doctors cared about Phil and were doing the best they could, given what their profession understood about mental illness at the time and the limited number of treatments available. Without being overly harsh or fatalistic, they grasped the seriousness of Phil's condition and the uncertainty of his recovery. Dr. Billig, in responding to the question about brain surgery, confessed that after treating Phil for more than five years, he was "somewhat at a loss" about the best course of action. The shock treatments seemed to have lost some effectiveness, he said, but a brain operation, while successful in some cases, was usually recommended for psychoses "of a somewhat different type." He nonetheless told my grandfather that it was worth exploring further, and passed along the name of a specialist in Washington.

Two weeks later, another Highland psychiatrist, Dr. Joseph Goldstein, sent a report to Ann Arbor stating that he and others on the staff did not consider Phil a suitable candidate for a lobotomy:

> *The operation as a rule is hardly to be considered seriously for one who has been making a fairly good hospital adjustment, such as Phil has been doing. It certainly usually is reserved for cases showing much more behavior disturbance. Also, it should be borne in mind that the operation, even with the most favorable response, tends to have certain side-effects, such as impairment in ability to plan, difficulties in initiative, tendencies to impulsiveness, child-like behavior at times etc., as well as, of course, certain risks and expenses associated with the operation itself.*

But as Phil's condition worsened early that summer, the Highland doctors changed course again. What had been deemed no longer effective (electric shock) or unpromising (brain surgery) were back in the mix. They told my grandfather that they had been using a "more intensive" form of shock treatment recently, and they explained, "By intensive, we mean decreasing the time interval between the treatments." There was no change in the total number of treatments or the intensity of each treatment. "It may possibly only have a temporary effect," Dr. Edward A. Tyler wrote, "but would give us some idea as to what we might expect from a prefrontal lobotomy, if that became necessary at a later date." The alternative, in Tyler's opinion, was to place Phil in the "locked section in the back hall." Some choice.

And so the cycle of hope and despair continued. Two weeks after my grandfather gave Highland permission to perform intensive electric shock treatments, he received a positive report from Dr. Tyler. There had been a "marked change" in Phil. He was now said to be "very friendly, cooperative, outgoing . . . again and neat and clean" and played "an excellent game of baseball on the Fourth of July." The optimistic outlook in this case was even shared by Phil himself, who wrote an optimistic letter to my parents—his sister and brother-in-law. It began:

> *Dear Mary and Elliott,*
>
> *How are you people after all these months? I sure would like to see you and the old homeland again before long, at least for a little while. I hope that you are all actually in good health and spirits and are enjoying life.*
>
> *The folks in Ann Arbor have undoubtedly told you something of what has been going on lately with me. The electric shock treatments which Dr. Tyler gave me are proving very effective in a real way (that is, a way that I can feel and understand).*

He was feeling better than at any time since he was a kid, Phil told my parents. In his unforgettable letter of despair two years earlier, he had refused to write about his daily activities in Asheville because they would only mask deeper feelings of hopelessness. Now he was eager to tell relatives what he was doing: how he hit a double over the center fielder's head and made only one error at second base and shot a bull's-eye in archery from forty yards out and couldn't wait to start pitching horseshoes again, just like he had done in his childhood, recalling the days in Jackson, Michigan, when he and his brother Bob would play at "the neighborhood courts down the street from Judy's toward E. Sharp Park"—and the time when he threw twelve straight ringers.

Phil's brighter outlook led to another visit home. A hospital caretaker put him on a Delta Air Lines flight to Detroit that landed at eight on the evening of August 11. For the one-week visit, the family was under instructions to "just treat him as though he had been in the hospital for a physical illness and was at home for a short period before his recuperation." He played golf, visited some college friends, and spent two days in Detroit visiting my parents. In a letter back to the doctors, my grandfather reported that Phil "talked freely about the electric shock treatments and seemed to be thinking some of the future"—all good signs.

Then, in November, another unfortunate turn. Phil was doing a lot of "fantastic thinking" and was said to be "entirely too philosophical in his thinking." Month after month of dispiriting reports followed. In early 1948 another of his doctors, B. T. Bennett, reported that Phil was "no longer receptive to the idea" of more electric shock treatments. The staff was now giving careful thought to a prefrontal lobotomy, but remained uncertain, Bennett said, because Phil exhibited two quite different disorders. His more debilitating behavior, which they called hebephrenia—characterized by delusions and inappropriate laughing— probably would not respond to brain surgery, they said, whereas the operation might be more effective in treating his obsessive-compulsive behavior.

My grandparents wrote back that as sad as the news was, they were grateful for the detailed explanation of their son's condition. They wondered what a lobotomy entailed and how much it cost. The price they got back was between $1,000 and $1,200, including hospital fees. As the year neared an end, Phil was examined by Dr. R. Burke Suitt, a brain surgeon at Duke, who concluded that the most effective operation would be not a lobotomy but a topectomy, which involved the removal of "a small amount of tissue on either side of the front part of the brain surface." If successful, it could "produce a relaxation of the patient's fears and tension, permitting him to express himself more spontaneously and relieving the general pressure under which he lives his life."

They operated on Phil's brain in January 1949, the year I was born.

He was flown up to New York City, where the operation was performed by Dr. J. Lawrence Pool at the Neurological Institute of Columbia-Presbyterian Medical Center. It took three hours. The next day, Phil was "reading magazines, books, and feeling much better," and within a week he made "an uneventful and happy" return to Asheville, where he was examined again and found to be "more spontaneous in expressing his feelings, and his repetitious and philosophical examination of his own thoughts were definitely lessening." There were few of the feared side effects. He took more interest in his appearance, ditching the beret he had worn during his delusional periods and expressing a desire for a new suit and hat. But one doctor, William W. Magruder, did notice that Phil seemed bored with the hospital routine. "If it is just being tired of five years of the same thing, that is good. If it is losing interest in his surroundings, that is not good."

Which was it? His parents visited Asheville in late March. Phil told his doctors that he thought the trip was too short, that everything seemed rushed, but that he enjoyed the company. If he did, his parents could hardly tell. "When Mrs. Cummins and I were there . . . we could not talk to him at all," my grandfather noted in a letter to the doctors a few weeks later. Yet within a few weeks, Phil was sociable enough to begin working outside the hospital at a frame shop in downtown Asheville. Reports from the owner, Gene Rezutto, that summer indicated that Phil was an excellent employee. With the exception of a few seizures, treated with Dilantin, the rest of 1949 was relatively stable for Phil. He took a vacation to Kill Devil Hills, North Carolina, with "an attractive companion," and made another trip home, where my grandfather noticed what he called a "sweet reasonableness" interrupted only by a moment of high tension "due possibly to the three harum-scarum children who were visiting." My grandfather was particularly heartened by the way Phil made decisions during the stay, including setting up an appointment with the dentist and making his own arrangements for the return to Asheville.

By this point, as I read letters in the box, I was rooting so hard for Phil that I could not bear more disappointing news, but here it was: May 16, 1950, a letter from Dr. Magruder to my grandfather and the line "Things have not gone as smoothly with Phil as I had hoped they would." He had visited Phil at the frame shop, and found him "not working but standing gazing at a picture." He seemed utterly unresponsive to the people around him. Mr. Rezutto said that Phil was becoming increasingly difficult to work with, exhibiting "a great deal of inappropriate laughter and behavior." He refused simple requests, treating them like orders, which he hated. He was let go and returned to the hospital grounds. And that is how it went for the next eight years—brief periods of hope and temporary freedom followed by relapses, with no permanent breakthroughs. He worked in the cafeteria until the head dietitian complained that he was inflexible. He tried selling hosiery, but could not get many orders. He went to a training program in Kansas City for a month, and finished among the top ten in a class of fifty-five students, but no jobs resulted. When he filled out an employment application for United Airlines, he added a supplemental page that began by noting that "due to nature of fathers' work during twenties and thirties, we moved from city to city quite often, consequently I attended an unusual number of elementary and high schools"—and then went on to list the schools and dates in meticulous detail. No job there either.

The letters end in 1958. He was by then nearing the end of his second decade in the hospital. Seventeen years lost—from before Pearl Harbor to the approach of JFK's New Frontier, virtually all of his twenties and thirties. Finally, when my grandparents moved into the new house at the farm, he left Asheville for good and came home to Ann Arbor. That is when I got to know him, when I was sent down to bed in his mystical basement hideout. Saying "when I got to know him" is not quite right. I thought I knew him, because he was my blood uncle and he treated me with respect and I liked him, and as I grew older I even romanticized him. But I didn't have a clue until I looked through that box of papers that Aunt Jean sent me. I am haunted by one letter. Not the 1945 letter of despair to his father, which is heartbreaking enough, but the note that he sent to my parents two years later, the one in which he remembers throwing twelve straight ringers.

That image makes me weep, much as my mother wept in Manhattan. I can hear the iron clang of a horseshoe hitting a rusted pole and thudding to earth, a winner. And I can see Phil chuckling softly, nothing inappropriate about his laughter, and squinting his eyes. Here he is the unbroken child, not doomed, not incapacitated, not with nothing to say, brilliant and athletic. My uncle. Many years after he left Asheville, I saw him toss consecutive ringers at the horseshoe pit between the peach orchard and the vineyard at my grandfather's farm. I wish that I could freeze that moment forever and say, This is Phil, as he grasps the horseshoe at an angle and loops his arm back and strides forward and the crescent sails in a perfect arc toward home.

31

The Sweet Long Days

On the afternoon of my tenth birthday, in August 1959, my friends and I rode our bikes down to Vilas Park in Madison, Wisconsin, to play with my favorite present. It was a new baseball, which came in the mail after my parents sent in a coupon from Red Dot Potato Chips along with a ten-dollar check. I remember how giddy I was when I first rolled the ball around in my hands and read the markings on its shiny white cover. There, in cursive scrawl, were the signatures of the great Milwaukee Braves: Aaron, Mathews, Spahn, Burdette, Buhl, Covington, Bruton, Crandall. Three Hall of Famers graced that ball, yet the thought of stashing it away in a drawer for safekeeping or mounting it for display never crossed my mind. Baseballs were for playing, and this new ball was the only one we had, so we took it down to the park and used it to play five hundred.

Five hundred was the least inventive of the many games we played, but one of our mainstays nonetheless, because it allowed us to chatter and tease and hang together yet still be ruthlessly competitive. While one guy hit grounders and flies, the rest of us congregated in a heckling mass out in the field, moving in or back depending on the hitter's power, scrapping and blocking and tripping one another to field the ball. You got twenty-five points for snagging a grounder, fifty points for a one-bouncer, a hundred for a fly, and minus the same amounts

for an error. The first to five hundred hit next. For anyone shudder-
ing at the thought of mindless boys ruining a collector's treasure by
pounding the prized signatures on the birthday baseball into unread-
able smudges, it should be noted that the game ended swiftly, before
any of us reached five hundred.

Winkie saw to that. Winkie was Madison's best-known resident, the
elephant at the Henry Vilas Zoo. She lived by herself on the western
edge of the old-fashioned zoo, whose small cages and limited spaces
must have been an outrage to animal rights advocates, although they
gave the place an accessible charm. Like the rest of the city, Vilas Zoo
had a free and unimposing air. It was situated right in the park, with
no fancy entrances separating it from the expanse of grass, dirt infields,
and picnic tables leading out along the Lake Wingra lagoon. All the
diamonds were occupied on that long-ago August afternoon, and five
hundred did not require bases in any case, so we found our own playing field between a big elm tree and the Elephant House. Without considering the consequences, we placed the batter down by the big elm
with the high green bars of Winkie's outdoor cage looming far behind
the fielders like the outfield wall at Milwaukee County Stadium.

My friend Frank Roloff batted first and last. Frank was strong and
nearly blind in one eye. His performance against live pitching was
uneven, but when he got hold of the ball, it really flew. I can still see
him tossing the ball in the air, whiffing, picking it up, tossing it again,
whiffing again, picking it up, tossing—crack! Bobby Freed and Dave
Roloff and Johnny Richards and I all look up as the birthday ball soars
over our heads, bounces a few times, and rolls through the green bars,
coming to a stop near a bale of hay. And there stands Winkie, her
wrinkled gray trunk looping and swaying, looping and swaying, until
finally she cradles the foreign object in a curlicue of rubbery trunk and
picks it up and stuffs it into her mouth. She chews a few times and the
ball comes hurtling out, landing on the cement so tattered and mis-
shapen that it does not even bounce. Just splat! Like soggy shredded
wheat. And that is all there is of my prized present, and the guys are
laughing, and finally I comprehend what has happened, and why, and
how typically careless I have been, and though it hurts I smile along,
until soon we all fall to the grass in a fit of mass hysteria, giggling and
snorting about how Winkie ate my baseball.

When that memory came back to me recently, my first impulse was to wonder where my parents were and why they didn't stop us from playing with the autographed ball. Then I realized that the reality of my childhood, the dominant theme of my youth, was that my friends and I grew up almost free from adult pressure or influence, good or bad. It wasn't the anarchy of *Lord of the Flies,* and there was nothing whimsically fantastical about it like *Peter Pan,* it was just the way we lived in Madison during our baby-boom youths of the late fifties to midsixties. Time let us play and be golden then, as Dylan Thomas wrote—or maybe it was our parents who let us.

There were no soccer moms or Little League dads. We defined and lived in our own world. Our landscape covered a square mile or two framed by the tunnels at Camp Randall Stadium on the east, the diving board at the Willows on Lake Mendota on the north, the reservoir at Hoyt Park on the west, and Vilas Park and Lake Wingra on the south. Within that territory we were native scouts who roamed free on our bikes (one speed, foot brakes, wobbly handlebars). We knew every shortcut, every grouchy old lady and loose dog to avoid, every patch of grass that could become a football field, every brick wall that could serve as a backstop for a game of broom ball, and every backboard where we could play H-O-R-S-E, the winner earning the right, in our fantasies, to kiss Ellen Dillinger or Sally Ylitalo.

I certainly have nothing against the parents of today who spend their weekends in minivans hauling gangs of uniformed kids from one organized sport to another, who slip out of work early on weekday afternoons to watch their daughters or sons compete. They are usually doing it as an expression of love, trying to show that despite their busy lives they can find quality time for their children. Some might even be motivated by what they see as a deficiency in their own childhood, wanting not to repeat the cycle of an absent father who never watched a son's game. When my own son played baseball, I tried never to miss it, and one year I became so obsessed with showing him I cared that I attended virtually every practice. Yet I hold absolutely no grudge against my own parents. I know they loved me. It was just something about that time and place that allowed them and the other parents to stay away with no apparent psychological bruising on either side of the equation.

Childhood in Madison was for children. There was no Little League in our part of town, the near-west side. We played in the city league, which was overseen benignly by the recreation department. No adults were acting out fantasies of being major-league managers or general managers, benching and trading adolescents. The umpires were high school boys. My friends and I put together our own team, which usually left us short on pitching but long on camaraderie. We set the lineup, hit the fungoes, ran the infield practice, and passed out the schedules and jerseys. Our uniforms were inexact, to be kind. Some of us wore spikes, some tennis shoes. Dan Siebens, our best athlete but already a bit of a bohemian, once showed up in sandals, which came flying off as he rounded first on a double. I don't know if any of us had heard of stirrups or sanitary socks. Our pants were jeans and khakis, all patched or with holes in the knees. But we all wore the same beloved jerseys.

And how fine those jerseys seemed. A few days before the start of the season, the captains would pick up a pile of them at the rec office on West Washington, and that is when we would learn what our colors were, who our sponsor was, and how we would be identified for the rest of the summer. The jerseys were made of soft knit fabric, and they usually had collars and half zippers. Once the jerseys arrived, our mothers had no need to wash shirts the rest of the summer. We wore them virtually every day, game or no. They were our gang colors, in a sense. You could tell friend or foe at a distance as swarms of red and black or green and white or maize and blue pumped and glided through the elm-shaded streets, gloves swinging from the handlebars of our bikes. The sponsors' names were on the backs, all local businesses from the neighborhoods: K&N Water Softeners, Findorff Lumber, Bowman All-Star Dairy, H&R Variety (we called it Hock and Run), Klitzner's, Klein-Dickert, Oscar Mayer, Octopus Car Wash, the Hub.

In all the years we played, I don't think we ever met an adult from one of the sponsors unless they happened to be in the family. My dad, who loved baseball, rarely saw me play. I remember once when he came to a game at Vilas. The only way I knew he was there was because our third baseman, Mike O'Meara, caught a glimpse of a familiar profile, raised his glove to cover his mouth, the way big leaguers do when they are telling one another what the next pitch is going to be, and called out to me at shortstop, "Hey, Dave, is that your dad standing over there behind that tree?"

That image has stuck with me over the years and I recall it wistfully, thinking back to the sweet long days when our parents let us live in our own world, and make our own mistakes, even if it meant that Winkie ate my baseball.

32

Crossing the Water

My parents left Wisconsin forever last Saturday morning at dawn. Their ashes were contained in two urns in the trunk of my car—my dad's made of solid wood, my mom's of intricate cloisonné. The August morning sky was high and cloudless, so soft and blue it hurt, like the sound of a melodious cello hurts. The world never seems more achingly fragile than on a late-summer day when you can sense something slipping away.

Mary Cummins Maraniss, my mother, had died in January at age eighty-four, and Elliott, my dad, had died at eighty-six a year and a half earlier. In one of his final assignments, the old editor had told us that he wanted to be buried not in Madison or Milwaukee, where he had lived most of his life, nor in Coney Island, Brooklyn, where he had grown up, but in Ann Arbor, where he had met my mother seventy years ago when they were students at the University of Michigan. There was a family plot there, her family's, at Washtenong Memorial Park and Mausoleum along Whitmore Lake Road on the northern edge of town. That is where my wife, Linda, and I were now headed, with the urns nestled safely in the trunk.

My brother, Jim, once taught me that life is composed of sensations. Days and weeks and months pass by, routine and quickly lost to memory, and then a moment comes that reminds you of who you are and why you are alive, and small details that normally go unseen in the random chaos of daily life suddenly take on deep visual and metaphorical meaning. So it was on this final journey to Ann Arbor. The trip began Friday afternoon when Linda and I loaded the car and drove away from our summer home in Madison to Milwaukee. In a sense, we were retracing the route my parents followed in 1983, when they had surprised us all by deciding to leave Madison and retire in Milwaukee. But more than that I could feel that we were starting to close a larger circle, one that had begun a half century ago.

Our family had first come to Madison in 1957, when my father was hired as a reporter at the *Capital Times*. Madison then was a godsend for us. We had bounced around for several years, moving from Detroit to New York to Detroit to Ann Arbor to Detroit to Cleveland to Bettendorf, Iowa, until we finally found some stability thanks to William T. Evjue, the progressive newspaper patriarch who had plucked my dad from a dying labor-movement newspaper in Iowa and given him a chance at a new life. We had moved into a big green rental house on Chandler Street near Vilas Park just as the Milwaukee Braves, led by the great Henry Aaron, were playing their way to a National League pennant and then a World Series championship over the New York Yankees. Now, fifty years later, on the first leg of the trip to Ann Arbor, Linda and I were stopping in Milwaukee to meet the very same Hank Aaron for the first time. Aaron had invited me to speak at a charity event he was hosting at Miller Park. My father had a deep admiration for Hammerin' Hank. Part of it had to do with the way Aaron hit the ball, and played right field, and ran the bases, but it also had something to do with the Midwest.

Elliott was a refugee from the East Coast and all of its pretensions, and for the rest of his life championed the heartland with the zealotry of a convert. He often said that Aaron was the greatest, but did not get the recognition he deserved because he played in Milwaukee, not in New York or Los Angeles. I felt Dad's spirit that Friday night at the .300 Club at Miller Park when I finally got to shake Aaron's right hand, and I know exactly what Dad would have whispered if he had been there with me: *"Jesus, what wrists."* Even at seventy-two, Henry Aaron had the big, soft hands and powerful wrists that had slammed 755 baseballs over the outfield wall.

The wake-up call came at a quarter to five the next morning at the Pfister Hotel. Linda and I were taking the six o'clock ferry across

Lake Michigan from Milwaukee to Muskegon, the second leg of our journey to Ann Arbor. When I had booked the ferry in July, I thought it would be something different, a summer adventure, and a welcome relief from the grinding, merciless drive around the arc of Chicago— but I didn't realize how appropriate it would be for this trip, or how deeply it would touch me. Not long after we parked our car belowdecks and found our seats, I walked out to the rail at the stern of the *Lake Express* and stared hypnotically at the ship's wake.

Then the feelings washed over me. I was looking backward, literally and figuratively. My parents were forever leaving the state that had shaped all of our lives. It was in Wisconsin that my father was able to prove his talents as a reporter and editor, where my mother reared four children and became a noted editor in her own right at the University of Wisconsin Press. They had arrived together and were leaving together, Mary and Elliott, sweet corn and bagels, Scots-Irish and Jew; he always looking for his glasses, she always looking for the right word.

My brother, Jim, my sister, Jeannie, and their spouses were waiting in Ann Arbor. Jeannie had made the arrangements at the cemetery. Jim had added his inimitable touch, suggesting that the headstone for Dad include his newspaper nickname, *Ace.* Our son, Andrew, their oldest grandchild, was also waiting along with other grandchildren and cousins. Hours later we would gather in a circle in the shade of a tree a few yards from the sunlit burial plot and sing ("This Land Is Your Land," "Union Maid," "Red River Valley") and tell stories that would mean nothing to strangers and everything to us, about the athlete's-foot inspections at Detroit's Rouge Pool, and the grease stains on our shirts that reminded us of Dad, and the forgiving look on Mom's face when Jim lost the five dollars that was supposed to buy groceries for dinner, and the children's book Dad wrote but never got published, called "Uncle Pudd," about a big house with rooms that could have anything you dreamed of; Jeannie's room was full of Kentucky Wonder beans.

The ferry ran slow—one of its four engines was out—but I had given us a three-hour cushion so we wouldn't have to worry about making the mid-afternoon burial. To the west, over Wisconsin, the moon appeared high in the deep blue sky. To the east, over Michigan, I could feel the warm rays of a soothing morning sun, softened by the breeze of the great midwestern lake. My parents were crossing the water, heading home and leaving home at the same time.

ACKNOWLEDGMENTS

My acknowledgments are usually too long. This time, with the most people to thank, I will make them too short. Thanks to everyone at the *Washington Post,* Simon & Schuster, the *Capital Times, Sports Illustrated,* all my friends in Washington, Madison, New York, Austin, and elsewhere—and most of all to my family.